# GOOD

## FOR THE

# MONEY

# GOOD
## FOR THE
# MONEY

## MY FIGHT TO PAY BACK AMERICA

—————————◆—————————

## BOB BENMOSCHE

with Peter Marks and Valerie Hendy

ST. MARTIN'S PRESS   NEW YORK

GOOD FOR THE MONEY. Copyright © 2016 by Bob Benmosche. Foreword copyright © 2016 by
Sarah J. Dahlgren. All rights reserved. Printed in the United States of America. For information, address St. Martin's Press, 175 Fifth Avenue, New York, N.Y. 10010.

www.stmartins.com

The Library of Congress Cataloging-in-Publication Data is available upon request.

ISBN 978-1-250-07218-4 (hardcover)
ISBN 978-1-4668-8357-4 (e-book)

Our books may be purchased in bulk for promotional, educational, or business use. Please
contact your local bookseller or the Macmillan Corporate and Premium Sales Department at
1-800-221-7945, extension 5442, or by e-mail at MacmillanSpecialMarkets@macmillan.com.

First Edition: April 2016

10  9  8  7  6  5  4  3  2  1

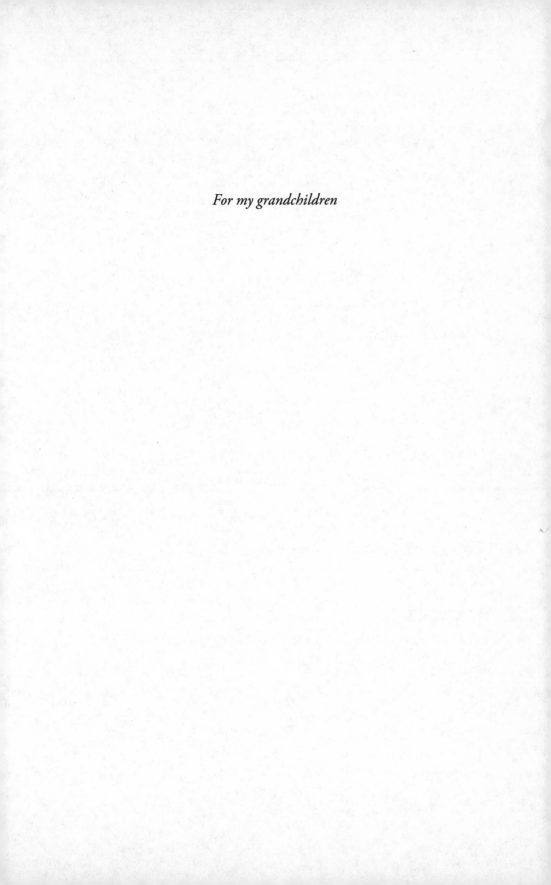

*For my grandchildren*

# CONTENTS

# ACKNOWLEDGMENTS

WE HAD THE PRIVILEGE OF spending many hours with Bob, his family, friends, and colleagues in assisting Bob with this memoir. Bob was a great storyteller, a big personality, and an American original. Helping us to tell the story of this singular leader and of one of the biggest business turnarounds in American history were those who were in the room as events unfolded. We are indebted to all of them.

In particular, we'd like to extend our gratitude to Bob's family for their generosity and, as Bob's illness worsened, their forbearance under ever more wrenching circumstances. His wife Denise, son Ari, daughter Nehama, daughter-in-law Clair, and sister Jayne all added vital depth to Bob's story, through photos, diaries, and personal accounts. His longtime companion, Lisa Weber, offered insight into both his professional and personal life.

Just as crucial were the observations, memories, counsel, and supporting material provided by people who knew intimately the story of Bob's leadership through the crisis: first and foremost, the valiant trio of Jim Millstein and Kenneth Feinberg, at the U.S. Department of the Treasury, and Sarah Dahlgren, the point person for AIG at the New York Fed. Don Nickelson, Thomas Bianco, Joe Jordan, Joe Reali, and Maria Escobar were invaluable in providing context for the stepping stones of Bob's career, and

Michael Grad was a superb resource on questions about the rescue. MetLife archivist Daniel May provided important context and historical photos.

Bob's oncologist, Dr. Abraham Chachoua, did us the great service of speaking to us, with the family's consent. We are grateful, too, to the many AIG associates of Bob's who gave their time to help us understand the parameters of his achievements. Gerry Pasciucco, who spearheaded the unwinding of AIG's Financial Products division, assisted greatly in understanding the complex challenge that Bob took on.

Bob's colleagues in AIG's executive offices—many of them instrumental in creating the turnaround strategy and then executing it—also deserve thanks: Peter Hancock, Brian Schreiber, David Herzog, Tom Russo, Bill Dooley, and Jeff Hurd.

Christina Pretto, who headed corporate communications for AIG and worked closely with Bob, deepened our understanding of many facets of the story. Peter Bahra and Jennifer Cher were tireless in their assistance with archival photos. Exceedingly generous, too, were Jim Ankner, Rob Gifford, Elaine Witt-Owens, Jon Diat, Ted Nevins, Mark Clowes, Betty Bell, Larry Mark, Jennifer Waldner, Jaime Nunez, and Robert Caffrey.

Our profound thanks go to Leah Spiro, Bob's indefatigable literary agent, who first came up with the idea for the book and from then on shepherded the project all the way through to the finish line. Tim Bartlett, whose editing wisdom enhanced the project at every turn, made just as vital an impact; indeed, there would have been no book without his savvy guidance. Our appreciation extends to the resourceful photo editor Kathy Moore; to Tim's gracious assistant Claire Lampen; and to public-relations whiz Mark Fortier and his team.

Additional thank-yous are due Christine Ledbetter, Glenn Skwerer, Carol Vogel, Lee Beltzer, Ben Brantley, Brittany Bell, Laura Gallagher, Melissa Tafe, Abbe Bates, Susan Wohleking, and Lizzie Marks for their help and patient ears all through the writing process.

Finally, we eternally owe our love and thanks to Bob Benmosche, for his extraordinary candor and honesty, and for entrusting us with his remarkable story.

# FOREWORD

I FIRST MET BOB BENMOSCHE in the summer of 2009. It was almost nine months after the government had bailed out AIG. The company was spiraling: battered in the press, condemned by Congress, beset by low morale, with customers and employees looking for the exits. The previous CEO had resigned that May, and Bob had been chosen to take over. I was leading our AIG efforts at the New York Fed at that time, and Tom Baxter, FRBNY General Counsel, and I were asked to meet with him before he took over.

While I'd been warned that Bob was not your average CEO, it went far beyond that. The Bob I met on that day was unique, at least in my experience, in a number of ways. I'd never met anyone more direct—he didn't mince words in expressing his views on what had occurred to date and where he thought mistakes were made, and he gave assurances that his version of a "bull in a china shop" would break some glass. I'd never met anyone with more energy—he spoke with his whole body and used nearly his entire range of voice that day to make sure we got a clear picture of his vision. And I'd never met anyone with less of a filter—I learned more about Bob's personal life in the short walk out of the building that day than I knew about many of my close friends.

My first reaction to the new CEO? Holy crap, what are we getting ourselves into?

But as Bob began to talk about the company, I realized that this man was just what AIG needed—someone who would come in and shake things up, get people within the company out of their "woe is me, I'm AIG" mentality. Bob had a vision for what the company could be, but was also someone who wasn't afraid to meet head-on the public outcry and Congressional uproar at the time. And right away, Bob did that. He may not have done it in the most tactful way (and that wouldn't be the first time), but he made it clear that he was fighting for the future of the company, its employees, its customers and, ultimately, full repayment to the government.

Bob took over at a time when all of us where facing unprecedented situations: there was no "playbook" for how to resolve a trillion dollar financial company. People expected a quick sale and a quick government exit, but this was impossible. There was great pressure to do it all fast, but that simply wouldn't work—it would require a strategic plan and time to execute. This is where Bob earned his salary again and again—by holding the company and the government to his plan. He would threaten to quit—on more than one occasion—when he felt he lacked support. Indeed, on one day, when compensation was being debated, he almost quit several times! I was sitting there with some board members during the back and forth, and again and again he came back to the importance of sticking up for a principle. He was trying to make a point, but he was deadly serious, and that gave him credibility. People took him seriously.

We're lucky that Bob was able to tell his story before he passed away. On one level it offers all of us—corporate leaders, government regulators, politicians—a clear vision of what to do, and, as importantly, *what not to do* during times of economic panic. Among the lessons that emerge:

- Governance really matters when it comes to big companies. Clearly AIG had significant failings in this regard before the crisis, and Bob knew how to fix it and did fix it. The company operates much differently today than it did before the crisis.

- Leadership makes a difference. Bob embodied great leadership skills; he was a master at communicating with his employees on an emotional level and breaking down complex ideas into simple principles. Great leaders inspire with great stories, and Bob always had a story. Among my favorites: "Mom's on the roof," which you will read more about later in these pages. Bob shared this story many times, as a way of making the point that all news, good or bad, should be shared as soon as it's known—and not held back to avoid a bad reaction. He also liked to tell the story of Sandy Koufax, who decided not to pitch Game 1 of the 1965 World Series because it fell on Yom Kippur. Koufax stuck to his principles, and, for Bob, his story was about standing up for what you believe in. Great leaders also help people understand where they're coming from by explaining things in a clear and transparent way. And they are able to connect with people at all levels of the company—Bob knew people's names, what they did, and he continually thanked them. Bob had all of these traits.
- Transparency and trust are critical. Bob believed in transparency, whether it was with the government, with his employees or with the public. And it was that level of transparency that built the trust and the working partnership that was necessary for Bob's plan to work.

You are about to read one of the great comeback stories in business history; its importance isn't yet fully appreciated. When AIG paid back its government loans with interest in December 2012, it was more than just a company meeting its obligations. It was a once-great company getting a new start. It was one of the great symbols of failure in the crisis coming back to life. And practically speaking, a world in which AIG actually failed and had to be wound down completely would have been catastrophic. And AIG would not have been the only damage in that scenario. AIG's connections to businesses—big and small, here and abroad, to retirees and savers, and to millions of insured Americans meant that AIG's failure would have damaged more than just AIG.

Politics did not allow people in the government to thank Bob publically for his service, something that he often mentioned. I'm confident, though, that everyone involved with the turnaround at AIG acknowledged privately the incredible service he performed for AIG and for the country.

I was no longer involved with AIG when I heard that Bob had cancer. The last time I got to see him one-on-one was in the summer of 2014, when we got together for lunch. I wanted to get some advice from Bob on how to think about my career and next steps. Bob was—as he always was—supportive and challenging. He was always looking for the next challenge for leaders he wanted to develop. It was a low point for him—his mind was as sharp and energetic as ever, but his body was failing: he couldn't eat or walk up the stairs. I saw him again at his retirement party a few months after that, and witnessed a final Benmosche performance. Person after person got up to say nice things about Bob, and then it was his turn. Without acknowledging all of the accolades, he immediately launched into a pep talk: "You all have to give your support to [incoming CEO] Peter [Hancock], you have to keep making things happen." He was motivational, inspirational, sometimes hectoring ("I don't want to hear any more of your shit!"). That was classic Bob—supportive, leading—and that was the last time I saw him.

—Sarah J. Dahlgren

# GOOD

### FOR THE

# MONEY

# ONE

# THE GOOD NEWS IS,
# YOU'RE NOT PARANOID

THE TRUTH WAS, I DIDN'T need the job.

I was content in retirement, living in the house of my dreams on Croatia's Adriatic coast, puttering around in my flip-flops, tending to the little side business we'd started, growing grapes for our own wine. But stepping back into the arena appealed to my sense of patriotic duty. Becoming CEO of American International Group—known by its universally reviled initials, AIG—would be an important service to the country. AIG had almost taken down the entire global economy as a result of the role of one of its divisions, AIG Financial Products, in the calamitous subprime mortgage market. Now, it was reeling under the weight of the astronomical $182 billion in bailout funds it owed the taxpayers. The company was in such disarray that it had burned through four CEOs in four years, the last one hounded out after a humiliating dressing down by Congress.

I would be CEO No. 5 in that line. Lucky me.

Sure, I knew that wading into this situation would be messy. I just hadn't fully calculated the magnitude of the mess. In fact, on Monday, August 3, 2009, my very first day in AIG's offices in Manhattan's Financial District, the groundwork was being laid for an attempt at neutering my leadership. I would soon find that a powerful faction within the company was opposed to the direction in which I planned to take it. Hanging in the balance was the fate of what was then the world's largest insurance company, a firm with a trillion dollars in assets and dealings in 130 nations.

Well, as the saying goes, no good deed goes unpunished. I didn't want to start the job until October. But officials at the U.S. Treasury Department—now owners of 79.9 percent of the company's stock—had other ideas. October? Impossible! The new CEO had to start when the man he was replacing, Edward Liddy, departed on August 10. So I agreed to their timetable. I arranged to start at AIG on August 3, a week before Liddy's departure, on an unofficial basis. That way, I would spend some time in the first half of August getting to know employees in the various units of AIG around the United States, take the end of August to honor my commitments in Croatia, where I had retired to start a vineyard, and then return full-time to AIG on September 8.

Not everyone was thrilled, me included. I still didn't even have a salary and compensation package nailed down. But I made it clear I wasn't going to alter this plan.

Little did I know my "vacation" in Croatia, which had the blessing of the government officials who urged me to take the job, would soon be fodder for an attack by my enemies on the board and elsewhere. Within days, news of the trip would be leaked to the media as evidence of more AIG profligacy, of the sense that the company—already on the defensive over its desire to pay contractually mandated executive bonuses—just didn't get it.

Oh, I got it, all right.

It was the first salvo in a campaign from within the company to try to smother my leadership in its infancy, and scuttle the plan I was formulating. My goal was simple: for AIG to defy the odds and pay back America, in full. I knew that AIG was still a tremendously valuable company that had been dragged down by a couple of divisions that made really bad bets on mortgage-backed derivatives. These toxic contracts had become, in Warren Buffett's colorful phraseology, the financial world's weapons of mass destruction. By no means, though, did they reflect on the worth of the rest of the company. I intended to clean up the derivatives mess so that AIG could re-establish itself as one of the world's premier insurance companies—and a mighty profitable one at that.

My ideas ran counter to those of some in the upper echelons of the firm. This faction wanted to unload huge portions of the company as fast as possible, at what I knew to be ridiculous, fire-sale prices. They had the backing of the Wall Street bankers who had made a fortune—$100 million at least—in consulting fees working for AIG and who were poised to make a lot more through commissions on the rapid sell-offs. Adding to the absurdity was that these were the very Wall Street vultures who had sold AIG the toxic derivatives to begin with! I have spent a veritable lifetime in the financial industry, so when I say that the buzzards were circling, ready to swoop in on AIG's highly prized insurance entities and real estate holdings, I know of what species I speak.

Not even the U.S. government seemed averse to selling AIG units at bargain prices. The prevailing philosophy in Washington was, let's recoup whatever we can as fast as we can. No less a figure than Treasury Secretary Timothy Geithner, one of the architects of the bailout, first as head of the New York Fed and then as a member of President Obama's cabinet, privately expressed his strong doubts over AIG ever paying back its debt.

My feeling was quite different. I believed AIG could pay the government back—I wouldn't have taken the job if I didn't. I also figured out quickly that those at AIG who didn't share that belief wanted me silenced, discredited, and shunted aside. Which reminds me of an old joke: A guy goes to his psychiatrist, and the doctor tells him: "I've got good news and bad news for you. The good news is, you're not paranoid. The bad news is, they're out to get you."

I hadn't pinpointed who specifically was out to get me. But by the time the story leaked in Bloomberg News the following week, with the headline "Benmosche Said to Start AIG Tenure With Croatian Trip," I'd begun to get an inkling.

Over the next five years, I would do battle on many fronts in my fight to make the American taxpayer whole after AIG's errors during the subprime debacle. Well before my tenure as CEO ended in September 2014, I'd made good on my vow: AIG had not only paid the country back, but also had settled the account with a $22.7 billion profit.

But there were bitter battles along the way. One pitted me against AIG's own board of directors, an entity that normally would be expected to support management's plans. They were led by their formidable, newly installed chairman, Harvey Golub, a former CEO of American Express Company, with whom I would lock horns over how to run AIG. I also had adversaries outside of AIG, namely some craven politicians who were making our jobs harder by publicly slinging mud at us and in the process putting the lives of AIG employees at risk. A battle, too, had to be waged in the public-relations arena, with some influential media types who thought us an easy target and found allies within the company who leaked inside information to them, further sowing anxieties about me and the company.

As tough as these struggles were, they didn't faze me. It wasn't even the worst corporate backstabbing I had experienced; that distinction went to my time in the 1980s and early '90s at the brokerage firm Paine Webber, where I was well schooled in Wall Street's cage-fight mentality. Even there, my foes had nothing on the cruelest and most intractable enemy I've ever had to face: the cancer with which I was diagnosed in October 2010, a year and two months after I got to AIG. The disease was supposed to end my life quickly. It didn't, thanks to some amazing medicine. But it's an adversary I continued to fight with every ounce of strength in my six-foot, four-inch body.

From those very first days at AIG, however, I was prepping for the fight, even if I was still only starting to get my bearings. First, though, I had to begin to deal with another insidious problem: morale throughout the company was dangerously low. The daily onslaught of bad news and negative commentary had taken its toll on a workforce that felt little compunction about staying; they weren't even sure if AIG would continue to exist. So I made it my first order of business to reach out directly to the employees, to let them know that the new sheriff in town was on their side. On my second morning, Tuesday, August 4, 2009, I called a "town hall" meeting at AIG's corporate headquarters at 70 Pine Street to lay out my philosophy, to say some things that AIG's workers had not been hearing from their leader, maybe ever.

"The fact is," I said, warming to the room packed with hundreds, "you are AIG, and it's time we stopped being embarrassed by it. And it's time that the people in Congress stop talking about you as the problem. Because you're the solution."

The attacks on AIG had gone beyond angry rhetoric to outright threats. The children of some workers in Connecticut were beaten up at school and some employees were being harassed online and confronted in person. I needed them to hear me loud and clear on the issue that is—let's face it—foremost in the mind of every worker, everywhere. "I just wanted to assure all of you that my first priority is getting your compensation right, making sure that from myself on down, all get paid competitively, so that you can come here every day and get fairly paid for what it is that you're doing."

I also referred to the divestiture plan that had been worked out by departing CEO Liddy and his restructuring expert, Paula Reynolds, a plan I had absolutely no intention of following. I did not say that outright, as Liddy was standing there and I had no details to present. I did offer a preview of my thoughts, though. "I am not a liquidator," I said. "I don't liquidate things. I build them." The relief in the room was palpable, especially as I sought to calm the audience's apparent nerves with some off-the-cuff humor. In the first minute of my first address before an AIG audience, I got a laugh when I explained, "I am not your dentist, and I am not going to ask you to open up wide and we're not going to start drilling, so we ought to relax just a little bit here."

It wouldn't be long before some of my words at that private gathering also made their way into the press: Bloomberg News quoted me (accurately) as having said that the government was creating "lynch mobs"—not the most sensitive phrase I could have come up with. The leaks bolstered my belief that a campaign was being mounted to pre-empt me by people with intimate knowledge of the company and the workings of the media. That those leaks may actually have served my purpose, by making me seem like someone politicians didn't want to mess with, was beside the point. The unauthorized disclosures were confirmation I was at the helm of a porous organization, some of whose more than 100,000 employees harbored hopes of my undoing.

As the doctor said: "The good news is, you're not paranoid . . ."

The task that lay before me amounted to one of the most challenging of my career, a working life that had been tested before by high-stakes pressure and internal strife. Still, I could tell that this job was going to be a new kind of challenge, one that would call on every aspect of what I've learned about leadership.

In the course of telling this story, I'm going to impart as many of those leadership lessons as I can. They are not, though, lessons of the business-school variety. I've never been to one. Never, in fact, enrolled in a single business class, ever. These are ideas gleaned from a life in business—with an emphasis as much on the life part as the business.

You'll discover in these pages, too, that I'm a full-fledged believer in the amazing things this nation can do when you give people freedom to act. If they choose to act responsibly—and most people in this country do—it's incredible what can be achieved. My desire to join AIG at this juncture was tied up in this idea, in a faith in the talent of the workforce and in convincing them that they had the freedom to act. I wanted to draw on their initiative to help propel us forward. From the outset, I was convinced we could accomplish what would seem incredible things, in spite of the tough conditions, in spite of a corrosively negative environment.

I think, too, that I had given myself a larger purpose: to make the renewal of AIG an example of American resilience. To provide evidence to the world that America was still strong, that we were still a capable people. The company's return to health would reaffirm that. It would say that our identity as a can-do culture remained valid, that both collectively and individually, we could still make a difference.

Now, you may wonder why a guy who had been contentedly trudging around in shorts on a terrace on the Adriatic Sea would want to parachute into this particular minefield. The insurance business isn't the sexiest in the marketplace, but this insurance company had managed to land in the middle of the world's hottest financial story. And not for good reasons. The once widely admired firm was now perceived as so dysfunctional that when writing about it in his memoir, Henry Paulson, President George W. Bush's Treasury secretary, declared: "AIG's incompetence was stunning."

Looking back at the magnitude of the mess I agreed to take on, I do at times think I might have spent too much time in the midday Croatian sun. Because AIG at that moment looked to much of the world like a corporate ghost ship, navigating toward its doom. Providing financial security for millions of policyholders was the company's bedrock mission, but it was not at this point what it was best known for. As a result of the miscalculations before I was on the scene, and egged on by some political demonizing, AIG was now one of, if not the most, despised companies on the planet. Facing mounting obligations it couldn't meet as a result of its bad bets on the mortgage markets, and deemed by federal regulators too integral to the nation's financial health to be allowed to slide into bankruptcy, the company had received a massive, and massively unpopular, government bailout. To keep AIG going, the Federal Reserve loaned the company billions and the Department of the Treasury pumped in billions more throughout 2008 courtesy of a new vehicle created by Congress, the controversial Troubled Asset Relief Program, or TARP, as it came to be known.

Those loans, purchases of AIG assets, and other instruments amounted to an almost unfathomable figure, $182.3 billion. It was by far the most money any publicly held company received; more than Citigroup, Bank of America, or any other among the better-known corporations that contributed to the disaster. No wonder average Americans—many of them living in houses newly under water, or terrified about losing their jobs in a tanking economy—had dark thoughts when "AIG" was mentioned. Those initials, in fact, were all many people knew about the firm. It seemed to a lot of them that this New York–headquartered company with a not-very-clear identity—AIG, after all, was the name of a nebulous parent holding company for dozens of other insurance and financial entities—was being propped up just as their own household security was crumbling. I was angry myself, and not simply because as I watched the crisis unfold I developed serious misgivings about the way the government was treating the company. In a long business career, capped by my retirement in 2006 as CEO of another insurance giant, Metropolitan Life Insurance, or MetLife, I'd invested wisely and amassed some wealth. And that, too, was to some extent disappearing in the crisis.

I, like millions of other Americans, had been a mere spectator to these events up to the time my phone rang in my home in Dubrovnik in the spring of 2009. A search committee led by AIG board member Dennis Dammerman, who had worked alongside Jack Welch at General Electric, was looking for the fifth CEO since Hank Greenberg's 2005 departure.

"Take it!" was my son Ari's blunt reaction, when I told him that feelers were being sent about my interest in running AIG.

It was actually not the first time I'd been approached about the job. In September 2008, with the meltdown in its early stages, Christopher Cole, an emissary from Secretary Paulson, had asked me about it. At that chaotic moment, the Dow Jones Industrial Average was in free fall, losing 440 points on September 17 alone; the just-announced AIG bailout was not reassuring the markets. I knew Cole and Paulson from the days both worked at the investment house Goldman Sachs, although I didn't have fond memories of my prior contact with Paulson. (I recall having dressed him down once when I was CEO of MetLife, over the way Goldman was advising on a job for us.) I had no intention, by the way, of becoming CEO of AIG if they offered me a dollar a year, as Liddy would later agree to do. As I often said, "I'm easy but I'm not cheap."

And as I always do with big decisions, I consulted my closest advisers, namely, my family: my businessman son; my daughter Nehama, then finishing up her rabbinical studies; and my wife, Denise, from whom I have been legally separated since 1999, but with whom I maintain a warm and close relationship. I also consulted my longtime companion, Lisa Weber, an executive whom I'd known since our days together at Paine Webber.

"You're the right man for the job!" they all declared, adding it would be good both for me—and for them. I thought I was doing pretty well as a retiree, but in their estimation, I was restless and in need of something more stimulating than overseeing the bottling of my own Croatian red wine.

Denise was very emphatic about this. Although we weren't together all the time, she could see, when we were, that I was growing bored. "You know, you have to do something," she said. "You can't just sit here and look at the water." There was also the huge hit I was taking financially on the meltdown; my millions in MetLife stock options—the nest egg that allowed me to take a retirement at sixty-two in the first place—were losing value by the day. If AIG went down, I could envision the entire financial system going with it.

But still, I wasn't entirely sold on the job, not if I wasn't going to be fairly compensated. Too much work. And anyway, in that go-round Paulson tapped another Goldman Sachs alum—Liddy, who had been on the investment bank's board.

I continued to watch the crisis unfold from the sidelines, though, and what I saw was frustrating to the point of being torturous. From an early age I'd been a deep believer in a free market as unfettered by government intervention as possible. Solid regulatory bodies were needed, certainly. But here was the government going beyond even a role as private-industry safety net, and insinuating itself into the fundamental mechanisms of the company: regulators now had a say in AIG's executive hiring and pay. They sat in on every board meeting. On top of that, politicians of every stripe were having a field day, publicly berating AIG's leadership whenever they had the chance, running down the company's reputation and as a result creating additional impediments to AIG's recovery.

The federal government had committed nearly $200 billion in taxpayer money to AIG. It was now both the company's creditor and its majority shareholder. Of course, I understood that having taken an action of this unprecedented magnitude and put this much of Americans' money at risk, the federal government should receive some control over the company. But then, it would also make sense for the government to do everything it reasonably could to help the company succeed, and that included both defending its decisions and expressing its support. And those in charge should have recognized this. Like any investor, the government first and foremost should have wanted its stake protected, and like any lender, should have done everything in its power to ensure it got its money back. But the government was effectively investing in the company, then in the next breath telling the world that the borrower wasn't worth doing business with. Was this any kind of sound strategy? Some members of Congress seemed intent instead on a strategy of corporate sabotage. They were making it harder for AIG to regroup and start making money again. In such an environment, how did anyone think it would ever pay the taxpayers back?

To me, one of the lowest ebbs occurred on March 18, 2009, when Liddy underwent questioning that bordered on humiliation by a Congressional panel, the House Financial Services Committee, charged with overseeing legislation on banks and other financial institutions. It was excruciating to watch and seemed a devastating turning point, in terms of breaking the company's spirit. Though Liddy had no part in what brought AIG low—remember, he had joined the company in September 2008, after the catastrophic derivatives deals had been put in place—he was the only target available to the politicians. He was grilled about the reports that in the midst of the turmoil, employees of AIG's Wilton, Connecticut–based Financial Products unit had been awarded $165 million in retention bonuses, a financial incentive used to ensure key employees remain in their jobs during, for example, a crucial business cycle, or a negotiation.

It's not that people weren't rightly enraged. The debacle at FP was horrific. A unit created in 1987 to generate new revenue streams during a period of soft returns in the insurance industry, FP had by 2007 become for the company a kind of suicide pill. I and the rest of the world would come to learn that FP had been gambling big-time by insuring investment banks' securities—many of them bundles of subprime mortgages—through a financial instrument called a credit-default swap. As the subprime mortgage crisis deepened, and the banks faced vast losses on these holdings, FP found itself drowning in obligations it couldn't begin to cover.

The problem was, to "unwind" these toxic swaps, employees with deep knowledge of them had to be retained. These were the same people to whom AIG was contractually obligated to pay the bonuses. To the outside world, it seemed unfair—even criminal—that the people who in effect helped melt the core and expose the financial system's fuel rods were being rewarded, and handsomely. But the intricately assembled instruments required expert handling if the damage was going to be repaired. And aside from the fact that many of FP's employees had no role in the bad swaps—only 125 contracts out of the tens of thousands written were in fact responsible—the bonuses were part of their legally binding compensation packages.

The stage for Liddy's shabby treatment in Washington had been set a couple of days earlier. Andrew Cuomo, at the time New York's attorney general (and not too long after, its governor), fanned the flames by revealing details of the controversial compensation: seventy-three AIG Financial Products employees received bonuses of $1 million or more in 2008, as part of their 2007 compensation. "Something is deeply wrong with this outcome," Cuomo said. He proceeded to express his outrage by subpoenaing the company for the names of the recipients. The purpose, apparently, was to shame them into returning the bonuses—which many did—but the effect, of course, would be to subject them, amid the public hysteria, to extraordinary vilification, even danger. President Obama chimed in, saying the AIG bonuses were an indication of a culture of "excess greed." And the media piled on, too, predictably, backing Cuomo up in the eagerness for retribution.

At the House committee hearing, the chairman, Representative Barney Frank, took up Cuomo's cause, demanding Liddy provide the names of those getting the bonuses. In response, Liddy did exactly the right thing. He read aloud from the death threats that were being received by people at AIG. Like this missive:

"All the executives and their families should be executed with piano wire around their necks. I'm looking for all the CEO's names, kids, where they live."

Mind you, anger was an understandable reaction. What was hard to take, at least for me, was the vengeful stoking of that anger by our leaders.

Unfortunately, Liddy went further:

"I've asked the employees of AIG Financial Products to step up and do the right thing," he told the committee. "Specifically, I've asked those who received retention payments in excess of $100,000 to return at least half of those payments. Some have already stepped forward and offered to give up 100 percent of their payments."

Now, this drove me absolutely nuts. From my living room in Croatia, I stared at the TV, incredulous at what I was hearing. "Tell them, Ed, that they *earned* those bonuses!" I shouted. "Stand up for your people! Tell them that they earned it!" Part of the problem was the terminology being used: in most people's minds, bonuses are what you are paid above and beyond your salary. In our business, though, they're built into a pre-approved compensation package. That's why I say these employees were entitled to the money, regardless of the company's dire straits. As I would later explain to Ken Feinberg, the government's "pay czar" at the time for executive compensation, a better term would have been "variable salary"— meaning the portion of the wages a worker was entitled to if they performed to the agreed-upon level. And most of them had, according to their contracts.

It seemed to me that giving in to the lust for blood was precisely the wrong thing to do, because it further demoralized and alienated the very people you were depending on to help fix the mess. I'd already made up my mind by this time that kowtowing to Washington was bad policy, no matter what the circumstances.

Liddy—who had taken over as AIG's chairman and CEO for the princely sum of $1 a year—pronounced himself done after this awful spectacle. Less than a week after the hearing, AIG announced that he would be stepping down.

A few months later, I was in. Among those who had urged my hiring, I would discover, was Greenberg, the legendary AIG CEO who'd been forced out of the company under difficult circumstances in 2005, and whom I'd gotten to know and respect over the years as his competitor at MetLife. But before I accepted the job, the people in charge of finding Ed's successor had to look me over. And I had to see if I could work with them. Aside from the AIG board of directors' search committee, headed by the upstanding Dammerman, the key operative was Jim Millstein, who recently had been installed as chief restructuring officer in the U.S. Department of the Treasury. An expert in rebuilding troubled companies, Millstein had been recruited for the job in the early days of the Obama administration by Geithner.

Millstein, a savvy New Yorker, would become one of my staunchest allies in the months and years that followed, and a largely unsung hero of the struggle to set AIG right. We met early that summer in the Park Avenue offices of Spencer Stuart, an executive search firm, and I liked him on the spot, and thought he felt the same way about me. He explained his belief that the new CEO had to be both strong and adroit and most importantly, a motivator. He was looking for a leader with "the right stuff"—someone who was self-confident and wily enough to contend with all the grief that in this job was sure to come his or her way.

The images of Liddy's appearance before that committee were seared into my skull. "You don't need me," I said. "The way Congress and all these people are piling on, treating this company like a piece of shit. Why don't *you* do it?"

"You know," Millstein replied, "I'm a restructuring guy. I can fix this balance sheet. But at the end of the day, it's going to require somebody who can get this company to stand up and fly right, to make the people proud of their work again, to be energized to come back into work. That's what you do for a living. You run big companies and you've done it successfully. So you should do this with me."

He was right: my skills were a good match for the assignment. I like to think that a skill I honed over my executive career was emotional intelligence, the ability to figure out what incentives people required to feel part of a bigger mission, and want to work harder to achieve it. My experience at MetLife had given me a lot of confidence, too, in my abilities as a maximizer of corporate value: I had an intuitive feel for what things were worth. I'll give you an example. Early in the financial crisis, and well before I took over at AIG, I knew Federal Reserve Chairman Ben Bernanke was going to be on *60 Minutes,* and I figured he would vow not to let the banks fail. Anticipating that (correctly), I immediately started buying stock (for my grandchildren) in the tanking behemoths Citibank and Bank of America, which were selling for a few dollars a share, and would soon be selling for many times more.

On a grander scale: When I was promoted to chairman and CEO of MetLife in 1998, it was an $11.5 billion company; by the time I left eight years later, it was worth $40 billion. I was certain I had a lot of know-how to share.

The pros of taking the job grew on me as I reflected on the significance of the task. Leadership is in many ways a service, and in this case, I could be providing one not only for AIG, but also my country. I saw a lot going wrong in the nation, the place where my kids live and my grandchildren are growing up. (Although I was living several months a year in

Europe, I hadn't cut ties back home, spending the rest of my time in Florida and the Northeast.)

If the problems raised by the financial crisis were not fixed, I reasoned, a lot of what we'd grown up to know and expect was going to vanish. If AIG did indeed fail—and in the summer of 2009 many people in government and the financial press were still writing it off—the prospects of recovery for everyone else were bleak. If we didn't get this company back on its feet and pay back what it owed and help to restore confidence in the system—in American business—then the economy, I believed, wasn't going to bounce back. We were going to be in deep trouble for a long time.

But based on Liddy's experience, I had nagging concerns about what, as AIG leader, my relationship would be to the company's biggest stakeholder. "Listen," I said to Millstein. "Before I even take this opportunity seriously, I want to meet whoever is really in charge of AIG in the government. I need to meet the key decision makers and decide whether they really have the stomach for me."

"I'm happy to introduce you to whomever you think that is," he said.

And so began a not-so-romantic courtship, a process that was instructive about the way Washington works. A week after our New York introduction, Millstein escorted me into Geithner's office in D.C. I think both of them imagined it would be one of those benign meet-and-greets, where we'd chat amiably for a bit and talk generally about the challenges ahead. But I had other ideas, stuff to get off my chest. And so I derailed the bland cordiality, immediately launching into what Millstein later described, to his horror, as a "lecture." I told Geithner that the bonus issue had gotten completely out of hand, and that I held both him and the president responsible, in their own public comments, for the way in which the FP people were hung out to dry.

"The way this has been handled is a disgrace," I said. "These people are trying to keep a company alive, to pay back your money, and you treat them like this? You want people to do the job and you don't want to pay them? That's ridiculous! At some point it doesn't pay to come to work anymore!"

I confess it: I was obnoxious. Geithner was clearly livid. He looked as if he wanted to throw me out of the room. And Millstein was flabbergasted. His jaw, he would later say, felt like it dropped "to my belt buckle." But I was content. I wanted it understood before any formal offer might be made that I was not going to tolerate being pushed around by the Treasury or Congress. And I'd wanted Geithner to hear it from me.

The meeting settled down after that, but it left a sour taste in Geithner's mouth.

"I can't believe you did that," Millstein said to me as we left.

"Well, I felt strongly about it," I replied.

From there, we walked out of the Treasury, across the plaza to the White House, for a West Wing meeting with the administration's other point person on the crisis, Larry Summers, the former Harvard University president who had been appointed President Obama's director of the National Economics Council. I wasn't sure what to expect from Summers, who, a few days before Liddy's March humiliation by Congress, added his own two cents. Appearing on ABC's *This Week with George Stephanopoulos*, he'd said: "There are a lot of terrible things that have happened in the last eighteen months, but what's happened at AIG is the most outrageous."

As we waited in the vestibule, Millstein was summoned by a Summers aide. Waiting behind the door, Millstein would later confide, was Summers, who already knew about my little tirade in Geithner's office.

"Well, I heard that didn't go well," Summers said.

"Larry, I would say that's a fair assessment," Millstein replied. "I think Bob did his level best to piss the secretary off, and I don't think the secretary for a second hid that he was pissed off."

Summers told Millstein he wasn't sure Geithner would support my being hired now. ("Too aggressive," the Treasury secretary is reported to have said about me.) Even so, Millstein stuck his neck out, telling Summers I was "the right guy" despite my gruffness and, as I would later learn, asked him to sell me on the job, and clue me in on Washington's peculiar power culture.

During the meeting that followed, Summers gave no inkling that he had doubts about me. His friendly manner betrayed none of the hostility toward AIG that he'd expressed in his public remarks. He indeed did try to sell me on the job, telling some stories about his own early experiences in government, and at the same time advising me about how if you didn't learn to play by Washington's rules, Washington would eat you up. He also emphasized the important opportunity this represented, for me to serve my country—an argument that was for me, an army veteran who served in South Korea, a compelling one.

I didn't let that sidetrack me, though. I stressed again to Summers that the abuse heaped on AIG over the bonuses was disgusting.

Summers confided that both he and the president agreed with me in principle. "The president called me up," Summers recounted, "and said, 'Larry, listen to me. You may think the bonuses are contractually right. You may think it's the right thing to do for a whole bunch of reasons. The fact is the American people don't and Congress doesn't, and if you continue that line, you are going to get Congress to figure out how they can run the country. And the worst thing that could happen to our country is if it's run by Congress and not the administration. So we have to criticize AIG. We need to satisfy the people and their anger, and it's purely political.'"

I didn't like this line of thinking at all, although it didn't surprise me. It encouraged mob rule, a bending to the need for blood, and it suggested to me they were arguing from a position of political weakness. And if Summers and Geithner couldn't even come together on whether I was the right guy, what roadblocks could I expect after I started the job?

"I don't know why you want me," I said to Summers. "I don't think you guys can handle what needs to be done. Because," I added, "I am going to have to be provocative."

Summers assured me that in the end Geithner's reservations would not be an obstacle. I was "the guy"—a sentiment echoed by Feinberg, best known as the special master of the September 11th Victim Compensation Fund, and who had been named special master (or "pay czar") for executive compensation under TARP. In that capacity, he would have to approve any salary I received from AIG—and unlike Liddy, I had no intention of being an unpaid volunteer. Emboldened by Summers's support, I pushed hard on the issue of my own compensation over breakfast with Feinberg in D.C. a few days later.

"Bob, the anger of this Congress is real," Feinberg warned.

"Ken, I heard that from Summers," I replied impatiently. And then I said, bluntly, "Oh, and by the way, I want you to understand something. You might want to talk to your boys over there, because I'm not coming into this job for less than eight figures. Otherwise, they can stick it up their ass. I am not working for a buck like Ed, okay? I want at least $10 million. I want to make a statement. But it's not about my pay and we don't want to politicize my pay. I don't want any bullshit and I want it decided before I start."

I had already talked this over with my son Ari, and we debated back and forth how much I should ask for. "What do you think about one, one, and one?" I asked him, meaning a million in salary, a million in stock, and another million in stock options.

"I'm really not sure," Ari replied.

I thought about it some more. "You know, maybe I should go two, two, and two." And the more I considered the sum, the more I was convinced I was underselling myself. "You know what?" I said to Ari at last. "I'm going to ask for three, three, and four and a half"—$3 million in annual salary, $3 million in stock, and $4.5 million in stock options. Remember: I don't come cheap.

Feinberg's mandate was to approve the compensation for the twenty-five top executives at each of seven companies governed by TARP's salary oversight provisions: four were related to the auto industry bailout; the other three were Bank of America, Citigroup, and AIG. He was a little taken aback by the number I was seeking. He said it was more than double what anyone else was getting, under his office's supervision.

"Couldn't you go for something smaller, maybe seven million?" he said.

I was adamant. "Nope. Ten. I'm worth it."

He backed off. I'd get my asking price. *Wow*, I thought. *They really need someone to start fixing this mess, and pronto.*

I had a few other requirements, one of them being liberal access to the corporate jet, and another, that I didn't want to commit myself for long. "I'll do it for about a year, two at the most," I told Dammerman. And of paramount importance: I did not want to be consumed in endless dialogue with Washington. For that reason, I went along with Liddy's proposal that the positions of CEO and board chairman, traditionally held by one person at AIG, be split. It was just as well that I didn't have to deal with all the political crap. Harvey Golub, a former CEO of American Express who joined the AIG board of directors earlier that year, was tapped for the chairman's position. He pronounced himself fine with dealing with Washington, although I'd learn very shortly that we were not a match made in boardroom heaven.

In the meantime, I needed to let AIG's workforce know the new top guy was not some remote, beaming figurehead in a nicely tailored suit. They had to believe that I'd be a leader who listened, one who when he spoke didn't sugarcoat the truth, hide behind corporate clichés. If there's anything I loathe, it's the business person who looks at you with a pasted-on smile, spouting the company line or nodding in completely unconvincing agreement—what is known, in one of my favorite expressions, as "grin-fucking."

So in that very first town-hall meeting, I tried to speak the truth. No grin-fucking by this CEO! I would share as much as I could about what was going on. Liddy introduced me to the assembled employees. He spoke generally—and enthusiastically—about the plan he and Reynolds had dreamed up, which included spinning off several AIG franchises that would "become public companies unto themselves." He was extremely gracious in his remarks about me: "Bob Benmosche is someone that you all will enjoy working with and for. . . . He knows the industry well. . . . You'll just enjoy his style and his openness and his willingness to mix it up with you all."

I wasn't going to mix it up with Liddy in this forum by challenging his characterization of Reynolds's plan. But I also wasn't going to pretend that the status quo would stand. "I have an obligation to all of you to think about this organization differently," I said. "We're going to have to create more discrete businesses and then when we get the fair value for those businesses, for the enterprise, that's when we're going to sell them. It's not going to be before.

"I'm appalled at how much pressure has been put on all of you to just sell it no matter what, because the Fed wants out or the Treasury wants out. If they want out in a hurry, they shouldn't have come in, in the first place."

I explained that my desire to depart from AIG tradition and have the CEO and board chairman functions divided grew out of a need to focus on rebuilding—and my distaste for politicians. "Somebody has to go to Washington and talk to them," I said. "I'm not doing it. . . . It's unbelievably consuming, and the return for the effort is very small. All those people wanted to do in those hearings was to be heard. They had no desire to listen."

I noticed that some eyes rolled the minute I brought up delaying the sell-off. The reaction was not surprising. But I wanted the employees to understand that AIG's recovery would be managed by us. In the upper ranks of the firm, the shape of that recovery was still nebulous. There were people at the senior levels of some AIG franchises who had ideas of spinning off their entities through IPOs, initial public offerings of stock, in effect becoming CEOs on their own. Many of these were foolhardy schemes that would have severely damaged the company. These entities would never have found sufficient support in the capital markets and some would have just collapsed. This freelancing behavior would have to be shut down.

My main objective was to try to give the workers back their backbones. "This is just god-awful, what they did to all of you," I said. "I can't tell you how angry I get, and I said to all of the key people in Washington I met over the last two weeks, I said, 'Why in God's name would you want me to be your CEO? I'm angry about everything you did. There wasn't anything you did right!'"

"So I don't know who's listening right now," I added. "But I hope it's just AIG people, and you don't tell everybody. . . . Try to keep it among ourselves for a while."

Fat chance.

# TWO

# WE'RE NOT DEAD, AND YOU'RE NOT DEAD, OR WHAT HE DID IS CRIMINAL

"BULLSHIT!"

This was the esteemed Treasury secretary of the United States, speaking about AIG. And more specifically, about a prediction by Jim Millstein, his man in charge of protecting the taxpayers' investment in the company during most of my AIG tenure. Millstein was expressing to the secretary his conviction that the company would make good on the billions upon billions in government funds we'd been given to get our house in order.

"Bullshit! You're not going to get all my money back!" Geithner scoffed.

"Yeah, we are," Millstein responded. "In fact, we're probably going to make a profit."

"There's just no way. If you told me in September of 2008 that we were going to get all of that money, and all the extra money we put into this on top of that, back, I would have told you, you were out of your mind. I still don't believe it, Jim."

"Well, you'll see. It's going to depend on the stock market and where things trade, but I think you're going to get all your money back."

Getting all the money back. Geithner may not have seen this as doable, but I did. We had a chance, I thought, if we did it my way. And doing it my way was going to require a major adjustment in the unfortunate course AIG was then on, a direction that had been encouraged by some in Washington and adopted by an unwieldy AIG management structure groping for an answer. Because when I got there, the plan basically was just stripping AIG, piece by piece, like a house in foreclosure, and selling the furniture and the fixtures for whatever price they might fetch.

It was probably easier to think of liquidation as a solution than to conceive of a scenario in which a smaller, more reasonably structured AIG could both pay off its debts and become profitable again. Because in terms of the size of the rescue, we were in uncharted terrain; a year before, AIG had come within hours of insolvency, arousing fears it would take the rest of the financial system down with it, as the venerable investment bank Lehman Brothers collapsed and mortgage giants Fannie Mae and Freddie Mac teetered. With banks no longer willing to extend AIG credit or lend it money to meet its obligations to clients and employees, the Federal Reserve Bank of New York had stepped into the vacuum as its lender. It put in place a variety of loans and "special purpose vehicles," i.e., entities that held corporate assets to shore up the company, to the tune of about $93.6 billion. Treasury would follow, providing another $67.8 billion, to buy 79.9 percent of the company's stock. AIG was authorized to draw even more than that—to a total of $182.3 billion.

Geithner was not the only one who harbored the suspicion that taxpayers would never again see these billions. A belief the country would get stiffed was widely held in 2009, and persisted long after; Geithner had the aforementioned conversation with Millstein in the late spring of 2010. And given what had happened, the suspicion was neither difficult to understand nor entirely unjustified. Mind-boggling amounts of taxpayer money had been committed not only to AIG, but also to banks like Citigroup and Bank of America, as well as to the government-backed mortgage giants Fannie Mae and Freddie Mac. With Main Street taking a hit, you couldn't blame people for their lack of faith that Big Business would do the right thing with their money. Early in 2009, a measly 14 percent of respondents to a CNN poll thought the bailout money was helping. Three years later, the opinion needle still had not budged: a 2012 Harris poll found, for instance, only 15 percent of Americans thought that the rescue of "insurance companies" had helped the economy.

Of course, by "insurance companies," the pollster meant one insurance company in particular, the only insurance company embroiled in the financial crisis. Founded in a two-room office in Shanghai, China, in 1919 by Cornelius Vander Starr, the firm that later was named AIG would by the 2000s become a $1 trillion conglomerate of global businesses selling property and casualty, mortgage, commercial, and life insurance. It would indeed grow into the largest insurance company in the world and it had, in its eagerness to grow further, branched out into the financial-services and asset-management businesses.

Getting the public's head around the idea that an insurance company could become a keystone in the world's financial structure, one that had to be saved at any cost, was never successfully achieved over the course of the crisis. In part it was probably because most politicians didn't understand how the economy worked—even President Bush, at the outset of the crisis, questioned how this could possibly be. The widespread head-scratching about AIG's role clearly fed the popular mistrust about whether the rescue was worth it.

The negativity, which was pretty relentless before I got to AIG, did not abate. One could hear and read all the time about the skepticism over where the money was going. Some of the chatter was irresponsible: maybe you recall the publicity-stunt artist Michael Moore showing up at an AIG office building in Lower Manhattan with crime-scene tape to make a "citizen's arrest" of AIG's board of directors, an event that showed up in his 2009 movie, *Capitalism: A Love Story*. Far more credible sources were sowing doubts about AIG's handling of the money, too.

The *Wall Street Journal*'s widely read "Heard on the Street" column opined in an item headlined "Ensuring Trouble at AIG" that the "dysfunctional situation" at the company "could end very badly for the taxpayer." The *New York Times* concurred: "The odds that taxpayers will even get their money back, let alone a return, still look long," it declared. *The AIG Rescue*, a 283-page report issued in June 2010 by a congressional oversight panel headed by Elizabeth Warren—soon an Obama Administration official, and after that a senator from Massachusetts—noted ominously: "It remains unclear whether taxpayers will ever be repaid in full." Skeptics could be found everywhere, from the top echelons of government to the boardroom of, yes, AIG.

We'll get to the implications of doing business in this atmosphere, as I lay out in forthcoming chapters just how we managed to prove the naysayers wrong. But this begins to give you a taste of what we were up against on a psychological level, and more to the point, what I was up against, when I first walked through the doors of AIG's executive offices. Although I was welcomed into the AIG fold with the mixture of expectation and wariness that accompanies any new leader, I wasn't of a mind to enter 70 Pine Street grin-fucking my way through the building. This was partly because I had only just begun to figure out this Balkanized operation, and because I simply did not know whom I could trust.

Millstein, who segued to the public sector from his role as a corporate restructuring whiz at Lazard, the financial advisory firm, would prove to be a reliable, even irreplaceable, ally at Treasury. I was also extremely fortunate that his counterpart at the Federal Reserve Bank of New York, Sarah Dahlgren, a senior vice president in charge of monitoring the Fed's relations with AIG, was just as intuitive, forthright, and encouraging. Feinberg, the pay czar, would be the third member of this essential trio. Although I was leery of the government's intrusions in our operations, I knew that maintaining open communication with these front-line players was only going to help in the long run.

At AIG, I would have to begin to assemble a team with which I was comfortable. Ultimately, that group would consist of some experienced

AIG executives, such as David Herzog, the chief financial officer, and Brian Schreiber, a key executive in investments, as well as people with special expertise I brought in from other financial institutions. One of the latter group would be Peter Hancock, a risk expert who in late summer of 2014 succeeded me as AIG's CEO. For the time being, though, I was going to have to get the feel of this unusual management assignment: I was at the wheel of a Fortune 500 vehicle loaded with people from in and out of AIG, who thought they should share the driver's seat.

One of my legacies, I hope, will be the spreading of the message that within any organization, leadership is indeed a shared responsibility. That idea must become part of the entire operation's DNA. People must feel they have the freedom to do all kinds of things, including make mistakes, or they will never succeed. It's why at AIG I created a seminar on leadership for the company's top three thousand managers. "Leading Leaders," as I called it, was a training program that I conducted for the company around the country even after I retired.

Embedded in the program is the notion that leaders lead by empowering others. "It's your turn," I always tell the managers, "to make heroes."

It was my intention, in August of 2009, to begin that process myself, of finding the people I could make the heroes of AIG.

In accepting this assignment, of course, I knew there were dangers. The outcome of my years at MetLife was deeply satisfying and financially rewarding. That would have served as a fine capstone to my career. This new chapter I was beginning: Would I come to regret it? If I wasn't the right fit, if the company foundered, the result would be on my watch. We've all seen ballplayers who stick around after their peak, with mediocre results. Would this be my one season too many?

On the other hand, AIG was held in incredibly low esteem to begin with. How much, really, was there to lose? And my intuition told me there was still value in this company. It just wasn't being tapped. With this notion in mind, I set about asserting my style and vision. If that meant ruffling feathers, so be it. I wasn't going to shy away from making the hot seat hotter.

I made it clear that I would be doing it my way right from the get-go. At the beginning of my "unofficial" first week, I was ushered into a meeting on the eighteenth floor of the headquarters building on Pine Street with Ed Liddy; Anastasia Kelly, the corporate general counsel; and two of the top corporate communications executives, Nicholas Ashooh and Christina Pretto. A press release announcing my appointment had been prepared. As part of the customary rollout, the PR people were eager to have me speak to the reporters covering the AIG beat for the major business news outlets.

"Okay," one of them said. "Once we issue the press release, we'll put you on the phone for five minutes with the *Wall Street Journal*, the *New York Times*, and the *FT* [*Financial Times*]."

I didn't have to think long for a response.

"No, you won't."

"Excuse me?" one of them said.

"That's your job, not my job," I said. They looked unhappy. They explained that the press was expecting to hear directly from me. At this point, though, I really saw no reason to reveal anything to reporters, just to satisfy their desire for a few quotes. Though having nothing to say rarely stops people from running their mouths in public, I truly didn't see any advantage at this moment in opening mine. "We're issuing the press release," I added, "and that's it."

Early that evening, my cell phone rang. "Bob? It's Christina. I need to follow up with you," Pretto said, sounding nervous. Absent any comment from me, the *Journal*, she explained, would be publishing a news story, part of which would implicitly question whether I was out of my depth, whether I was prepared to deal with Congress and all the other stakeholders in this complex affair.

Pretto's urgent tone reminded me that going forward, the important players included some stakeholders without portfolios, namely the media. It would be the start of a steep learning curve regarding how the press operates, for good and for bad, in the midst of a hot story with global implications. I had to come to grips fast with the transition, with being thrust onto the biggest stage of my life. On this day, it suddenly felt as if my independent streak, the very quality I had been recruited for, might be used as evidence against me.

"Listen," I said to Pretto, my voice rising for emphasis, "you tell them I have a background in brokerage. I have a background in insurance. I have a background in banking. And we're going to work this thing out, okay? Good-bye."

The *Journal*'s story on Tuesday, August 4, as it turned out, played it pretty much down the middle. It pointed out that as CEO of MetLife, I had successfully taken the company public. It grudgingly noted that my "deal experience could prove useful." And it touched on the array of possible bumps in the road ahead:

"Mr. Benmosche will have to navigate AIG's unusual corporate structure, which includes both a board of directors and three trustees who represent the government's nearly 80 percent stake in the company. More broadly, the job in effect answers to multiple overseers in Washington, including members of Congress who have expressed outrage and frustration with the cost of the AIG bailout . . . AIG also faces potentially controversial decisions in the near term, including whether to continue paying bonuses to employees in that unit and executives elsewhere in the company."

The article ended with the quote Pretto put together after our phone chat, and it was just right. "An AIG spokeswoman said Mr. Benmosche 'has worked in the insurance, brokerage and banking industries and is here to do his best for AIG stakeholders, including its clients, employees and the U.S. government.'"

The smile with which I greeted Pretto when I saw her at a meeting at AIG the next day was meant to convey: "You're good." (She'd soon be promoted to head of AIG's entire global communications operation.)

The markets responded positively to the announcement, too. By the middle of the week, AIG's shares had risen by nearly 60 percent, from $13.50 to $22. The stock—which was selling for only 50 cents a share in March—had been making a gradual comeback all that spring and summer. And now the numbers were shooting up, a sign that expectations were indeed rising.

That same week, the AIG board named its new chairman, Golub, who had joined the board only a few months earlier. His appointment fulfilled Liddy's recommendation—one I would come to regret signing off on—that the duties of CEO and chairman of the board be divided. For public consumption, Golub and I sounded made for each other. "It is critical that we preserve and protect the value that has been built over the course of decades in AIG, a unique global franchise," Golub was quoted as saying. "Harvey is a terrific partner, and we are very much looking forward to working together," I added.

Still, the reporting by the *Journal* and others in those early days only hinted tangentially at a larger problem. AIG was being picked apart from the outside, but it was being pulled apart from within. The combined pressures of governmental scrutiny, public mud-slinging, managing the payback, and charting a sound future were traumatizing and fatiguing the company. Some people at AIG didn't even believe it had a future. The firm had been posting eye-popping losses: $62 billion in the last quarter of 2008—"the largest such loss of any company in U.S. history," said the *Washington Post*. Cumulative losses would top $100 billion by the first half of 2009.

The amount of the government rescue was staggering for anyone to contemplate, its structure a numbing, evolving jigsaw. In any two news stories, the reported number of how much we had borrowed never matched. (I have to admit that when filmmaker Moore stood on Wall Street, pointing a microphone at startled traders and asking, "Can you explain a derivative for me?", he was getting at something real about how little Americans grasped of what was going on.) Part of the reason the figures were so difficult to nail down was that regulators had to continue to improvise all through 2008 and 2009 as the ramifications of our part in the subprime mortgage crisis came into ever-fuller focus.

I got the sense right away that beyond the psychological straitjacket the debt burden imposed, problems had been compounded by the decentralized way the company was structured. Its various operating units seemed to think of themselves as independent tribes. The lack of a strong, corporate center served as encouragement to executives heading some of the units to use a vulnerable moment to make grabs for more control. At the same time, the panic-driven atmosphere was leading to a hasty unloading of major assets, under a misguided belief that selling them quickly was the only possible way out of this mess. And the lousy economic conditions were making it even more difficult to sell off anything for close to its real value.

A case in point had occurred a few months before I started: the June 2009 sale of 70 Pine Street, the Art Deco gem in the Financial District that had been AIG's headquarters since the mid-'70s. At sixty-six stories, it was the fifth-tallest building in Manhattan, a limestone and granite symbol of the firm's enduring stature. It and an AIG building across the street at 72 Wall were sold to South Korean investors for the rock-bottom price of $150 million. Letting it go for a song left a bad smell, an odor of desperation. A month before, the company had also sold its grand Tokyo headquarters, a fifteen-story building in the Otemachi district, overlooking the Imperial Palace. This priceless real estate—on a historic parcel granted to AIG by General Douglas MacArthur during the American occupation after World War II—went for a higher price that was still considered a steal: $1.2 billion. And after taxes, AIG only reaped about $500 million.

The shortsightedness of the Manhattan transaction was made yet clearer two years later, when the South Koreans flipped our headquarters. By itself, 70 Pine went for $205 million to a developer who converted it into luxury apartments.

I would have put the kibosh on the sale of both 70 Pine and the Otemachi building, but I was too late. (We did continue to lease office space in 70 Pine for some time after.) I was going to put the brakes on other such deals until I got a sense of what really needed to be sold, and at what moment it would get us the highest possible return. I knew that the firm was fully in the grip of this fire-sale mentality: it was all laid out in the plan hatched by Liddy and Paula Reynolds, recruited by him to lead the restructuring.

In light of my own plans for AIG, the title "Project Destiny" would prove to be highly ironic. Project Destiny wouldn't be our destiny, not at all.

After that first town-hall meeting, I started a campaign swing across the country, talking to as many of the company's employees in as many units as I could. On Monday, August 10, I startled the employees up in the Wilton, Connecticut, offices of the notorious AIG Financial Products—no CEO had bothered to visit in years, they said. Over the next few days, I'd visit with employees in Kansas, California, Texas, and Florida. The most tumultuous of those events—and the one that would get me in the hottest water, courtesy of another leak to the press—occurred on Tuesday August 11, in Houston.

That day, I addressed the employees of American General, a domestic life insurance branch and one of AIG's 200-odd operating units, from life-insurance and property and casualty insurers in Asia, Europe, and North America to such unrelated businesses as ILFC, a company that leased jumbo jets to airlines around the world. Like many thousands of other AIG employees, those at American General were anxious and frustrated and eager to hear what the future might hold.

I'm not big on prepared remarks, and I'm not a natural public speaker, either. But over the years, I've honed a skill at talking extemporaneously, at relaxing in front of a crowd, at just being myself. And on this day in Texas, standing before a sea of worried faces, all of them hoping to hear the truth, I was prepared to give them some.

This also happened to be the day Bloomberg News reported its exclusive about my "Croatian trip," set to begin a week later. While the bare facts were true enough, the article was a cheap shot. It left the impression that by traveling to Europe—where apparently there were no such things as phones or e-mail—I was not treating my new responsibilities with the proper urgency. The reporter even reached out for comment to, of all people, an "executive recruiter." "It's probably not a propitious time for an incoming CEO to begin with a vacation," the headhunter observed.

The story unfortunately was likely to cause grief for Millstein (who of course had cleared the trip, reluctantly). I wasn't upset, though. The article in the end proved helpful because it let the world know I didn't give a hoot what the Washington bureaucrats or Wall Street big-shots or the media thought. It was my saying, in effect: "Fuck you, I'm going to do what I want whether you like it or not." This salty summation may come across as smug. But it was exactly the persona I wanted to project. Some people, like Dahlgren at the Fed, understood what I was up to. About me she would later say: "You needed someone who would not be afraid to say 'F-you'—and I mean to everybody."

I was announcing who I was. And as I always say—and I will say again—to be effective, you have to bring your authentic self to work. This was me, doing that.

I was doing that in my remarks in Houston, too.

"The reason I want to spend my first couple of weeks here at the company out meeting all of you," I said, "is to listen to you and to begin to let you know that we're not dead. And you're not dead."

Since the beginning of the crisis, the employees had heard no such reassuring words. I wasn't going to coddle them—that's not my style. Another of my mottos—and as you'll read, you'll find I've got a lot of them—is, "If it ain't broke, break it and make it better." But I sensed they were feeling they worked for a broken organization already. And it incensed me. Which is why I said the things I said that day, words that later got the media all worked up, and a lot of people who now reported to me very upset and urging me to issue a public apology.

Because I told the crowd I thought the attorney general of the state of New York, Andrew Cuomo, was unfit for his job.

My exact words were: "He doesn't deserve to be in government, and he surely shouldn't be attorney general of the State of New York. What he did is criminal. You don't create lynch mobs to go out to people's homes and do the things he did."

This was in response to a reasonable, if difficult, question from the audience: "How will you be able to get the very critical Congress and attorney generals to stop trashing us and attacking us every time we do anything?"

My answer came from the head, but also the heart. I referred to the browbeating Liddy received back in March. "I would never, ever, ever let anybody in Congress—and I feel badly for Ed, I've known Ed a long time and I've told him this personally, and I understand the pressure he was under at the time—I would never, ever let them talk to me the way they talked to him. I would have told them what to do with this job, and I would have said it on TV. 'You can stick it where the sun don't shine!'" And then I started in on Cuomo, whose grandstanding in wanting to name names I found so reprehensible. Protesters had in fact begun showing up at AIG employees' homes. The threats so terrorized some families that they had to send their children to stay with relatives.

"The worst thing that will ever happen to him is when he and I meet in the room and I close the door and all of the people disappear," I said. "So how am I going to deal with him? The question is, how in the hell is he going to deal with me?"

This was a wildly popular statement in that room, as you might imagine. Applause and cheers went up. It was cathartic for these men and women to have someone not only stick up for them, but also seem willing to call the big boys out. Sure, I knew the audience I was playing to, as I tried to explain later, after I began to realize just how transparent was the fishbowl in which I was now swimming.

It takes a healthy ego to bear up when the backlash comes. You're not always going to get pats on the back for exposing your true self, especially when your honesty is used against you by those who don't share your vision, don't like your style, or just plain feel threatened by you. And besides, the discomfort provoked by my saying I was headed to Croatia had nothing on what happened after I got there.

Villa Splendid was the name we gave to our home outside Dubrovnik, overlooking the Adriatic. I'd fallen in love with the area while on a business trip for Paine Webber back in 1986, and when I returned in 1999 on a wine lover's crawl, I was told by a local grower about the estate, once owned by the treasurer of the king of Yugoslavia. The eight-thousand-square-foot house and the surrounding grounds were in shambles when I paid about $1 million for them in 2001; the place was for a time used as a disco, and then had been hit by bullets when soldiers were housed there during the warfare over the breakup of the Yugoslav federation in the early to mid-1990s.

I spent the next few years refurbishing the stone house and cottages on the property. It now truly is splendid, my favorite place on earth. While my children and grandchildren visit occasionally, it operates at other times as a high-end bed-and-breakfast. Learning that a prized local grape may have been the precursor to California's Zinfandel, I decided it would be fun to grow my own. So in 2006, I bought two plots of land on the picturesque Peljesac peninsula: a two-acre vineyard in Dingac, and a larger, twelve-acre tract in Viganj.

I had promised to be there in August 2009 for our first-ever grape harvest, on vines we'd imported from California. The event was of special significance because it represented a return of the Zinfandel variety to this wine-growing region of the country after an absence of more than a century.

I know, it smacks of the concerns of a 1-percenter. But I'd been very clear before I took the job that not being able to make this trip would be a deal breaker. It was emotional for me, as I'd grown to love the earthy, hardworking people of the countryside outside Dubrovnik.

Which is where a man with a TV camera found me shortly after I arrived in Croatia for the harvest. It was a gorgeous, sun-baked August day on the steep slopes of my vineyard in Viganj. I was out there with a pair of garden shears and a plastic pallet helping to collect the grapes that would be used to produce our 2009 Zinfandel, with renowned Croatian winemakers Marija and Boris Mrgudic, under our own Benmosche Family label. Standing amid the local residents observing the harvest was the guy with the mike. He asked if he could interview me.

"Who are you?" I asked, figuring he was covering the harvest for some local TV station.

He told me he was Boris Cerni, and that he worked for Bloomberg, based in neighboring Slovenia.

"Are you going to do the same as your predecessors, selling units of AIG at fire-sale prices? Or, how do you plan to fix AIG?" he asked, pushing the mike at me.

I didn't consider the "optics," though the resulting pictures didn't exactly show me sipping piña coladas by a pool, either. It was sort of funny, actually, that the tagline Bloomberg would run under the shot of me schlepping the grapes up the hill was "Benmosche Vacationing in Croatia." In any event, Cerni asked a question, and I answered.

"The most important thing to remember is that AIG is still the largest insurance company in the world," I said. "And it's made up of over 100,000 really high-quality people. And so my first charge is to get the company to operate at the level it used to operate, being world class and one of the best there is in the industry. The fact is, we owe the U.S. government a lot of money and we're not going to be able to pay it back just by our profits, and so we will sell some of the company off, but only at the right time at the right price.

"The government is working with us, they want us to do things in a very prudent, smart way. It's important we pay back the government, but at the end of the day, we have . . . groups we have to deal with in the U.S., Asia, and Europe, and we also have to recognize that we have employees, we have customers in those countries and regions of the world. And then we have the people we owe money to. So you will see us make AIG a little smaller—it is too big for any one person to run, it's huge—and you'll see at the end of the day we believe we'll be able to pay back the government. And our hope is we'll be able to do something for the shareholders as well."

He asked other questions, and I answered those, too. I emphasized I wouldn't be rushed into selling anything. Echoing my remarks at AIG, I said: "I don't liquidate things, I build them."

Like many of the things I was saying publicly, my remarks were aimed at a specific audience—not Congress or the general public, but at AIG's employees and investors. The interview ended up having an impact. Our stock continued to climb—a function, I thought, mostly of impulse buying by day traders. By August 21, the day after Bloomberg posted Cerni's video, it was nearing $33 a share, almost triple where it had been at the beginning of the month.

And then, things got nasty. Bloomberg had the recording of my August 4 town-hall-meeting address at AIG in New York. The first story, on August 20, was an amalgam of remarks I made to Cerni in the vineyard and excerpts from my earlier talk to the employees. My effort to tell employees we were in this together was now used to further an impression that I was dictating to the government.

The following day, in a Bloomberg story out of New York headlined "Benmosche Accepts AIG Job After Friend Chides U.S.," more of my August 4 remarks were excerpted. I was quoted as saying I had turned down the AIG job "three times" because I was "angry" about how Congress and the Obama administration had treated AIG. It also quoted me as recalling, as I was deciding whether to take the job, that a friend in Croatia had said to me: " 'How does it feel, here we are moving forward, and you guys are becoming socialists?' " The article went on to report that this made me "think about the motivation I had to do this job."

This was an artless compression of a longer philosophical conversation I had recounted, regarding how the bailout looked from abroad. I, of course, felt burned.

Yes, reporters do what reporters do, some a lot better than others. It was galling, but I wasn't the only one getting pissed off.

Millstein called me in Dubrovnik. My candid commentary about how I would be running the company was not playing well with his superiors. The impolitic tone of my remarks about Washington was freaking them out. And the backdrop for my pronouncements—on a sparkling coast thousands of miles away, in anything but business attire—was adding to the feeling that I was prone to wandering way off the reservation.

"Are you crazy?" Millstein said. "You've got to stop talking!"

I tried to explain to him that the interview with the Bloomberg guy had taken place days earlier, and that the other comments were from the recording of my talk to AIG employees when I was in New York. Millstein was reading them as if I had just spewed all these words in one gulp.

"Jim, it's a tape from my first week on the job," I said. "It's a leak from the camp that wants me out of there."

I told him there was more on the tape, if Bloomberg chose to run it.

Millstein sounded stricken. "You're kidding me," he said.

I felt bad for the bind he was in. Millstein was perceived in government as the expert who picked Benmosche. And here he was, having to explain the combative things I was saying, to the people who felt they'd saved AIG from oblivion. Mine was not the only professional reputation on the line here.

But the control of this story couldn't be handed on a plate to Bloomberg News. (After this episode, I refused to speak to them for two years.) Strategically, I thought it was important to get my initial plans on the record through other outlets, preferably via reporters in Europe, who had more distance from the mortgage crisis and might be more willing to listen.

So I invited to Villa Splendid reporters from Reuters, based in Belgrade, and the *Wall Street Journal*, from Hamburg. Adam Tanner from Reuters came first; he in fact owned a vacation cottage on an island across a channel from my vineyards.

Over the course of his three-hour stay, I showed him around, a tour resulting in an article on August 27 that mentioned the "massive villa's" million-dollar price tag and that I'd spent "several times that amount in rebuilding the house and gardens," and that I "used many imported materials, including imported Italian tiles, and added Viking stoves, an 18th Century French tapestry, a well stocked wine cellar and a huge 1922 Persian rug."

I showed him the villa's twelve stylish powder rooms, and when I took him into ours, I said: "Every bathroom is like a piece of art. Women go wild when they walk in here."

This observation did not endear me to Denise or my daughter Nehama.

Millstein didn't love the article either, but at least it wasn't a sandbagging. The *Wall Street Journal* piece the next day was even more on point. It accurately reflected my view that we could wait for quite some time, as long as three years, to sell or spin off some of our large businesses in Asia, such as American Life Insurance Co., or ALICO, and American International Assurance Co., known as AIA. This was a very different narrative from the one outlined in Project Destiny, which I was doing my utmost to smother.

And then, four days later, on August 31, Bloomberg News struck again. "AIG's Benmosche Says Cuomo's Bonus Tactics 'Unbelievably Wrong,'" the article said. It reported my remarks from the Houston town-hall meeting three weeks earlier. The story included long verbatim quotes from my recorded remarks. It did not go over well at headquarters in New York with the communications team, or, for that matter, the board of directors that had just hired me.

"Bob," declared the apoplectic communications people, "for God's sake, you can't say things like that about the attorney general! We've got to work with his office. You're going to have to apologize."

I refused to apologize for the content of my statements—only the tone. A statement was drawn up to that effect: "Mr. Benmosche now recognizes that the New York attorney general resisted public pressure to discuss the names of AIG employees during the controversy in March regarding compensation, and with emotions running high, he noted the importance of all parties to proceed with care and sober judgment."

What Cuomo had done in March, actually, was merely retract his threat after some of the employees had agreed to return some of the bonus money. ("If a person returns the money, I don't believe there's a public interest in releasing their name," he said at the time.) From my perspective, the bonus money should have been paid, and it was wrong to ask these workers to return it.

This led to the follow-up headline by Reuters: "AIG CEO Regrets

Sharp Criticism of Cuomo." The story included my explanatory remarks, which I really don't consider an apology. "You can characterize me as a goon. Or you can characterize me as somebody who is attempting to deal with a complex issue of a very demoralized employee force, and said those things to them in confidence to reassure them that they no longer have to be afraid."

My reference to "lynch mobs," though, was overheated and just plain stupid. I repeated the analogy, in stronger terms, in an interview subsequently and had to retract it, again. I understand the unfortunate connotation, and realize that my hyperbole got the better of me. When my adrenaline gets pumping, I can go too far. I plead "human." Taking it out of context, of course, made it sound more horrible, and so that one extreme example from my talk destroyed the message. In this case, the remark also drew a rebuke from no less a figure than Elijah E. Cummings, an African-American congressman from Maryland, who opined that I should resign. (After I made amends, we became friends.)

I was learning, at the impressionable age of sixty-five, that my voice was a hugely powerful tool in this new job, by leaps and bounds the most visible office I'd ever occupied. I sensed, too, that it made some people nervous, people who were counting on me to guide this lumbering, capsizing vessel to calmer waters.

Millstein, too, was getting some Washington feedback that ran counter to the prevailing "Benmosche may be crazy" narrative. As the last of the Croatia stories was running, he received a call from a senior press adviser in Treasury who sounded as if he was in a good mood.

"You're laughing; that's a good sign," Millstein said, in a later recounting of the conversation.

"The stories are horrible, but the guy's a genius," the senior adviser, speaking about me, told Millstein. "He's totally inoculated himself. He's proven he'll say anything. So they could call him to testify and he'd give it right back to them. And that's something they will never do."

"Wow," Millstein said. "I don't know that he did that intentionally, that he understood Washington that well, but I get it."

Still, doubts about me lingered. The press guy asked Millstein if, after this spate of stories, "Would you have [still] hired this guy?"

Millstein would as a result be an isolated figure in Treasury for a while. The attitude there was if I worked out, he'd be praised. But if I didn't he was on his own.

I certainly could relate to this feeling. Before leaving for Croatia, I had put the kibosh on Project Destiny—the plan that was supposedly the Way Forward for AIG—in a dramatic fashion that I will describe to you shortly. I was now both the disrupter and the builder. And, like Millstein, I owned whatever path we were on. There'd be applause for the whole team if this bore fruit, but if it didn't, I, too, was probably on my own.

The doubters and the saboteurs stiffened my resolve. Given that the American taxpayer was our banker, it seemed all the more imperative to me that AIG replenish America's pocketbook. Nothing would be good enough, until we showed we were good for the money.

# THREE

# ALWAYS TAKE THE TIP

DEBT IS A FOREIGN CONCEPT to most kids.

It wasn't to me. I became fully versed in it at the age of ten.

I had no choice. My father died suddenly when he was fifty, leaving my mother with four young children and loans to repay. The amount of the obligation was pretty breathtaking for the early 1950s: a quarter of a million dollars, roughly $2.2 million today.

We lived at the time in an apartment above a bar and grill that we ran, called the Fireside, about four miles outside the village of Monticello, New York, in the heart of the Catskill Mountains. Named after Thomas Jefferson's Virginia estate, but pronounced with a soft "c," Monticello is the seat of Sullivan County, the home at the time to Grossinger's, a hotel popular with generations of Jewish vacationers and synonymous with the entertainers of the Borscht Belt. The county later became known as the location of Max Yasgur's farm, the site in 1969 of the Woodstock music festival.

My parents, Daniel and Lillian, moved to Sullivan County from Brooklyn in 1949, when I was five. They bought the bar-restaurant and thirteen cabins, arranged in a horseshoe on Route 17, that were rented to tourists during the summer and to businessmen and truckers passing through the area in the colder months. It was woodsy country life, so isolated that our nearest neighbor was a farm a half-mile away. Our apartment was pretty cramped, with me and the other kids, my older sister Judith and my younger siblings Jayne and Michael, sharing a bedroom directly over the bar.

I have a few vivid memories of my father, who oversaw the cabins and for a time worked in the kitchen of the Fireside. Because he was a meat-and-potatoes kind of guy, steak was a specialty of the house. He was also a portrait photographer on the side, and I remember the pleasure of watching him in the darkroom he'd built in the attic, developing the film and hand-painting the black-and-white photographs, a popular technique at the time. He must have gotten good at it, because he also held down a part-time job with the local newspaper, the *Sullivan County Democrat*, snapping pictures for its "Man on the Street" column. He'd ask a question of random passersby, and the paper ran their answers with their photos.

He was pretty strict, and not afraid to use the strap occasionally. He could be an extrovert with other people, but he had a hidden side, too. I'll tell you just how hidden: his father was a rabbi—and I didn't even know I was Jewish.

How can this be, you may well ask, when my grandfather, Herman Benmosche, was not just a learned Jewish man, but also a highly regarded leader of the Jewish community in Norfolk, Virginia, at the turn of the twentieth century? My grandfather pursued Jewish studies in Germany, then moved to London and served as a rabbi there before immigrating to the United States in 1894. Two years later, he became rabbi at Norfolk's Congregation Beth El. A man of wide-ranging tastes and talents, he was also an opera composer. One of his operas, *Haddassah, the Faithful Jewess*, "a grand opera in four acts," was praised by newspapers in Virginia and Washington, D.C.

His father, my great-grandfather, Moshe, was a Jewish soldier forced at a young age to join the Russian army, and fought in the Crimean War. To avoid a similar fate as a conscript for his own sons, he and my great-grandmother fled Riga for Cairo, where Herman Benmosche was born. Grandpa Herman recounted his and his father's exploits in an edition he called *Personal Diary of a Young Man's Journey.*

"In Cairo, Egypt, young Benmosche was born," Herman wrote, referring to himself. "His father served the tyrannical Emperor Nikolai the 2nd for 25 years." The diary is filled with vivid descriptions of the trials they faced in the mid-nineteenth century, including a passage about the arrival of Moshe and his pregnant wife, Sarah-Rivkeh, in Cairo after a five-week trek. In a flowery prose style, Herman noted that "in a land of different customs and habits, without a language capable to make himself understood, or understand those in whose midst Moshe expected to make his home, he had found himself rather in an embarrassing position. . . . The thought of having taken his wife from a good home into a foreign land was very aggravating."

So my family had a rich and colorful Jewish legacy that was never mentioned in the household of my youth. And I, being so young and without any other strong Jewish influences around, never asked. (Did I mention that my middle name is *Herman*?) Later on, a story was told to me that offered an explanation for my father's silence on the subject. At Grandpa Herman's funeral in New York City, an argument broke out with the gravediggers: their pay was short a dollar, and they demanded the money. My father, Herman's youngest child, was incensed. The rabbi was widely known for his charity—"a ministering angel among the poor and needy" was how he was described in an account in *Norfolk, Virginia: A Jewish History*—and here his memory was being sullied by pettiness. In front of everyone, my father pulled out a dollar and threw it angrily on the ground.

He clearly took it as the culminating event of a deeper betrayal. "I will never speak about religion again," he declared. And he never did.

I know I frustrated him. I wasn't the easiest kid, to put it mildly. My sister Jayne, five years younger than I, and with whom I remain close, will tell you that I was always looking for what I could get away with. Like the time a guy pulled up to the gasoline pump we had, and while he went inside to have a drink I painted his car white. I don't think it was a malicious act: the car was rusty and in need of sprucing up! My father didn't appreciate my pranks. One time I must have really ticked him off, because I recall sending a note downstairs. In big letters I wrote: "I am sorry that I upset my father. May I please come down? Yes? No?—Please circle the right answer." There are warmer memories, too, of him in the car, showing me how to drive. He'd position me in front of the wheel, in his lap, and explain how to keep the car steadily in the lane. Sometimes, when we drove together from Monticello to Sheepshead Bay in Brooklyn, where he kept a small photo studio, he'd have me recite the names of the upstate towns as we passed through them: Goshen, Chester, Harriman, Middletown . . .

My mother I had a soft spot for, and she for me. She was a practical woman, tough and savvy about running a business. She was also a kind person who wore pigtails all her life. She worked with my father in the restaurant and the cabins, but geez, if you got on her wrong side, forget it. On one occasion, a chef she'd hired tried to pull rank on her. It was his kitchen, he said, as he showed Lillian out the door. No, she replied, it's my kitchen! And out of a job the chef quickly found himself.

In all the decades I've spent in business, I still think she taught me as much about it as any person I've ever known. It was she who impressed upon me the value of a dollar and the need to remain ever vigilant about results. She dispensed to me my first doses of common sense. I can give you any number of examples, though one that stands out occurred when I was a teenager and starting to be of some use around the front desk, of our second motel. That day, the lesson was in how to guide customers to the decision you wanted them to make, a story I like to call, "Give them the pen!"

A man and a woman walked into our office and asked if we had a room. I was behind the desk and apparently, my salesmanship was lacking, because I said, "Yes," instead of "Yes, we have vacancies." More to the point, I didn't do what was required to close the deal.

"You should have handed him the pen," she said, taking me aside. "And you should have handed him the registration card, and while they're holding the pen, you ask, 'Do you want a room with one or two beds?' But you have to give them the pen!"

"Mom," I said, "they hadn't even decided whether they wanted the room or not."

"You give them the pen!" she exclaimed. "*Then* they decide!"

It was as if a lightbulb were being switched on. I had to help them help me make the sale.

"So they're holding the pen," she went on, "and they say: 'By the way, what's the rate?' But you never tell them the rate unless they ask. And many of them never ask. If they do and when you tell them, they think it's too high, well, they've already got the pen in their hand, right? The paper's there to sign—what are they going to do, say 'I'm sorry, it's too high'? It's very hard for somebody to do that, to put down that pen, once it's in their hand. So, son, give them the pen when they walk in. Make them say, 'No, no, wait a minute, I have a few more questions.' Make them *refuse* the pen!"

The guests made me aware that lives changed and relationships sometimes took inexplicable turns. There was, for instance, one couple who stayed with us for a week every year, whose arrival my mother looked forward to because the woman was such a lovely person. The trip was apparently their big splurge for the year. And then one year, the man showed up with another woman. "Hi, Lil," he said to my mother. "I want you to meet my wife." My mother told her what a pleasure it was to meet her, as if it was the most normal thing in the world for this man to be with someone else. In fact, my mother was devastated to discover that the woman she'd taken such a shine to over all those years had been his mistress. (This was the 1950s, remember.) After checking them in, she ran upstairs and cried her eyes out.

I took away from this encounter my first inkling of what professionalism means. The key point was my mother's poker face. In a service business, it would be fatal to let your own expectations of people get in the way. We were there to serve the clientele who walked in, and nothing more. As far as anyone could tell from our behavior, how they conducted their lives was their own concern, and none of ours.

One other story: A guest needed help with his luggage, and my mother dispatched me to do bellhop duties. As the son of the owner, I demurred when he offered a tip. My mother asked me when I returned how much he'd given me. I told her that I'd explained that as part of management I couldn't accept anything.

"Couldn't accept?" she thundered. "What's the matter with you? We're in the business here of making money, you understand me? *Don't you ever, ever turn down a tip!*"

Like in the old E. F. Hutton commercials: when my mother spoke, you listened.

Encouraged by how they were doing with the restaurant and cabins, my parents in 1954 decided to expand by building a new motel. Of the two, my father was the more entrepreneurial; he also had an idea to start a dude ranch on a four-hundred-acre property in another part of the county. They acquired the land for the motel, to be called the Patio, on High Street in Monticello. He planned to bolster traffic by attracting the patronage of state employees with business in the area, and charging them a lower state-approved rate. After buying the building materials for the 1950s-style, thirty-six-room establishment on credit, they were in hock up to their ears. The plan was to get construction finished that spring, in time for high season. Unfortunately, the motel wasn't completed until fall, and without the expected income, they were even more strapped.

In early December, calamity struck. My father suffered a minor heart attack. The doctors approved his release from the hospital, as long as he promised to rest, which he said he would do in the new motel, under the watchful eyes of the staff. He didn't keep still for long, though. An insurance company called; they had a job for him, taking pictures of the scene of an accident at one of the resort hotels in the area. It was money, and we needed it.

While he was driving to the job, his heart gave out. A distant relative of ours happened to be driving by and spotted my father's car on the shoulder, my father slumped over in the driver's seat, barely alive. At a fire-house in nearby Fallsburg, rescuers administered nitroglycerin. But it wasn't enough. He died that day.

After school, I walked over to the motel, where a plumber was work-ing; my mother was nowhere to be found. "Did you hear what happened to your dad?" the plumber asked.

"No—what happened?"

"He died today."

"No kidding," were the words that came out of my mouth. I had no tears. Rather than sorrow, a surge of anger came over me.

"Look," my mother said, when I finally found her. "Your father passed away, and we're going to have to figure everything out." I have no mem-ory of what my sisters and brother were doing, or anything else. Only my mother's words remain with me. "You're going to have to be brave. There's nobody here to take care of you. You need to go to school tomorrow." That was the sort of tough customer my mother was. Not unduly harsh, but not a coddler, either, even at a moment like this. I chalk it up to the enormity of the disaster that was facing her. Figuring out how we were going to survive was more on her mind than my feelings. I was expected to be able to take care of myself, and I did.

So I did go to school that day, although I cared about what was going on in class even less than usual—which is pretty hard to imagine. On a more profound level, the day was the start of an entirely new life, in which the concerns of the adult world became real to me in a way they never had before. It was the start of being responsible—sometimes, anyway.

My mother suddenly found herself alone with four kids, ages three to twelve, and an even more stress-inducing dependent—that quarter-million in debt. My father left no will, no life insurance. Financially, we lived in the moment. Decades later, after I became head of the nation's largest life insurance company, I could cite this to employees as evidence of the vital necessity of our work.

There was no bailout plan in place for the Benmosches.

With our spanking-new operation, we looked to the world as if we were doing well, but the reality was we were constantly gasping for breath. Keeping up with our payments became a family affair, especially for me, as the oldest son. I would become more and more involved in running the businesses, even as I took on other part-time jobs in the following years. My mother's brother, Julius, would also step up and become an integral part of our lives, helping us manage the motel and becoming a second father to us.

Other aspects of our lives changed: my mother started observing some Jewish holidays, and I, learning something at last about my heritage, decided to enroll in Hebrew school. At thirteen, I even celebrated that traditional Jewish coming-of-age ritual, my bar mitzvah.

I also learned at this stage of my life that few things can erode one's sense of well-being and confidence more quickly than owing a humbling amount of money. For evidence, I only had to see the strain it was placing on my mother. Over the next few years, it would affect her health to such a degree that I worried she might not survive.

On one occasion, when she was stricken with a painful angina attack and had to go to the hospital, I was left in charge of the Fireside restaurant. I must have been thirteen. "Don't worry, Ma, I'll take care of it," I said reassuringly, as an ambulance came for her. "Just do the best you can," she replied, a bit warily. Truth was, my knowledge had gaps. During a breakfast rush, when I was both waiter and cook, a guy came in and asked for eggs and white toast. *Okay*, I thought, *that's a little odd, but if that's what he wants.* So I went into the kitchen and put the bread on the grill, pulled it off very quickly, turned it over, and pulled it off again. When I brought the order out, the man says, "This looks very nice, son, but you didn't toast the bread."

"But you said you wanted white toast," I explained. "If I toast it any more, it's going to be brown."

In a working person's life, there are big lessons and small lessons.

In other ways, I was trying to grow up fast. I had started smoking at age eleven, and by thirteen, I was driving by myself. Yes, without a license. Once my duties were done cleaning up the restaurant kitchen,

Uncle Julie would toss me the keys to his car and let me take it for an evening spin as a reward.

So here was this cocky thirteen-year-old, motoring in the twilight on the winding back roads of Sullivan County, with the radio tuned to a top-40 station, feeling as if the darkening byways belonged to him. I'd light up a cigarette, roll down the windows, and with the music blaring, revel in the adult pleasures, trying in my immaturely mature way just to enjoy the ride.

For a guy who ended up a leader of the insurance industry, this may look like a cavalier relationship with risk. But I wasn't reckless, just eager for independence. I was actually a very careful driver, and knew to be cautious on the curves, to anticipate cars that might be on the wrong side of the road. My instincts for self-preservation were so keen that I never got into trouble for these nightly excursions—never once got pulled over by a cop. This bore out one of my mother's observations about me, that my mischievous side hid the fact that I was actually born ninety years old.

To help us make money, I worked as a stock boy in a local supermarket. "It's boring stocking shelves," I told my mom.

"You got a better job?" she replied. "No? Then do it." There's an important business lesson here, one I would repeat often years later, after I fully grasped the scope of its meaning: Play the hand that's dealt you. If there's a less-than-perfect opportunity, but it's the only one on the horizon, you grab it and make the best of it you can.

It was at the store that I met my first serious girlfriend, Debbie, a relationship that decades later would have an impact on me in the form of an emotionally enriching revelation. In the meantime, I continued to help out in our businesses. When my mother had another angina attack, and I had to tend the bar at the Fireside, there was an incident—my first encounter with the world of government regulation. I was fourteen at the time and tall for my age, but still clearly underage. A gentleman with a stern look on his face approached me as I stood at the end of the bar.

"Where is Mrs. Benmosche?" he asked.

"She was taken to the hospital," I said. "Who are you?"

"I'm with the Alcohol Beverage Control board. Who are *you*?"

"What do you mean, who am I?" I said, indignantly. "I'm her son."

This wasn't welcome news to him. "You're a kid. Why are you standing at the bar?" he demanded. "You're not even allowed to be in here. And if your mother's in the hospital, who's the bartender? Are *you* the bartender?"

I wasn't sure what to say. Of course, I knew that a minor serving alcohol was illegal and could get us shut down. At this precarious juncture for the family's livelihood, that could spell ruin.

"No—I'm the bartender!" came a voice from behind me. It was one of the bar's regulars, who overheard the conversation, and God love him, came to the rescue. "I was over here, talking to my friends," he added, as he strode behind the bar. The ABC guy was skeptical—in fact, he went to my mother's bedside at the hospital to demand answers. Fortunately, the matter was resolved, through the offices, I was told, of one of our state legislators, with whom someone in our extended family had a relationship. But it was an uncomfortably close call.

As I finished my freshman year of high school, we started to make some headway at the motel, even if I myself was headed a bit sideways. Earning money made sense to me, but school really didn't. I was allergic to homework and still bitter about my father's death, and bullheaded in general about doing what I wanted. (When I was a little kid, I so hated the badly fitting new shoes my mother bought that, to her horror, I used to hide them in the woods.) Between my rambunctiousness and total lack of interest in my studies, my mother and Uncle Julie decided I needed direction and discipline. And so in my sophomore year, I was shipped off to military school.

The New York Military Academy in Cornwall, New York, about an hour's drive west of Monticello, was as regimented as my previous life had felt unfettered. There were lots of rich kids there: I remember a whole group of fabulously wealthy boys from Cuba, the sons of rich exiles from Fidel Castro's revolution, when I arrived in 1959. And Donald Trump was in the year behind me; decades later he told me he remembered me, though

I didn't remember him. Unlike a lot of my peers, I had no trust fund. The people who sold us the early American lobby furniture for the motel had sons who had graduated from the academy, and spoke highly of it; knowing the school would be a huge financial stretch for us, they offered me all of their sons' uniforms for free.

So with hand-me-down threads, a job in the academy's dining room, and a restless spirit, I began this new chapter. Having been a Boy Scout, I was somewhat prepared for this more orderly existence, and overall, I will say that it was a great experience for me. It toughened me up physically—I wrestled and played football—and it bolstered my sense of independence. But I got into a lot of trouble. I still hated schoolwork; it bored me to no end. "I don't know how you learn to make money, doing all this bullshit," is what would go through my mind. My lack of interest was reflected in my grade average, barely a C. And though smoking was verboten, I refused to stop. I was brazen about it, taking drags as we were lining up for roll call. Before the inspecting officer noticed, I would swipe the butt from my mouth and stub it out in the calluses of my hand.

I smoked a lot—half a pack a day, in cartons I smuggled onto campus after trips into town—and naturally they'd end up catching me, eventually. I worked off the infractions by marching, and I was in trouble so often that over one Easter vacation I wasn't allowed to go home. I had to stay on campus by myself and march for something like eight hours a day. It wasn't that I enjoyed breaking the rules. I just didn't give a damn about them.

Earning money, though, I did care about. In the dining hall, I bussed tables three meals a day, keeping close track on index cards of how much I was owed. After meals, I stuck around to make a little more, stacking plates coming out of the dishwasher. I became a whiz at this highly specialized skill; decades later, I could empty a dishwasher like nobody's business.

It didn't bother me, working when the other guys didn't have to, but I was aware, and even a little ashamed, when I was reminded of how little we had compared to these other preppie soldiers. To my everlasting regret, I let these feelings show one time when my mother visited. Taking care of my younger brother and sister, and working at the motel, she found it hard to get away. She was also giving money to her poorer relatives. ("Mom, we don't have a pot to piss in. What are you helping these people for?" I asked. "This is family, and this is what we have to do," she answered.) Well, she was able to make the trip to Cornwall this one time in the dead of winter in a car that today looks like a classic but back then looked to me like crap, our 1948 military-style Willys Jeep. It was a frigid ride from Monticello, even with the jeep's canvas top on, and she arrived all bundled up in multiple layers of bulky outer clothing. I was embarrassed. The other parents showed up in limos and furs. Why couldn't she look like everybody else?

I was too much the self-conscious adolescent to simply appreciate that she'd come all this way for me.

"Why did you show up here like this?" I demanded, as she got out. Then I added coldly: "I can't believe one of those relatives you give all the money to couldn't bring you here."

My mother didn't let my cutting remark upset her. She smiled and said in a quiet voice, "Don't you worry about me. I'll be right back."

With that she disappeared into the ladies' room, and returned a few minutes later, in a beautiful outfit that she'd brought along. She'd known the world she was walking into, and what my expectations would be.

All these years later, I can still see her standing there, looking radiant. The shame of my sullen behavior that day comes rushing back, along with the powerful wish that I could take back the way I greeted her.

I gradually grew up a bit in military school, learning to be a team player through football, and to be disciplined through drilling and exercise. I was Lineman of the Year as a senior, and was promoted to platoon sergeant—my first real stab at leadership.

And in the summers of my junior and senior years, I came home to my first serious job, working for the Coca-Cola company. Since we knew someone in the state Labor Department, I was issued the special working papers I needed, and I started on a delivery truck at sixteen. A year later I was old enough to drive a small truck—yes, with a bona fide driver's license—and was given my own route. At eighteen I moved up to the bigger rigs.

The money was good. It helped pay my school tuition, and for the first time, I even got to put a bit in the bank. The work meant something to me, too. I felt a sense of accomplishment at the end of the day, getting things done. That's what the other drivers told me I was, a GSD. A guy who Gets Shit Done.

With Uncle Julie and my mother running the Patio, business started to improve. The construction in 1958 of Monticello Raceway, a half-mile standardbred racetrack, brought some more visitor traffic to the area, and skiing was becoming a big draw in the Catskills. Good thing this was happening, because the old, two-lane Route 17 was replaced by a new, modern version, known as the Quickway, that bypassed our cabins and the Fireside. So with the customer volume dropping, we sold that property and used the money to help retire some of our debt.

Wonder of wonders, it appeared I was going to graduate from the New York Military Academy on time in the spring of 1962. I wasn't sure what to do next. I toyed with applying to West Point, but my grades weren't close to good enough. I was just an okay football player, so that wasn't going to get me in anywhere, either. The headmaster was eager to help me find a school because the academy prided itself on sending every kid to college. So he brought me into his office to suggest I try Alfred University.

Alfred? I thought. What kind of name is that for a college? It actually was a well-established liberal arts university in western New York, best known for its programs related to ceramics because of its proximity to the headquarters of Corning, makers of glass and ceramic products.

I made it clear to the headmaster in my own delicate way that I was not acquainted with the school.

"You have to be kidding me," I said. "What the hell is 'Alfred'? This isn't a joke?"

My reaction wasn't the one the headmaster was looking for. But he arranged for me to apply all the same, and though what-the-hell-is-Alfred wasn't impressed with my academic record, I was accepted on the headmaster's say-so.

Despite my indifference to academia, I started out on reasonably good footing, although there were gaps. I decided to major in math. It wasn't because I was so interested in the subject; I just thought that's what smart people did. To qualify for the major, I had to take calculus. The professor was so pleased with my performance, he gave me an F-minus. I wasn't aware they had a grade that low. In any event, I discovered it was tough to get through calculus without studying.

I stayed in touch during college with my girlfriend Debbie from our supermarket days. Over winter break at the beginning of 1963, we went out on a date in my mother's Opel one frigid night, an evening so icy that when we got back to her house, Debbie's father suggested I sleep over. My memory of what happened that night is to this day a little foggy. But we did end up in bed together. A few months later, Debbie (which is not her real name) called. She was pregnant and pretty sure I was the father.

How does an eighteen-year-old react to this news? Well, I wasn't ecstatic. Starting a family seemed laughably impractical. But I wasn't going to do what some guys would do—just walk away. I went to see her, sat down with her and her parents, and explained that while I wasn't prepared to get married, my family would see Debbie through the pregnancy. We agreed that she would stay with my older sister in Boston, and then we'd see that the baby was adopted by people who were in a better position to love and take care of a child.

The baby, a girl, was born in the fall of 1963. After the adoption, Debbie and I continued to date, but we grew apart. We both started seeing other people; during this period, in fact, I met Gael, the woman who would become my first wife. We met on a train leaving Alfred, where she was also a student.

While I never got to see the baby, I would meet my daughter many years later. Her name was Beth, and she tracked down Debbie and me separately. I first heard that she was reaching out through a family lawyer, who called to prepare me for the news. I was not upset; in fact, I was the opposite. "Oh my God, I thought you had no clue," the lawyer said.

"No, I'm happy," I said, adding that I'd long ago told my wife and children. I was by this time married to my second wife, Denise, with whom I'd had Nehama and Ari. (My son was around eleven when he found a box of pictures of the baby that I had hidden in the basement. "Dad, you wore a condom, didn't you?" he demanded, after I explained the circumstances. "Ari," I replied, "if I'd worn a condom this wouldn't have been an issue!" I vividly recall Ari's zinger: "Dad, how could you have been so stupid?")

Later on, Ari's sister Nehama greeted the news with more aplomb. "Beth was born on my birthday," she declared, "and so I'll get to share it with my half sister!" For Denise, it was a little more complicated; she herself was adopted as a child and because she had run into some serious health problems, had been searching in vain for her own birth parents.

I received my first letter from Beth in 2004 or so. I'd often wondered what happened to her, and so an agonizing mystery was solved. (A DNA test confirmed that she was my biological child.) It made me feel complete, somehow. She has two sons and lives in California, and after we met, I took her family under my wing. They really became part of my life, and when I was on the West Coast, I made a point of visiting them at their home at the edge of a wetlands, overlooking the Pacific Ocean. Eventually, I would pay for the educations of her boys—my grandsons. The older one, who looks a bit like my younger brother, Michael, decided he wanted to go into the military and enrolled in his college's ROTC, the Reserve Officers' Training Corps program.

Learning that bit of information took me back to my own college days. At Alfred, I had enrolled in ROTC, too. Military school had made more of a mark on me than I could have anticipated.

My academic career would come to an end successfully at Alfred, from which I graduated in 1966 with a degree in, believe it or not, mathematics. The university was not entirely finished with me, however. Nearly half a century later, Alfred invited me to be its commencement speaker. On May 17, 2013, I was awarded an honorary Doctor of Business degree—the only time in my life I'd come close to being called doctor. But I did have some wisdom of a practical nature to impart to the more than 350 graduates receiving their diplomas that day in Alfred's McLane Center. I told them about the struggles of my own family: the debts that nearly buried us, the jobs I took on at a tender age as a truck driver and dishwasher. I advised them to seize opportunities and plan for rainy days.

"If you have no choking chain of debt around your neck, you don't have to be obligated to do things that don't make sense," I said. "If you do not have that financial freedom, you find yourself trapped in life."

These are words I believed in, words I live by. And of course, invoking them brought me back to my memories of the woman who gave them more meaning for me than anyone else ever has.

"My mom taught me in life, don't take yourself too seriously. And I don't," I told those students. "What she said was, in life, people will kiss your buns on the way up, and they'll step on your throat on the way down. Don't forget who you are. Don't forget who you are at your core."

It's thanks to her I never did.

# FOUR

# THE GSD GUY

DON NICKELSON POSED THE QUESTION as I sat in his Manhattan office, interviewing for a job for which I really had no business being considered. "What is the one characteristic about you," he asked, "that both your friends and enemies would agree on?" It was 1981, I was thirty-seven, and Nickelson was then the president of the consumer markets division of the brokerage house then known as Paine, Webber, Jackson & Curtis, soon to be just Paine Webber. A colleague at the investment house, Thomas Bianco, who had worked with me at Chase Manhattan Bank, where I remained, thought I should come meet the top people there to discuss job possibilities. Nickelson struck me as my kind of guy, charming, friendly, easy to talk to. So I responded to his question in my natural, grin-fucking-free manner.

"I think they would all agree that I'm going to piss off a lot of people, and most people don't have the stomach for that," I said. "But if you can deal with a lot of noses out of joint and some angry people, I'm going to get the job done."

It was an assessment of my abilities I'd been hearing long enough from those I worked for that I was starting to believe it. Organizations needed doers, men and women in a position not just to recognize a problem, but also to be willing to stick their necks out to fix it. I'd had this collection of impulses since I was a kid, to be the hardest worker, to cut through the baloney, to make things happen regardless of the risk—I was the GSD guy on the Coca-Cola truck. My brain wasn't wired for long hours with a book, but it was good at tackling complex business issues and pointing employees in the direction of a positive outcome. I had an intuition for both the worth of a buck and the value of a worker, what motivated people and kept them motivated. As I pointed out to Nickelson, in the cause of getting things done, I had no fear of holding anyone's feet to the fire.

A needlepoint sampler given to me by a friend has some tongue-in-cheek wisdom in it. "When you have them by the balls, their hearts and minds will follow," the inscription reads. It occupies a place of honor in my rec room. One of my other strengths evolved out of the financial independence I courted, enabling me to walk away if, for whatever reason, the work or the conditions became unbearable. I call this "fuck-you money." We'll examine this lofty concept in due course.

My leadership style is also rooted in my military background. In college, participating in ROTC was an important discipline-building experience, even though I wasn't 100 percent sure at all times I wanted to complete the training. In 1964, at the beginning of my junior year, I expressed my doubts to my colonel about remaining in the corps, which gave out scholarships in return for a commitment of two years' service in the U.S. Army, starting at the rank of lieutenant. I suddenly wasn't as keen on devoting my initial years out of school to active duty, considering that I could have been trying to make money in the private sector.

The colonel tried to set me straight. "You're one of the best leaders in this group," he told me. "If you finish ROTC, graduate Alfred, and spend two years in the army as an officer, you'll establish your credentials as someone who is responsible, who does service for his government, and who is a leader." His other argument was an even more pragmatic one: the Vietnam War was escalating; the selective service draft was calling up more young American men all the time. He warned me that if I left the corps and was drafted into the army, I'd enter as a private, rather than as an officer.

I graduated from Alfred with the rank of second lieutenant. While at Fort Monmouth on the Jersey Shore, I was assigned to the Korea group as an adviser in communications. That led to my posting in mid-1967 to an army garrison in Daegu in south-central South Korea. Some of my New York–bred stubbornness paid off during my army experience. On one occasion, I was assigned to lead a convoy through a small South Korean town. The mayor, objecting to our plan, refused to let us pass. It was a tricky diplomatic impasse, but with a mixture of swagger and plain talk I made it clear we were coming through whether he liked it or not. He backed down, we drove on, and I had further confirmation that the leadership skills I'd absorbed at the New York Military Academy and in ROTC were not going to waste.

Luckily for me, that was about as exciting as my tour of duty got. The more consequential event was my marriage to Gael, on a short leave back to the States in early '68. We returned together to my bachelor's quarters in Daegu, where for the duration of my tour we slept on a single bed.

As for my fuck-you money: that resource was an essential part of my career planning from the moment I was honorably discharged from the army late in 1968. Gael and I returned from Korea and headed back to Monticello; her hometown of Tuxedo, New York, wasn't far away. I had already saved $10,000—I was a frugal guy, the experience of watching my mother agonize over her bills having seared into my gut the need to count my pennies. It is even truer today—in an age when students leave school with outrageous loans to repay—that starting out with a clean financial slate, and maybe even with a little bit socked away, is an incredible leg up.

Fuck-you money was my hedge against bad bosses, untenable work situations, and sheer boredom. It was my get-out-of-jail card, even if it wasn't free. The hitch was that you had to be willing to use it. If you could do that, fuck-you money was a down payment on freedom.

It was also, in a conceptual sense, a first step into the business in which

I would eventually make my mark—insurance. Psychologically, it would remain an essential tool for me all through my working life and especially at AIG. Fuck-you money gave me the confidence to talk to my adversaries and my handlers the way I needed to, and the assurance that I could walk away anytime the frustrations pushed me to the edge. And several times at AIG, they just about did.

You have to have some feel for the squirrel's life to amass enough fuck-you money. In my twenties, when we had very little, my care with a dollar was, to me, a virtue, even if it drove the people close to me crazy. Gael, for one, found my attitude about money exasperating—like the time I came home to find a set of decorative wooden spoons hanging in the kitchen.

"Why would you do that, buy these spoons?" I ranted. The point of this purchase baffled me. Looking back, though, I have to wonder: What was I thinking? I mean, I was getting worked up over a five-dollar set of spoons! And Gael, in fact, was making a bit more than I was at the time. In the ensuing years, as I've become more successful, I've also become more flexible about spending when I'm convinced of its importance, or the advantage of doing so. Still, this trait has been useful throughout my career. It's kept me vigilant about costs wherever I've worked. And it has also helped shape my macro view of compensation: how absolutely essential it is that a person in charge of setting wages be scrupulously fair to the people who work for him.

Our first jobs took Gael and me in '68 to Washington, D.C., where we worked in research and development in computer-related companies. In college, I'd studied early programming languages, Fortran and Cobol; in D.C., Gael and I helped to develop early versions of personnel management software for the army. We decided after a year that Washington wasn't for us and so we found ourselves back in New York, where Gael got a job with a computer company, Information Science, and I tried to figure out my next step. My mother wanted me to work in the family motel business; I sensed tension between her and Uncle Julie, who was attempting to branch out into real estate but needed the financial backup the motel income provided. When we talked about my coming back, he asked whether that was really what I wanted to do. I realized his preference was that I not dilute the income stream further.

I was not at all sure where I was going in those days—certainly not on any conventional path to the top job at an insurance company. Most insurance executives rose through the ranks on the legal or finance side, or made their mark in investments, which are how insurance companies often earn the bulk of their profits. (Underwriting insurance policies needs to be kept in the black, but it is secondary on the plus side of the ledger: AIG, for instance, pays out millions in claims *every day*.) My path would not be through any of those well-traveled routes. I developed other skills: building on my experience in military communications, I was an operations guy in computers and technology. Instead of returning to the Patio Motel, I found a job with a New York firm run by former whizzes from General Electric who were capitalizing on a new idea, a time-sharing service that provided connections to computers by dial-in—the beginnings of remote access.

From there I moved in 1971 to a job with Information Science, where Gael was working as a computer programmer. In the corporate world, "personnel" was morphing into "human resources," and the building of computer systems to process employee records was at the forefront of innovation. I was hired to work with a variety of clients—Banker's Trust, Illinois Tool Works, Missouri Pacific Railroad—on automating employee records, creating inventories of workers' skills and performance. The military was pioneering all sorts of technology for keeping track of things that would be adapted later by the private sector: its development of systems to monitor satellites, for instance, would lead a half-century later to the widespread commercial applications for global positioning systems. This was yet another adaptation. Companies like Automated Data Processing, or ADP, were pushing the envelope in the sphere of payroll and other services. I was eager for my firm to get into the business not only of developing HR systems, but also to contract with companies to do the processing and computer maintenance for them. Because one of the problems with our business was that in terms of finding work, we essentially started at zero every month.

When Apple came on the scene a decade later, it seemed to have a similar flaw in its strategy. I thought it was strange that the company was not willing to lease its operating system to others. Not that it ended up in a bad place, but Microsoft at the time was cleaning Apple's clock, making a fortune by allowing other manufacturers to sell PCs with the operating system it had devised.

The assignments I had for a growing list of Information Science customers were stimulating. But the travel was brutal. It took a toll on my relationship with Gael and, after a while, on my mental faculties. The breaking point was on a return trip to New York from Charlotte, North Carolina, where we had a client. Now, routinely, I flew this route on Eastern Airlines, which would land me at Newark Airport. But my flight was canceled and I was rerouted on another airline to LaGuardia Airport—a perfectly reasonable detour, except that I associated LaGuardia with trips to customers in other cities. After spending the flight distracted by paperwork, I got off the plane and walked through the gate, where a woman, mistaking me for someone actually sane, approached.

"Excuse me, sir, where is this flight coming from?" she asked.

I drew a blank. "I'm sorry. I don't remember," I said, sounding to my own horror like the kind of New York asshole I tried never to be. It wasn't until I got out of the terminal that I thought to open my briefcase and look at my ticket. "Oh shit, I was in Charlotte!" I considered running back in to apologize.

It was one of those small events that contain a subtler meaning: I really did need to adjust my compass. By this point, my marriage to Gael was kaput, and my tolerance for living out of a suitcase had ebbed. The next day, I walked into Information Science's offices and quit. "This isn't for me anymore," I told my boss.

I didn't yet have a plan. But the fuck-you money allowed me the time and space to figure it out.

I had spent the next six weeks doing DIY projects and thinking about my next move, when the phone rang. A gentleman named Bernie Romberg with Arthur D. Little, a Boston-based management consulting company, introduced himself.

"I've heard good things about you," he said, explaining that he headed up information systems at the firm. "I need a project manager to help me with Chase Manhattan Bank. I need someone to work with them on capacity planning for their computers, so they can begin to forecast what's coming on stream, how much computer power they need. If you don't forecast it correctly, you could have a lot of excess capacity and a lot of overhead. And if you miscalculate you can't get your systems operating."

"Bernie," I said, "I don't know the first thing about what you just said."

He was not dissuaded. "That doesn't matter. The people I have working on it do. What they don't know how to do is get it done. And," he continued, "they tell me you're very good at getting things done."

There was that phrase again. The GSD guy. I got things done.

I agreed to a sit-down with Romberg, who flew into LaGuardia and met me at an airport bar. A bit of an absentminded professor, he forgot his money, so I paid for the drinks. I told him that to consult, I wanted twenty bucks an hour—worth roughly $110 in today's money—and he instantly said okay. "Shit," I thought. "I should have asked for more." He wanted me to start right away on a capacity-planning contract with Chase in New York. The bank sent me to a guy in their tech department, who looked a little like Howdy Doody, the TV puppet. I told him what I had told Romberg: "I don't understand why you think you need to pay me."

"Because I need somebody to help me get it done, because they won't listen to me," he replied. "They think I'm a space cadet." For the next few months I learned and then mastered the intricacies of capacity planning, then got the team on task and the job done. Arthur D. Little then hired me full-time, basing me in their offices in Fort Lee, New Jersey, to service the Chase account just across the Hudson River. Under Romberg's savvy guidance, my on-the-job education continued, as we shifted into other innovations like the building of computer databases. And I learned how a consulting firm like Little, which survives on the number of hours it bills its clients, generates revenue.

The instruction came in a phone call from Romberg. "I need you to stop what you're doing right now," he said. "You have to go to the piggy bank, because we're out of money."

"What do you mean, 'We're out of money'?" I asked. "We're a big company."

"We have a cash flow problem," he replied. "I need you to start billing hours right away."

"Uh, okay, but who the hell is the 'piggy bank'?"

"Chase! Chase is the piggy bank," he said. "Go to Chase, find work to do, and get on billable contract time."

So that's what I did. I knew the human resources people were having some issues with their computer system. So I called my contacts at Chase and I said, "You know, I've been thinking about your HR system, and since I do a lot of work in this area I think I could help you." I'm simplifying a bit here—but not by much. And the word came back from Chase that they did want me to consult on their HR tech capabilities. So I got the billable contract. Romberg was ecstatic.

Decades later, of course, I'd discover that for a host of consultants, AIG had become the piggy bank. The law firm Weil, Gotshal and Manges; Black Rock, the asset management outfit; McKinsey & Company, the global management consulting firm; the accounting giant Ernst & Young: collectively, they were paid about $100 million in 2009 by AIG, just to try to untangle the mess at AIG Financial Products. Knowing what I knew about consultants, I was infuriated by the massive amounts being paid out.

It was around this time in 1973 that I found myself at a dance class for singles at a country club in Spring Valley, New York, when a pretty young lady caught my eye. Denise Bar was a Spanish teacher living in Yonkers, also recently divorced. She apparently had her eye on me as well, because she dropped her dancing partner to dance with me. I invited her back to my house for coffee, which she drank, and left. A proper young Jewish woman.

We started dating. I continued to date other women, too. Denise will tell you that even after we became more serious, I explained to her that I wanted the freedom to see other people. Sure, we got along fantastically and I loved being with her. But I didn't want to settle down at this point, not after the collapse of my first marriage. This didn't seem to faze her. Many years later she would reveal to me how she always knew when other women had stayed the night at my place: one of the telltale signs was in the freezer. I, in my ceaseless economizing, bought meat in bulk. When Denise was over she would count the steaks. She could tell by the number of cuts that were gone whether I had been entertaining. An even surer indicator was in my housekeeping habits, evidence that could be traced back to my experience at the Patio Motel.

See, I learned in the hotel business that to be able to strip the beds in a room quickly, you didn't tuck in the sheets. They came off the bed much more easily. It was a ritual that followed me into adult life: I never tucked in my sheets. Whenever Denise slept over, she would get up in the morning and without telling me, tuck in the sheets and blanket on her side of the bed. If on her return the bed linen on that side was untucked—a sign that someone else had messed them up—she'd conclude I'd had a guest for the evening.

"What on earth are you doing?" I'd ask, as she tore the linens from the bed. "I'm not sleeping on the sheets that you slept in with someone else!" she'd declare.

For the life of me, I couldn't figure out how she knew.

Still, I was reluctant to get married again. But Denise stuck by me. When she was over at my place, she would even supervise my clothing choices when I dressed to go out with other women. (I favored polyester at the time. Mr. Cheapo, remember?) "You're going out on a date looking like that?" she'd say. "Your shirt doesn't match your pants. Go upstairs and change!" This was devotion. As Denise would later explain: "I was in love. I loved him and I didn't want him to look like a clown!"

At the same time, she made it clear she wasn't going to tolerate this arrangement forever. Every three months, she'd bring it up: "My dad is asking what's going on here," she'd say. And then: "I'll give you three more months; then I'm not going to see you anymore . . ."

I was still gun-shy because of the failure of my first go-round with wedded bliss. And marriage to me meant children. I was convinced that you had to have a lot more money than I was earning on a consultant's salary to support a family. It was the memory of a mother saddled with debt reasserting itself again.

The future of our relationship reached a turning point in 1975, when I was mulling moving over to Chase full-time, or taking a position at the Hay Group, a management consultancy in Philadelphia that wanted to hire me as head of its technology group, to help it get into surveys and the business of advising on worker compensation. I was on the fence. So, in need of advice myself, I was all ears during a conversation with a head-hunter for Otis, the elevator company. He was instrumental in helping me set priorities. I'd proven myself as a consultant, he said, but that would get me only so far. I lacked the experience of leading within a large organization.

"What you haven't proven is that you could lead a group of people from the inside, and get things done," he said. "And unless you can demonstrate your ability to get stuff done on the inside, your career's going to get capped real quick. Because there's a certain value to being a consultant, and that's as far as it goes. And then you start going backwards, because you become too expensive."

It was one of the most instructive bits of career advice I've ever received. I was hungry for greater success—Denise liked that about me—but my dearest desire was to make more money. That was always the goal for me, what motivated me to keep moving up. This sounded like a way to do that.

In terms of prestige and pay, the Hay Group was a step up but meant remaining on the consultant track. And going to Philly would have been a blow to Denise, who was teaching in a school district in northern New

Jersey. I was not keen on leaving her, and working for Chase did present the opportunity my impromptu adviser described. So I accepted the job as vice president in Chase's technology group. At the age of thirty-one, I was making $32,000 a year, plus $3,000 in profit sharing, and suddenly, some headway. It gave me the confidence to take the plunge again.

"I can't think of anyone I would rather have as the mother of my children," I told Denise when I proposed in November of '75. We planned to get married in Suffern the following April. Her father offered to give us $5,000 for the wedding, but here, frugal Bob reared his head again. "Denise," I said, "we can give that money to a catering hall, or we can use it to convert my garage into a beautiful rec room. We can have the wedding at my house." Which we did, exchanging vows before a rabbi as we stood in front of my fireplace.

I would remain with Chase for the next several years, building up my knowledge of HR and its systems—the go-to technology guy—and getting my first real taste of working for a large conservative company, brimming with tradition and office politics. With all the software and other technological innovations being introduced in the back offices of major companies, the seventies were a time of wild upheaval and corporate fighting for control among the people running operations groups, systems groups, and HR groups. I waded right into all that.

My domestic life was settling into something more traditional, too, only, wouldn't you know it, less than a year after we got hitched, Denise came up with the most surprising plan.

To give our marriage a sounder financial footing, she proposed that we get divorced.

Yes, this was the same Denise who couldn't wait to be my wife, and still very much wanted to spend the rest of her life with me. (I was the one who remained less than entirely on board with monogamy, as I told Denise early on.) But Denise also knew how enamored I was with saving a buck—hell, I'd furnished my house with stuff discarded from an AT&T office. We'd both watched a piece on *60 Minutes* about a problem in U.S. tax law at the time that amounted to an income-tax penalty for married couples. Knowing how much this sort of financial injustice infuriated me, Denise thought she'd make me happy if we joined other American couples who had found a way around the penalty. If we weren't married by the end of the year, we wouldn't have to file as a married couple.

It was just before Christmas, 1976. We were in Santo Domingo, the capital of the Dominican Republic, to visit my mother, who was staying with my sister Jayne, in medical school there at the time. Afterward we were supposed to fly on to Venezuela, where Denise had lived for part of her childhood. Her parents had moved back there for her father's costume-jewelry business.

In our hotel room, Denise was thumbing through a local magazine and came across an intriguing ad.

"Look, Bob," she said, "we can get a divorce here for four hundred dollars." The *60 Minutes* piece had described couples who divorced in the year prior to the April 15 filing deadline, and then remarried that next year, to avoid the penalty.

"Oh, you don't want to do that," I said.

"No, I really don't," she replied. "But I know I will never live through April 15th with you if we don't do it. But," she added, "I'll only go through with this if you promise that after it's all done with, and we're married again, you'll wear a wedding band." I hadn't worn one up till then.

"But I don't have the four hundred dollars," I said.

"Well, you can borrow it from your mother. You don't have to tell her what it's for."

I called my mother and told her I needed four hundred bucks.

"For what?" she asked.

"I'm going to get a divorce from Denise. It's about taxes. It's hard to explain." That was an understatement.

"You're an imbecile!" she said. "I raised my son to be an imbecile!"

She didn't deny this imbecile the money, however. Denise dialed the lawyer's number in the ad and, courtesy of her fluent Spanish, arranged for us to obtain a divorce, Caribbean-style—on Christmas Eve, no less. A guy in one of those old AMC Pacers, the little bubble-shaped cars, picked us up and drove us to San Cristobal, a city in the hills about an hour's drive from the capital. When we got there, it looked like a scene from some wacky film comedy: a country courthouse, with a couple of guys sleeping on the benches in front with hats pulled down over their faces. Chickens and stray cats wandered across the yard.

The judge who had been roused for this auspicious event looked us over as we stood there, holding hands. "Who's getting divorced?" he asked suspiciously, in Spanish. "We are," Denise said. He didn't quite grasp what was going on: "No, I need to know who the ex is going to be."

"We're going to be the exes!" Denise said.

He shook his head. "You Americans are crazy," he declared.

We followed him into an office, where he produced some documents for us to sign, and applied a bunch of official stamps. We gave him my mother's money, and presto! Divorced. The tax savings were about $3,000, by the way. They paid for the trip and then some. I was extremely pleased.

When we came home, we told no one—except the rabbi who performed the original ceremony. "Rabbi, we need to get married again," I said.

"What happened the first time?" he asked.

We wanted to remarry on our one-year anniversary, April 7, but the rabbi wasn't available that day. So we arranged for our do-over wedding to be performed in the rabbi's study in Spring Valley on April 11, 1977. We'd also learned Denise was pregnant with our first child, Nehama. "You know," the rabbi said, "I've married brides who were pregnant before—they just never admitted it!" The result was two marriage licenses and two wedding anniversaries, which in our private joke we referred to as 7-11. Soon after, Congress voided the penalty, sparing us from having to go through this again.

And I slipped that wedding band on my finger.

That gesture proved to be more than symbolic. I didn't want to be MIA in my own family. During my time at Chase, both Nehama and Ari were born, Denise left her teaching job to raise them full-time, and I made a rule for myself to be home every night in Suffern, an hour north of Manhattan, in time for dinner with the kids. I honored that promise almost every night.

I had rules at work, too: no breakfast, lunch, or dinner meetings; I liked to eat fast and head back to my desk. If anyone wanted to meet with me, my office door was always open. And I took an even riskier vow: not to succumb to office pressure and stay late just because some of my bosses did.

Not long after I started, a colleague noticed me with my coat on at what he considered an unreasonably early hour. When he called out, "Where are you going?" I replied, "I've got to get home. It's dinnertime."

"The senior vice president is still on the floor," he said. "If he sees you're not here, he's going to think you're not working very hard."

My reaction was not what he was expecting. "Let me tell you something," I said. "If that's how you're going to measure my performance, I'm going to fail big-time. So don't worry about it. I'm going home for dinner."

Where was it written that supervisors in our business had to measure their subordinates' work by how much of a marathon they made of their days? I recalled my mother starting her chores at home and in the motel at 6 a.m. and not finishing until something like 1 the next morning. The work never ended. Unless you're in dire straits, as we were, getting things done should not preclude having a life.

I told my team in the Technology Group: "If I hear about your marriages breaking up or your kids wondering where their parents were because you're here until late, that's not going to be good. If you think you're impressing me by staying till eleven, well, I'll have the completely opposite impression. Completely."

I meant it, and I kept to that philosophy, even though there were titanic tasks at Chase for an operations guy like me. In my more than six years with Chase, I had huge projects. Setting up the Human Resources Information System—a replacement for our obsolete payroll system (or rather, our 153 systems) for the 35,000 Chase employees—was one. We got it done in a year's time.

When those projects were finished, though, my own path at Chase seemed less clear. The politics there were intense, and I was pushed aside by some guys who were more willing than I to game the system and grin-fuck the big bosses. I ended up being given a very abstract assignment, and moved to another Chase building, where I shared a bullpen with seven other guys. I enjoyed the work—yet another problem to solve—but the momentum was not with me.

Which reminds me of a story. A guy goes out for a walk in Central Park and stops for a rest. Sitting on a nearby bench is a man who's reading a newspaper, a dog at his side. "Excuse me," the guy asks, "does your dog bite?"

The man looks up. "No, my dog doesn't bite," he says, and goes back to his paper.

So the guy sits down, whereupon the dog snarls and sinks his teeth into his leg.

"Hey!" he exclaims. "I thought you said your dog doesn't bite!"

"My dog doesn't bite," the other man replies. "That's not my dog."

In offices, as on park benches, you have to be vigilant about who is at the other end of every leash. So I was ready for a change. The way was shown to me by my erstwhile Chase protégé Tom Bianco, who had left to attend Wharton, the University of Pennsylvania's business school, and subsequently was snatched up by Paine Webber to be the assistant to the new CEO, Donald Marron. He suggested to me a trajectory that would, in effect, eventually lead me to AIG.

Bianco urged me to look into opportunities at the brokerage firm. Once again, I had to plead complete ignorance. They were looking for someone to build a "mission critical" product: Paine Webber's cash management account. "Tom," I said, "I don't know the first thing about Paine Webber. I don't even know what their business is. I have no background whatsoever in it, and HR is really where I want to go. I want to be in HR."

His reply has always remained vivid to me. "You know what you once taught me?" he said. "That before you make a judgment on an opportunity, you should understand it first."

In throwing my own advice back at me, Bianco was absolutely right. It reminded me of what I'd said years before to Bernie Romberg at Arthur D. Little, about not having the foggiest notion what capacity planning was, then getting over my initial trepidation and learning what I needed to get the job done. I could have stuck with Chase and had a decent if not stellar career in human resources. But I was only making about $50,000 after six years there. And I had other financial obligations. On the side, I'd gotten back into the hospitality business! On the prowl for new investments, I'd agreed in 1979 to rent with an option to buy the Monticello Inn, a ninety-six-room motel across the street from my folks' place, the Patio Motel. It wasn't the wisest business decision I ever made. The inn was a money pit, in terrible shape. The super-cold winter of 1981 hit me where it hurt. With wind whistling through the inn's badly framed windows, the oil bill alone was $5,000 a month. I was losing money on the inn even as I was trying to support my young family. Things were so bad that I had to ask my mother to float me a loan.

Bianco's words rang in my ears. I was a tech guy and the job Paine Webber wanted filled was in marketing—a discipline in which I had zero experience. But still Bianco was pushing me. The firm was years behind competitors like Merrill Lynch in setting up the cash management accounts, or CMAs—a type of account offered by brokerage firms, with checking and other services mirroring those offered by commercial banks. My marketing expertise may have been nil, but I was increasingly perceived as a guy who knew how to build a team that had the skills to successfully master and finish the project.

So I went to Paine Webber's offices in Manhattan and sat down with Nickelson, among others. And, as is my custom, I spoke candidly about my own abilities—including my go-my-own-way talent for pissing people off.

That night, I told Denise that I thought I had killed my chances with my bluntness. She was beside herself.

"I don't understand it," she said. "You've bought the motel in Monticello. It's losing money hand over fist. You've taken a lease out with an option to buy our neighbor's house with the indoor pool, and we can't even sell our own house because home mortgages are now at 18 percent. What are we going to do?"

She was right to be alarmed. I was watching my fuck-you money go down, down, down the drain.

Paine Webber, though, came through in the end. Nickelson and Paul Guenther—who would eventually become the brokerage house's president, and a key supporter of mine—offered me a job as vice president of the resource management account unit. It represented a hefty raise from Chase: I'd be earning $80,000, with a guaranteed $10,000 bonus.

I took it.

And over the next fourteen years, went for a ride on some of the most treacherous rapids of my career.

# FIVE

# THE HOT SEAT WAS
# MY SWEET SPOT

I MARRY MY JOBS.

That's how Denise would describe the intensity of my bond to my business life. My family meant the world to me, of course, and both Nehama and Ari can tell you that as they grew up I was there for them. Or maybe the more important point was that they were there for me. When they were little, the kids would wait for me to walk through the door before sitting down to dinner. Even if it was after 7 p.m., we ate as a family. Denise would give them a snack to tide them over and they'd do their homework or play. And then I'd arrive and we'd talk about what I did during the day, who I saw. My work really turned into a family affair.

When I traveled for Paine Webber, meeting with associates around the country, Denise almost always came with me. This is not the norm among executive spouses. She had given up teaching after the kids were born and began to study for a PhD, but she interrupted her routine when I went on the road. With Nehama and Ari in tow, Denise and I became quite the team around the country, working both sides of the room at various functions. Over time she knew almost as many Paine Webber people as I did.

"Omaha? I've never been to Omaha!" Denise would say, as I ticked off my latest itinerary. She always said she enjoyed traveling with me. But she had other motives as well. Mindful of my warning of long ago, that strict monogamy was not my thing, she came along to keep me on the straight and narrow.

Not that I didn't have more than enough to occupy me at Paine Webber, then the nation's third largest independent brokerage firm, with about 500,000 customers. I quickly learned that the bureaucracy there was brutal, and the aftershocks of the 1979 merger with the investment bank Blyth Eastman Dillon & Co.—a deal that almost broke the company— were still being felt. The merger was an attempt to grow Paine Webber beyond the retail stock brokerage business and into securities trading, mergers and acquisitions, and other aspects of the investment banking business. But the logistics of that process proved to be a nightmare, a huge drain on Paine Webber's employees and capital. And a number of key Blyth Eastman executives, blindsided by the merger, quickly left, making it harder for Paine Webber to successfully enter this highly competitive marketplace.

I was brought in to get a certain job done. Those words again. I realize now that they were as apt a description of why I was recruited for AIG as they were for why Paine Webber hired me. As with Chase and before that Arthur D. Little, I would show what a quick study I was. By then, I had pretty encyclopedic knowledge of the "back room," the operations side of business. I also had keen powers of persuasion; people responded to my taking command. I'm sure my physical stature was a factor, as was my, ahem, irresistible charm. Seriously, though, I became much surer and clearer about my leadership skills in my years at Paine Webber, realizing that I had particular talents as a communicator and problem solver. I imparted something ineffable: the sense that I was in charge.

"He sees the issues and he develops solutions for the issues," a colleague said about me in a multi-volume report on my abilities, conducted at MetLife by Kaplan DeVries, a leadership assessment firm, in 1996. "In doing it, he calls on everyone in the organization to respond and to give him their ideas. He has more aggressively than anyone reached out to the field force, to the managers and to the regional manager. . . . For example, he has these town meetings with all the salespeople in an office, or in a group of offices, or a region. He asks them how he can help them, what he should be doing. But he doesn't open it up to Q&As because he feels he doesn't hear from everybody that way. He goes around and asks each person: 'What's the major thing we should do?' He wants everybody to be heard."

One of my direct reports made a point about my willingness to provide space for people to take risks. "He gives you the opportunity to fail—I like that. He does not guide everything you do. He sets the direction, says what he wants to accomplish, and lets you put together the plans for accomplishing this."

This same person also commented on another attribute I'm proud of: my sense of loyalty. "He is supportive—this is a big one. He sets the direction, picks his team, talks out the direction and helps people understand there is a risk-reward ratio . . . Once we had set a direction and we were exposed, he supported me. If I need his support, I know I can count on it. I can get to him and he will be fair. He does not blindly support. He supports what is right."

I like to think these are some of the core traits that fed the belief that I always got my teams to the finish line, that I was an effective "closer." Not that the substance and style of my approach were perfect. "Very quick on the trigger," "A bit of a control freak," "The 'I-word' is very frequent": these were some of the tougher verdicts on my office behavior. In my own interview for the report, I acknowledged my all-too-apparent fits of impatience: "I have a difficult time dealing with empty-shirt types of people—people who talk a good game; great interviewers I call them, people who 'manage upward.'" I also owned up to a more unfortunate habit: "I think I may come across as someone who doesn't listen," I said. "I've learned to take more time to tell people why I won't do what they suggest, because I can cause a lot of resentment when I don't seem to listen."

My tolerance for criticism is no more evolved than the next guy's. But in the service of getting people to bring their best selves to the task at hand, I took to heart the more constructive observations of the people around me. There's no downside, after all, to acquiring more patience, or being a better listener.

And I needed all the personal artillery I could muster for what would turn out to be a fourteen-year run at Paine Webber, the longest I would ever work anywhere, and where the challenges streamed through like items on the stock ticker. If Denise was right, and I did get hitched to my jobs, this one promised to be one hell of a rocky marriage.

The place was a political minefield. The chairman, Donald Marron, seemed to me to be toxic; although I got along with almost everybody, I avoided building a relationship with him. The leadership model was less corporate than it was medieval: anybody who got close to him seemed to end up with their head chopped off, at least figuratively. Operationally, things were a mess. Paine Webber ran on what were to my mind antiquated systems ill-equipped to respond to the fast-changing market. And as I would discover, my first assignment pinpointed how lackadaisical the organization had been.

That job was getting the firm's own iteration of the cash-management account, pioneered by Merrill Lynch, up and running. When I started in January 1982, the brokerage house was way behind competitors like Shearson/American Express and Merrill Lynch, which already had CMA products on the market. We were, in fact, the last of the top five brokerages to launch one. These were accounts, linked to money market and other investment funds, that allowed you to write checks and draw out money. They also often were linked to a credit card, as ours would be to MasterCard. The advantages were easy access to your money and a higher rate of return than a regular checking account.

The dangerous precipice to which the Blyth acquisition took Paine Webber made the success of my initial project there even more crucial. Creating Paine Webber's Resource Management Account, as I named it, seemed an assignment tailor-made for me, precisely because it played to my greatest strength: getting shit done. And it appealed to me because it propelled me in a totally new direction. I was now reporting to marketing, a field in which I had zero experience. It was also a high-stakes venture that had to be set up fairly quickly—I was given a two-year time frame and a $3 million budget—in a company with a complexly bureaucratic culture that required skillful navigation. Paine Webber's late entry into the market only exacerbated the pressure.

The hot seat, though, was my sweet spot. I found the whole experience exhilarating. When there's a trouble spot in an organization, people often avoid it, hoping someone else will step up. I have always seen my biggest opportunities in these moments.

Leaving operations behind as my primary focus turned out to be a blessing. I was moving away from the bones of the organization and into its main bloodstream: designing a product, dealing with the people executing the concept, pitching ideas about how to sell it. This was fun, and a fantastic break from technology, which I'd come to feel was largely about people griping at you about which systems weren't working that day. I no longer had to worry about building computer code. I was now the client for the building of the code.

And because I knew the technology side, I had an unusual amount of insight into how the whole project could be built. Over the years, the range of departments through which I passed would be one of the pivotal cards in my hand as I applied my skills to ever more intractable business problems. My deeper familiarity did not always sit well with turf-conscious people in departments other than my own, of course, who on occasion saw me as a nuisance. This was the case with the operations people at Paine Webber, some of whom complained to Nickelson and Marron, who was still relatively new as CEO at the time, about my interference.

But the initiative I was heading up was deemed so critical that I was given extraordinary latitude. Operations was told to take a backseat, and if they didn't like it, they knew where the door was. As a result, at least one top executive was shown the exit.

Looking back, I have to marvel at how much responsibility was ceded to me, considering how new to the subject I was. I hadn't even begun to familiarize myself with some of the basic tools of the trade, like market research, the scientific collection of data on the reactions of potential customers; it was a friend from outside the company who suggested engaging a research firm to understand what was going on with the CMAs already out there, and to figure out how we might do it better.

So we looked at the cash management account offered by one of our rivals, a leader in the field, and what we came up with actually shocked us. It seemed there were real problems with confidentiality, especially for the wealthiest clients—our prime market. A broker in Los Angeles, for example, expressed the worry he was going to lose some of his biggest customers because the CMAs' monthly statements gave him access to an uncomfortable amount of client information. Instead of the traditional bank practice of returning canceled checks directly to the account holder, the CMAs listed the names of the people being paid right there on the statements, all of which the broker could see. This led to embarrassing possibilities. Brokers were now privy to, for example, the name of a person with whom a client was having an affair, or the famous shrink he was seeing. Who would ever want their investment account to be a peephole?

And even record-keeping itself was a problem: the systems were half in the twentieth century and the other in the nineteenth. Back in those days, transactions were logged in by hand, by operators who were instructed to record them as quickly as possible. They did not have time to decipher the illegible chicken scrawl on a hastily written check, so some of the entries went down as "payee unknown." This drove customers bonkers: "Hey, Bob, I'm so glad I opened that super new account of yours! It can't even tell me who I wrote checks to!" You couldn't say to people what you were thinking: "Next time, write more neatly!" Instead, the broker would have to retrieve a copy of the check—at the time a process that could take upward of a month. Gold-plated customer service this was not.

There were many disadvantages to a tardy entrance into the market, but the opportunity to fine-tune the introductory product was not one of them. Our Resource Management Account would in fact feature the

banklike service of returning the canceled checks to the clients, elimi-
nating the concerns about accurate record-keeping and privacy. I introduced other innovations, like issuing a debit card with the account, rather
than a credit card. Because money in investment accounts tends to be very
fluid, moving quickly in and out of transactions from day to day, I came
up with the idea of providing a $10,000 line of unsecured credit to qual-
ified customers. And perhaps most importantly, we signed a deal that allowed us to be the first in the industry to gain access to ATMs.

We had the system on line by the fall of 1982—under budget and a
year ahead of schedule. Our only problem with those lines of credit, in-
cidentally, would come with the accounts of some of the Paine Webber
brokers themselves. We opened accounts for all the brokers so they'd know
how to talk to their clients about them. In the bear market of 1984,
though, many brokers were being fired. So some of them went to the bank
and took out thousands of dollars as advances against those credit lines.
When it came time to collect, they gave us the middle finger and refused
to pay up.

At the end of that year, one business reporter did a write-up on the
swiftness of our launching the RMA. He described it as a "Pyrrhic victory." Now, I speak English, but not always the king's version. So I had
to look up "Pyrrhic"—"an empty victory." *That son of a bitch!* I thought.
I was so mad I went to our PR guy and ranted and raved about how we
should object to his characterization.

"Are you done?" he asked.

"Yeah, I'm done."

"There's nothing we should do, because you haven't done anything
yet."

"What do you mean?" I thundered. "I've done a hell of a lot!"

"Don't you understand? Nobody cares how much you think you've
done. You haven't sold anything," he said. "So you're out in the marketplace. Have you made any sales? People care about what you've actually
sold."

*Oh,* I thought. Okay, good lesson about how the business press works.

By 1984, the victory was Pyrrhic no more. We were No. 2 in the market behind Merrill, and by a year later, our average account size of $183,000 set the industry standard. The RMAs are still a successful product today.

"Congratulations," Nickelson said to me one day, as the RMA program was being put into place. "The book on you was you wouldn't last three months."

He was kidding, sort of. This was the kind of competitive ice I was skating on at Paine Webber. Almost everyone in corporate life gets caught in that kind of vise at some point, when you have to watch your back constantly. Denise recalled a time at a tennis tournament sponsored by the firm. Taking a break, the management team sat down together in the catering tent. One of the big bosses walked over and shouted: "You people, you're not supposed to be sitting together. You're supposed to be mixing with the clients!" It was those moments of unnecessary pettiness and hypocrisy you tended to remember.

But I did more than last at Paine Webber. With the support of Guenther and Nickelson, I thrived. My adaptive skills allowed me to continue to move, without fear, into new areas of the business. I was inventing a trajectory for myself that allowed me to consider, for the first time, really, how far I might actually go, and how much farther than I had ever imagined. In 1984, to counter an offer I was entertaining to depart for a job at Bank of America, Paine Webber promoted me to senior vice president in the marketing group. My responsibilities now extended to a whole bunch of products—the selling of IRAs, 401(k)s, pension plans, and annuities.

It was both an opportune and inopportune time for me to be branching out, because an economic downturn was compelling Paine Webber and other brokerages to reduce staff.

"We're going to have a bad year, and you've got to reduce your expenses now," Nickelson explained to us at a contentious retreat in Florida. This meant firing people—words no manager wants to hear. To quell the brewing discontent in the room, Nickelson posed a rhetorical question. "What happens," he asked, "when a dog has eight tits and nine puppies?"

He had our attention. Nickelson would later tell me he didn't recall relating this story, but everyone else in that room surely did. "So what happens if you don't do anything about the ninth?" he went on. "They all die. Because they'll all be fighting for those eight spots and one is always being left out. As a result, none of them ever gets a chance to feed enough, and they all starve. If you don't drown one of the puppies, all of them will die.

"So here's what I want you to do. Go home and drown a puppy. And save the rest of the company."

As harsh and shocking as this story sounded, it was absolutely on point. I would in time adopt this story as one of my own when I sought to impress upon managers the usefulness of ranking the performances of their staffs, of focusing on the top performers. "Celebrate their success," I'd say, "and stop crying about the people who don't roll quite fast enough."

I certainly saw myself as one of the fast-rollers. Another promotion came my way soon enough—though not one I'd sought—as chief financial officer of Nickelson's group, which ran Paine Webber's retail side. Number-crunching was not a task I aspired to in the least (that F-minus in calculus was still clear as day to me). Nope, being CFO did not thrill me. I was not the type to go weak in the knees thinking about tax laws and accounting standards.

"What did I do to piss you off?" I said to Nickelson, half-jokingly.

Nickelson explained that while he thought I had done well, "I really can't tell how good you are unless you report directly to me. I want to see what happens when you're on my staff." He added that this new position would require me to recruit some senior people myself. And hiring effectively, Nickelson said, was another test of a top manager's value.

In this new capacity, I was privy to a broader array of outmoded practices within the company. Too many departments still relied on paper records, a cumbersome and cost-ineffective way to do business in the computer age. In fact, we were having trouble keeping up with our brokers' transactions. On this score, the place was afflicted with a paralysis of nerve. When, for instance, I urged the senior VP in the margins department to confront the head of operations directly about the need to modernize, the VP looked stricken, like he was the Cowardly Lion in *The Wizard of Oz* and I'd told him to go get the Wicked Witch's broom. I said to him: "Look, you can't be successful in life unless you take a stand. Your department is so old-fashioned; it's all paper, paper, paper. You're not doing anything with technology. Tell him! Show some courage!"

He soon showed me what he got for speaking up. "Bob, I did what you said," the VP reported back to me. He handed me a copy of his assessment of the department's issues, which he'd given to the head of operations.

"This is good stuff," I said.

"I know," he replied, "but read what it says."

The note was scathing. "I don't know why you wrote this," it said, or words to that effect. "I don't know who said we had a problem, and I'm not aware of anything broken. And the next time you should ask me before wasting your time writing crap like this. We don't have any problems and don't ever do this again without talking to me."

"I appreciate your advice," the VP said, diplomatically. "But I think he's upset with me."

Not as upset as I was. I wasn't going to let it rest. The head of operations couldn't get away with this kind of backward behavior. I went to Nickelson and Guenther and I said: "This is just ridiculous. He's been doing things his way for thirty years. You need to figure out how to fix this, not me." And because I like raising the stakes, I added: "And let me know what you decide because I'd like to start looking for another job." It may sound as if I was overreacting. Well, fair enough. I was one of those guys who wore his feelings on his sleeve at work. I blustered. I was loud. Whether I was happy or unhappy, everyone knew it.

Soon enough, the VP of operations was gone. To replace him, they picked me. So I was moving up the ladder again in 1987, as executive vice president of operations, administration, and technology. It happened to come at a rough time for the company. The staff reductions were taking their toll; the firm had been losing market share. We'd let go of so many people at the low end that we didn't have the resources to keep up.

My new job was incredibly complex, which meant that I needed the people who reported to me to be on their toes at all times. So I was especially chagrined to discover that one of them, a worker with strong technical skills, was a serious alcoholic. The radical approach I took to the issue was entirely of my own doing, and it caused others to wonder about my style. I confronted him directly, and what's more, when I told him I was going to fire him if he didn't get help, I also dared him to take me to court.

"If you don't see a doctor by four o'clock today, I'm going to fire you, and you know, I have no right to fire you," I said. "And so when I fire you at five o'clock, you can sue me, and you're going to make a mess of my career. But that will probably take a couple of years, so make sure you have a couple of years to hang out, because I think I can get past this."

And you know, he went into rehab that day. I believe that I did him a favor (even if he didn't stay with the company after that). But my drastic and unilateral tactic was questioned. "Why would you do that? Without even asking anyone?"

No, I consulted no one. I asked permission of no one. It may not have been the smartest way to proceed, in terms of covering your ass in an organization that did not prize sticking your neck out. I didn't care. This was just the way I operated.

To effect a full-scale modernization of Paine Webber's back-office operations—and ultimately, to save money—I decided to move them from Manhattan to Lincoln Harbor, a commercial development on the Weehawken, New Jersey, side of the Hudson River, just outside the Lincoln Tunnel. It was unorthodox at the time, and not cheap—around $50 million—but it was also an opportunity to find the appropriate amount of space for the data center, for a third of the cost of office space in lower Manhattan. The bonus was distancing myself from the roller-coaster politics of Wall Street. It was September 1987, and my to-do list was out of control. In addition to updating the company's computer systems, my group was working on a special project for Nickelson, a report to the board projecting where the stock market was headed in the near and middle term.

Our conclusion? "We think the market is in for a 500- or 600-point correction, over the next twelve to eighteen months."

We never had a chance to present our findings. We'd gotten everything right—except the time frame.

On Sunday, October 18, 1987, Denise and I threw a buffet lunch in our home in Suffern for Paine Webber staffers—103 people (with spouses)—involved in installing a new payroll system in our financial services center and participating in a new training program, the operations managers' seminar. The latter was an effort to expose managers to parts of the company they'd never had the chance to explore. We took them onto the floor of the New York Stock Exchange for the first time in their lives.

"This party is a thank-you to two groups of people who have helped make this year successful for Paine Webber," I wrote in my invitation letter. The markets had been rattled that previous week by a sharp downturn, but the mood at the party that weekend was lighthearted, and I raised spirits a bit higher by giving pats on the back all around. "What we've achieved here is a new beginning," I told my guests. "We are finally fixing the company."

The head of the margins department came up to me with encouraging words of his own. Having gotten through a bad week with our systems intact, he was optimistic about the week ahead. "We're in great shape for Monday," he said.

Right.

Reams have been written about the confluence of economic events that led to Black Monday, October 19, the worst day on Wall Street since the great crash of 1929. As panic took hold, the sell-offs spread from stock exchange to stock exchange around the world, in a terrifying ricochet. The one-day percentage drop in the Dow Jones Industrial Average—more than

22 percent, representing 508 points—was the largest ever recorded, the equivalent of about a 4,500-point drop today.

Whatever havoc was wreaked elsewhere, the results caused pandemonium in my shop. Our job was to record and process the trades, but the orders were coming faster than we could handle them; as the *New York Times*'s Floyd Norris would later write: "The ticker tape rolling across the side wall was hours behind actual trading." In a business built entirely on speed, this was inconceivable. On the trading floor, Art Cashin, a Wall Street legend who headed up our operations there, couldn't believe what he was witnessing. "You saw prices disappear and you said, 'This can't be real,'" he'd recall years later on CNBC. Coming back from lunch that day, he spotted John Phelan, the New York Stock Exchange chairman, seated at a table on the trading floor. As he walked by, Cashin remembered, he placed his hand on his chest and recited for Phelan a Latin phrase. It translated as, "We who are about to die salute you."

Cashin voiced what many of us were thinking: "The world's over, isn't it?" he said to me. Given the way preprogrammed trading was set up at the time, it sure felt that way. As the market crashed, the pre-set computer programs, triggered by the on-the-spot prices, couldn't be stopped from automatically engaging in the sell-off; the system that ran trading for Paine Webber's retail group had no turn-off switch. My first thought, though, was that the worst possible response would be giving in to the panic. I didn't know where the bottom was, but I did know that the people around me were capable and that we had to methodically get things under control.

"Art, we'll make it," I said. "Just go back to work." Late that morning, I gathered my team. "Look, I don't know a fraction of what you know," I said. "What I need you to do is just do your jobs. Whatever goes wrong, just let me know. I'll take responsibility, I'll own it all. Just do what you need to do."

In the wire and order room, where all the trade orders are processed, things were out of control. I sent in extra people to help. The room's supervisor objected. "We need as many hands as we can get," I explained to him, and when he continued to protest I sent him to his office. "Don't come out," I shouted.

The frenzy continued for days; by the middle of that week, the Pacific Coast Stock Exchange, with which we normally did a lot of orders, couldn't handle the volume and shut down; our computers weren't programmed for this outcome and continued to make trades. So we were engaging in business that was quite literally going nowhere. I kept as cool as I could, projecting an air of "we can get through this." "Go get done what you know how to do," I told my managers. In the case of Pacific Coast, we went back and dealt manually with the data entry for every transaction.

The markets eventually settled down. The frantic pace subsided. In about three weeks' time, our shop caught up with the backlog. Our trading losses were in the neighborhood of $3 to $4 million, which considering the size of the event wasn't too bad.

The years that followed were productive for both Paine Webber and me, the most notable business development coming toward the end of my time with the company: the acquisition of the securities firm Kidder, Peabody in 1994. Far more personally meaningful was the arrival at the brokerage of a young woman who was destined to be an important part of my life. Lisa Weber joined the firm in 1988 from Merrill Lynch as a specialist in human resources—my old stomping ground.

We met on the treadmills in the gym in the Weehawken data center. We had an instant connection. Soon, I'd show up at her office to talk over business stuff, or just to chat. She was perceptive and quick on her feet.

But by the early nineties, the office politics had shifted in the company, and not in my favor. I stopped keeping track of the coups. Marron had inscribed a bronze plaque with the names of his management team, forty or so people he identified as having carried Paine Webber into the nineties. But by 1990, two-thirds of them were gone. Further, my job had gotten harder—there was endless whining about each new technical innovation operations introduced. With Nickelson in retirement, and a new guy who came over from Merrill Lynch, Joseph Grano, the heir apparent for Guenther's job, I saw few options for moving up. By the end of 1993,

I sensed something was coming to an end for me, a feeling I had to start over.

So I did the unthinkable.

I took a demotion.

At least that was how people close to me looked at it when I asked for the job of head of the southern sales division. I saw it otherwise: an opportunity once again to do something different. And to get the hell out of the way, because I wanted to protect my "golden handcuffs." My contract included an agreement that Paine Webber would pay me $5 million in seperation funds, a fuck-you sum if there ever was one, and certainly one in those days.

For all my years in the business, I had never been in sales. And in a company so heavily reliant on the brokers out there selling the products, that's where you earned the respect of the rank-and-file. So I went to Marron and asked him to put me in charge of one of the regional sales forces. He agreed.

As head of the southern regional sales division—1,500 brokers in eighty branch offices from Washington, D.C., to Florida to New Mexico—I would be on the road a lot and no longer in anything like the inner circle. It was challenging, new, and I looked forward to seeing what I could learn. Still, I wouldn't be reporting to the president anymore. I'd be reporting two levels down. This kind of downshift just wasn't done voluntarily in corporate life. But I never put much stock in following the manual. My family, however, with whom I always talked and then did exactly what I wanted to do, made it clear to me that they were not happy about this.

They imagined I was unhappy, too. I really wasn't, though. I've discovered it all comes down to what you mean by "happy." The reality of a working life is that the ups and downs occur in phases, and nothing is forever—not even life itself. I survived a few dangerous twists and turns at Chase, and again at Paine Webber I made it over any number of hurdles. Within these financial houses, trying on new hats was what made me happy. That and, of course, the money.

"You do what you have to do," I told Lisa. "And I'm going to do the best job at this that I can." I was still married to Denise at this juncture, but in the complicated life I'd made for myself, I was also with Lisa a lot of the time. As these things tended to happen, two of the guys who worked for me had previously held jobs at Paine Webber at the managerial level in sales that I was now assuming. I told them that if they wanted to get all bent out of shape about this, so be it. My intention, I explained, was that I would run things with them as if it were a partnership. Hiring and retaining the best brokers was a huge part of our jobs. "I'm good at solving problems," I told these two fellows. "You guys are good at recruiting. And together we'll get this done."

That was how I spent my last eighteen months at the firm. When the next big offer came, in 1995, from Metropolitan Life Insurance Co., it was past time for me to go.

Years later, when I was at AIG, Nickelson, who was now retired and living part of the year in Idaho and part in Florida, called to tell me that one of Paine Webber's brokers, a top earner from my time who was also now living in retirement in Michigan, was coming to New York and wanted to see me. I had no idea what it was about, but I agreed to have lunch with him.

It turned out he had no agenda; he just wanted to look me up. The path my life had taken after Paine Webber, he said, confirmed his belief that I'd make good. That was nice to hear. There are people you're only vaguely aware of who do wish you well, even at times you experience as difficult and stressful.

"Warren," I said, "thank you very much."

# SIX

# TAKING OFF THE COLLAR

"HE SCARES THE HELL OUT of people."

The 1996 Kaplan DeVries study of my leadership abilities had asked a member of the executive group at Metropolitan Life Insurance Co. how clearly my subordinates knew what was expected of them.

In other words, they knew. "Bob is now saying, 'I want to see your plan and I'm going to hold you accountable,'" this person, whose identity was shielded, went on. "I think he's got some people who are like the deer caught in the headlights."

When used with dexterity, fear is not a bad motivator, especially for people who aren't used to being asked for concrete results. Let me be clear, though: an office in which fear is the primary ingredient will not be a healthy place to work. But you also have to consider causation here. What is it that someone who works for you is afraid of?

My directness, for instance. Oftentimes, people don't know how to deal with someone who says exactly what he means.

"He does not chitchat," one of my direct reports told the interviewers. "If he had called you today he would not have started with something social. He goes right to the task. In a sense, it is refreshing, but it can be disconcerting."

Denise would certainly agree. She also found my one-track business mind disconcerting. When we went out socially with people, my conversation remained stuck in the office, and Denise often felt she had to pick up my slack: "These people are people," was how she'd put it. "They have families, they have children, they have grandchildren. Can't you ask about that a little bit?"

It was true. I was impatient with small talk. On the other hand, I did not hide behind it, either. "You don't have to 'interpret' Bob" was how I described myself to those leadership researchers. Looking back, I think that transparency was a hallmark of mine years before the word became fashionable.

"People may not like what I have to say, and may not like my personality, but if I say it, I believe it," I explained. "You don't have to worry about whether Bob is straightforward and honest with you." Then I added: "Some people may wish I were less straightforward and honest, and more polished about it."

So while my bluntness was generally considered a plus, it was not universally appreciated after I arrived at MetLife in 1995 as an executive vice president. I was both a disrupter and an agent of change. I had been brought on to shake up the passive culture. I was also a potential replacement down the line for the CEO, Harry Kamen, who'd hired me with all these things in mind.

I discovered quickly that I'd joined another struggling organization, this one desperately in need of having its pilot light relit. A series of management workshops I organized—akin to the Leading Leaders seminars I later ran at AIG—would soon identify a key problem. Managers at MetLife, a sleeping giant of an insurance company headquartered in ornate splendor at One Madison Avenue in Manhattan, felt as if they did their jobs in straitjackets.

It was a benevolent company, mind you, popularly known for its celebrity mascot, a comic-strip beagle you may have heard of by the name of Snoopy. But the company was a chronic underperformer, with too little emphasis on accountability. It languished in near-bottom-of-the-industry results in important Wall Street measures such as return on equity and return on assets. The firm's 41,000 employees enjoyed some generous if outdated benefits, like unlimited sick days. "The company for years offered free lunches and nap time," reported *American Banker* magazine. Nap time! And workers received toothless guidance when it came to such vital measurements of individual performance as job reviews. For example: I discovered that 87 percent of the workforce received ratings of "excellent" or "extraordinary." The remaining 13 percent had to settle for merely "good." Too good, in fact, to be true.

The firm was in those days a mutual—a corporate structure that meant it was owned by its policyholders, rather than by shareholding members of the public. Its 12 million policyholders in actuality, though, had little say in how the company was run. And since the mutual wasn't answerable to stockholders, it operated behind a veil; it didn't even issue quarterly earnings reports. The arrangement was cozy but severely hampered the organization's access to new capital and thus, in a competitive and consolidating industry, its ability to grow. With repeal looming for the barrier-enforcing federal Glass-Steagall Act, paving the way for financial-sector organizations like banks, brokerages, and insurance companies to compete in one another's businesses, MetLife simply had to become a better-fortified player.

I was a shock to MetLife's insular system, but Kamen knew the place needed fresh blood. He placed me in charge of what was viewed as one of MetLife's toughest challenges: stabilizing and rebuilding the sales force. My last position at Paine Webber, running the southern sales division, was ideal for my immersion—and credibility—on the selling side. As Tom Bianco, head of equity markets at the time at Paine Webber, put it to me: "In this industry, salespeople never trust you until you have one of these jobs, until you've sold or managed them. You never get taken seriously, because people don't think you know how it feels."

The sales side of Paine Webber was robust. MetLife was another story. It had gone through massive attrition—down to 7,500 agents from 12,500 just four years earlier—and had been rocked by allegations of shady selling practices. (In 1999, we paid $1.7 billion to settle class-action lawsuits related to the accusations.) My background in technology and information systems was also put to use in the integration of the operations of New England Mutual Life Insurance, the nation's twenty-seventh biggest life insurer, which merged in 1995 with MetLife, No. 2 in the industry behind Prudential Insurance.

My charge was a wholesale reorientation of the MetLife culture, away from a singular focus on making products to a broader goal of tailoring our services and policies to the needs of individual customers. MetLife had been focused so narrowly on the "manufacturing" side that it was effectively destroying its own sales force. I was hired to revamp all that, to make sure the company understood its primary distribution system was its salesmen.

I can't say it was my dream job. I knew I was not necessarily a good fit personality-wise at MetLife, because the culture was so button-down and clearly change-averse, though ultimately I did find there were more people rooting for me to bring them to where they needed to be than those who would have preferred I uphold the status quo. I was not anyone's stereotype of the aloof executive. I expected results and I said so. I had no patience for games or evasion. "You're dead if you lie to him," one of my direct reports said of me. This was absolutely true. My reflex was not to trust; a lie confirmed my default suppositions.

But if Chase was where I got my basic training, and Paine Webber was where I earned my purple heart, MetLife was going to be my truest battle testing yet. The company was going to call on all my accumulated skill as it plunged me into the most far-reaching financial challenge I'd had to date: taking a massive Fortune 500 company public.

Within three years of my arrival, I moved up from executive vice president to president to CEO. I was an anomaly at MetLife, a leader of the then-130-year-old firm who wasn't a homegrown company man. I hadn't taken the conventional route, making a long, incremental climb up the MetLife ladder to the top job. Hell, I wasn't even an insurance man; I'd never sold a policy in my life. The closest I'd come was running Paine

Webber's annuities and pension plan businesses several years prior, and before that tangling with an insurance company when I sued Sullivan County over oil leaking from county property and causing a stench at the money-sucking Monticello Inn. (I settled the suit for $200,000 and then let my option on the place run out.)

What I initially lacked in intimate knowledge of premiums and actuarial tables I made up for in organizational savvy and an ability to invigorate the staff.

And through the workshops I held, I gave the sales force the benefit of my philosophy of instilling independence in people, and encouraging them to pass this value on to other workers in their departments.

The buy-in for a hidebound outfit didn't occur automatically. "Excuse me, Bob," said a participant in one of my workshops. "I've been here thirty-one years. This is your first year at MetLife, and you don't know what it's like to work at this company, and I do. We have very set rules for how we do things," he added, and proceeded to paint me a picture of the buttoned-up MetLife way.

"It's like we're each a dog with a collar inside an electric fence. You don't go beyond your boundaries, because the minute you get close to them—" and here he imitated the sound of a buzzer. "And you, in all your wisdom, seem to be telling all of us managers that you've found a way to turn off the power to the electric fence. That it's safe to walk around. And that sounds really exciting, except you can't guarantee to us that some idiot in the home office won't find a way to turn the power back on. And when it comes back on, that could be really hurtful. So unless you can guarantee us that no idiot in the home office could ever, ever, ever turn that power back on, you're wasting your time in this class."

His analogy suited the occasion perfectly. It helped me to figure out what I wanted to get across: that it was up to them to take the initiative, that they had to persist in seeking to change the parts of the culture that didn't work. Still, that would take guts on their part, too. "You know what, Ken? You got it right," I said. "I can't guarantee they won't turn the power back on. But you know what this course is about? How to take off that collar.

"And some of you," I continued, "don't have the courage to take off the collar. You want that collar for safety. And so, until you have the courage to be a leader and take off your collar, I can't help you."

The reality was, a lot of those salespeople would never in a million years take off the collar. They were too wedded to the status quo, a fatal handicap in an industry desperately needing to adjust to modern realities, including the fact that life insurance was a receding priority for younger Americans, who were not inclined to think as seriously as their parents did about financial security decades ahead of time. Within a couple of years, 80 percent of those agents had left the company, and a whole new generation was brought on to replace them. There were other deficiencies in the company culture I had to deal with on a more one-to-one level, as I did in the case of a regional sales manager in Florida with an abusive manner. He verbally tore apart an employee for daring to suggest the need to improve the office décor for the sake of visiting clients.

A friend of the abused employee called to tell me the agent had been crying for two weeks over the incident. The whys and wherefores weren't as important as the treatment she received. Nobody deserves to be dressed down for making a perfectly reasonable suggestion.

So I called the guy and gave him a taste of his own medicine. "You know what?" I said to him. "If I ever hear of you talking to someone like that again, I'll fire you on the spot!"

I just could not tolerate behavior like this. That it was a male superior humiliating a female underling intensified my anger. (Lisa would always recite her view of me, that I am constitutionally incapable of abandoning a woman. Her theory was rooted in her own experience with me, as I remained married to Denise while also involved with her, all with my family's knowledge. At some level it goes back to my having felt at a tender age my mother's terror over the responsibilities she had to shoulder alone after my father died.)

The Florida incident didn't end there. Two days later, the regional manager's boss, the division manager, called. He clearly thought he was going to put me in my place. "How dare you talk to our regional guy like that!" he shouted at me.

At this point, I'd had enough. I fired them both.

As you can tell, I've never had any trouble taking off *my* collar. And I would be just as likely to do it with people I worked for as with the secretary of the Treasury.

This facility certainly was heavily in my favor when it came to charting MetLife's cloudy future. Kamen, who had taken over as CEO in 1993, dropped more than a few hints about my having an inside track on becoming his successor. My feeling was if it happened, great. "I am not out to be Harry's replacement," I said in 1996. We were beginning to make headway in retaining agents after the disastrous years of '94 and '95, and productivity was increasing as well; we experienced a 10 percent gain in 1997 in sales of new life premiums by agents integrated into MetLife from New England Mutual. This was where my focus was, though others saw me as more concerned about where I was headed.

"He will either be the chairman or he will go down in flames," a member of the executive group told the Kaplan DeVries interviewers. "What happens is that when someone operates like he does—damn the consequences and don't worry about the casualties and the issues and details— he goes for broke. If he hits the bull's-eye, okay, but if he doesn't, it will unravel. It is a bold, risky strategy."

From Kamen's perspective, it looked like my appointment to lose. "If this early assessment [of his performance and ability] is correct and he continues that way, I think he would be one of the primary contenders for the top job," he volunteered.

In the fall of '97, the path was indeed becoming clear. I was made president and chief operating officer, and early the following spring came bigger news. "Metropolitan Life Names Benmosche, a Former Securities Executive, as CEO," read the *Wall Street Journal* headline on March 30, 1998. The plan was for me to take over on July 1.

"Mr. Benmosche's promotion," said Bloomberg News, "shows insurers are abandoning a tradition of hiring leaders from their own ranks in order to fend off mounting competition from banks, mutual funds and securities brokers for consumer dollars."

"You're going to see a lot of new things under Mr. Benmosche," Mark Puccia, a Standard & Poor's analyst, told the Bloomberg reporter.

My rise at MetLife coincided with a difficult period for my family. Denise was diagnosed with breast cancer late in 1997. She astonished everyone with her recuperative powers; only ten days after her surgery, she was supervising a party for three hundred people that was thrown for me at MetLife after I was named president.

Our marriage was, at the same time, on shaky ground. We loved each other but, as happens in many marriages, life's stresses were taking their toll. We went through counseling and ultimately decided on a legal separation. It was important to both of us that whatever issues we were having did not divide our children, who were now in early adulthood. We continued to see each other, celebrate holidays together, and even go on some vacations together.

Meantime, the analyst who predicted "new things" at MetLife couldn't have been more correct. The changes, in fact, would be radical, in everything from the scale of our acquisitions to the legal and financial structure of the company. The mutual model was receding fast in the insurance industry, as survival increasingly meant growing and that meant acquiring other companies, which of course required infusions of capital. Prudential and John Hancock, two of our major rivals, were also pursuing reorganizations as public companies, a trend that led *Business Week* to conclude the changes in our business were "the largest single event in the equity markets" of the late 1990s. Together, the magazine said, our firms would be issuing $100 to $200 billion in new stock.

The question was how best to use "demutualization"—a mouthful of a term for what was indeed a monumental undertaking—to reposition ourselves in this brave new financial world. Joseph Reali, the legally trained finance executive who headed up our corporate structures department, researched various options for us to start the process. It was a huge project, requiring hundreds of millions of dollars and approvals from both state regulators and ultimately our own policyholders.

"This sleeping giant is no longer asleep," I told *Business Week*.

I'll leave the more arcane details to those who enjoy poring over the fine print of contracts. What's important to know is that I wanted to be able to offer MetLife to potential shareholders as quickly as possible, and to do that, I thought that establishing a mutual holding company would be a good mechanism. This would have allowed us to sell 49 percent of the company to the public, and leave the distribution of shares to the policyholders to a later date.

But New York state lawmakers—who would have to pass a law to authorize such an arrangement—were highly resistant. So we steered a path instead to a total demutualizing of the company, with one intriguing departure from the conventional route. A provision of existing state law allowed us to hold all the policyholders' shares in a trust, run by an independent trustee. This was an attractive option, because we simply had so many potential future shareholders—12 million of them. Going public would make us the company with the largest number of stockholders in the country. Some of our industrial insurance policies—a mainstay of MetLife's business in the first half of the twentieth century, for which workers contributed as little as five or ten cents a week—dated back to the 1930s. The costs of communicating with such an army of shareholders every time a prospectus or ballot had to go out were astronomical.

The advantage to the shareholder was a vehicle through which they could cash out at the price of the initial public offering, or sell their shares at whatever the market price was later on. Either way, through the trust, they would not be charged any commission on the sale.

Not everyone at MetLife appreciated this approach, or me. I tried my best to get people to relax a bit. One time, I brought Bianco to the employee cafeteria for a quick bite—I ate fast. Heads turned every which way. What the hell was the boss doing here?

"You're creating a stir," Tom remarked as we sat down to eat.

"I'm trying to show people I'm human," I said.

Still, some of those people viewed an impending IPO as a dangerous upheaval, and me as a threat so poisonous that they seemed to believe I was hell-bent on destroying the company. What many of the detractors really wanted was to preserve MetLife's shopworn, good-old-boy network. This was the atmosphere in which the knives came out for both me and for Lisa Weber, whom I had brought to MetLife from Paine Webber late in 1998 to work in human resources. She was married and nine months pregnant at the time of her interviews, a condition that fed the rampant rumors about the two of us. It got so bad that reports circulated at a MetLife conference in Hawaii that I was going to have to resign.

A *Wall Street Journal* reporter called before I left for Hawaii to say that they were running a story that would suggest I was the father of the child. My response was a conversation-ender. "I had a vasectomy fifteen years ago; I couldn't make anyone pregnant," I told the reporter. "You're barking up the wrong tree."

The story never ran. Still, I was furious at this intrusion into my private life. I was legally separated from Denise; my evolving relationship with Lisa had nothing whatsoever to do with my work for MetLife, or hers. But the whispering campaign was a worrisome sign of what lay ahead for both of us, and set in motion the circumstances of the life-altering decision I would have to make a bit farther down the road.

I decided to address the rumors head-on in Hawaii, telling the gathering that any account of my fathering a child was patently untrue. My booster, the ex-CEO Harry Kamen, was on hand, too. I greeted him with a touch of anxiety about what he might say.

"Let me give you some advice," Kamen said. "Just don't let the bastards get you down."

I smiled. His continuing support was a big shot in the arm. It gave me added strength for the heavy lifting ahead.

After receiving official okays from state regulators and our policyholders, MetLife issued almost 500 million shares of stock to its policyholders on April 5, 2000, sixteen months after announcing our proposed demutualization. Another 202 million were sold to the public at large, at an opening price of $14.25 per share that went up to $15.37 by day's end. The IPO—one of the largest ever, with lead underwriters Credit Suisse First Boston and Goldman, Sachs & Co.—raised us $4.43 billion. The positive effects of demutualization were just beginning.

By any measure, the reaction was enthusiastic. "A momentous day in the 132-year history of MetLife," I declared. "Not Just Peanuts," said one of the financial news outlets. And for people who'd been paying into life insurance policies with us for many years, it was a bonanza as well. Many were buoyed by what they saw as an unexpected windfall. The *New York Times* talked to Paolo Capoferri, an importer of Italian food from Bridgewater, New Jersey, and longtime policyholder. "This is like found money for me," he said, referring to the 206 MetLife shares he received. "It never crossed my mind that I might get some stock out of this."

I'd set us on a course with clear goals: a 15 percent annual increase in earnings per share, and an 11.5 percent return on equity. Meantime, MetLife had cemented my own financial security. In 1999, my compensation package totaled a little over $3.5 million, more than I'd imagined earning in my wildest dreams. Over the next couple of years, I'd spend some of it on real estate—most notably, to buy and renovate Villa Splendid, my Croatian property.

Back in Suffern, New York, a project was brought to my attention that had value to the community far beyond the mere brick-and-mortar. In 2000, a movement was under way by historic preservationists to save the Lafayette Theater, a one-thousand-seat Art Deco gem on Lafayette Street in downtown Suffern, a 45-minute drive from Manhattan. The mortgage on the movie house was in arrears and the building was now threatened with demolition. Ari came to me with a request from the organizers for a sizable donation—they needed $500,000 to buy and thus save it. I couldn't see tearing down such a vital feature of a town I loved. "Why don't you make an appointment with them for me, and I'll listen," I said.

The place was in disrepair: the roof leaked and the seats were in bad shape. But I saw an opportunity for us to make a civic contribution, and

for twenty-one-year-old Ari to take on a personally rewarding managerial role. "If you agree to learn how to run it, I'll buy it," I told him. So I
plunked down half a million dollars and now was the owner of one of
the country's dwindling number of great old movie palaces. We poured
hundreds of thousands of dollars into fixing up the place, and we would
soon be exhibiting first-run movies there. As a result, the downtown re-
tains a vital cultural anchor—complete with vintage Wurlitzer organ—
and we get to experience the pleasure of sustaining it.

One of the biggest kicks comes at Christmastime, when we open the
theater to local school groups that perform on our stage before showings
of family classics like *It's a Wonderful Life*. The wide-screen viewings pack
our house with filmgoers who travel from as far as New England and
Maryland.

I was continuing to renovate, too, at MetLife, where I was intent on
cutting some of the fat. Our palatial Manhattan office space, for instance,
had to go. "Can you believe this?" I said as I showed visitors around my
suite, which had a private bathroom as large as a conference room. Some
execs live for this kind of pampering, but it didn't have much appeal for
me. All I could think about was the money being flushed down the toilet. "All this has to go," I told people.

A negotiation was finalized in 2000 to lease most of our fifty-story
One Madison Avenue to a bank, First Boston. Looking for a less expensive and more suitable space, we announced a deal the following year to
move a thousand employees across the East River to Long Island City in
Queens. Eager to have us stay put—after I made it known I wanted to
move operations to New Jersey—city and state officials agreed to a package of incentives worth almost $31 million. Soon, we'd be moving even
more Manhattan workers to an outer borough.

This was more change than some at the company could bear (and some
of it would be undone a few years later by my successor). Even Snoopy's
fate wasn't certain. Charles M. Schulz's beloved *Peanuts* characters, and
Snoopy in particular, had been the popular faces of the company since we
first signed a deal with the cartoonist in 1985. But in the run-up to our

taking the company public, we were thinking about the various ways our image needed to be refreshed. My feeling was the commercials by the venerable advertising firm Young & Rubicam were too Snoopy-focused. Consumers needed more information about the solid institution being fronted by the mischievous beagle.

So while we kept the memorable slogan "Get Met. It Pays," we started running TV spots in 1999 that put less emphasis on *Peanuts* and more on MetLife's impressive history. As I told Stuart Elliott of the *New York Times*, "I was amazed how many things MetLife had done. I would go around telling people, 'Did you realize the Plaza Hotel was built with MetLife money? Or that in 1897 the company built a gym for its employees?'" Our civic footprint in New York City was deep and wide, extending most famously to two vast campuses of middle-income apartments built before World War II on Manhattan's East Side, Peter Cooper Village and Stuyvesant Town.

Snoopy appeared briefly in a new batch of commercials, which featured actors as MetLife agents, telling stories of how the company aided the country during World War II and the Depression.

Not everyone at MetLife, in fact, cared for our association with Snoopy; the folks from New England Mutual, in particular, disdained all that cartoonish cuteness. "They hated the dog," was how Lisa—by now our senior executive vice president and chief administrative officer— amusingly put it. (She was one of a number of executives who had come to MetLife from Paine Webber; another was the indispensable Joe Jordan, who had joined to run MetLife's annuities business and under me took over the insurer's retail division.) In the long run, though, Snoopy was too valuable a connection to sever. How many insurance companies could count on the level of brand awareness *Peanuts* represented? What price could a corporation place on that? In the selling of life insurance, continuity is a vitally important concept. Our ongoing relationship with Snoopy was a symbol of that sense of a durable bond. The Schulz family, of course, understood all of this, too. In 2002, when our ten-year deal was up for renewal, Schulz's widow, Jean—the cartoonist had died in

2000—drove a tremendously hard bargain, so hard, in fact, that Lisa had to warn the executive team that we might be losing Snoopy.

Word got out that I'd said, "We're not going to be held hostage by Snoopy." Now, I didn't want to lose Snoopy. This was a negotiating tactic. I mean, I was ready to lose Snoopy if I had to. But the fact of the matter was—even if I scared the hell out of people—I had a soft spot for Snoopy, and more importantly, for what he'd done for the company.

Negotiating new financial terms took us right up to the deadline. We finally hammered out a new deal an hour before our rights were to end.

The news-release headline flashed across Business Wire on December 11, 2002: "MetLife and Snoopy Sign Up for Another Ten Years."

Hallelujah, we saved the dog.

Lisa capably guided us through those rough currents. But as our relationship became more serious, so did the implications for us at work. I confided in people I trusted to get their sense of whether the potential conflict of interest could do us both damage. To underline that I had kept our personal lives separate from our professional responsibilities, I asked the board to hire outside counsel to examine my expense accounts. The determination came back that I had not billed the company for anything related to our private concerns. I made no attempt to hide my feelings for Lisa from my family. But I also realized that my dating a member of my executive team could at some point land me in hot water, and wasn't good for Lisa, either.

At the same time, I was getting older, and work was feeling less and less important to me. I really wanted to make a commitment to Lisa, figuring out what to do with our life going forward. Could we have a life going forward? And Denise and I were struggling with the nature of our relationship as well; we'd been in therapy over it for years. Why did Denise even want to remain a part of my life, when there was Lisa? It's a question she struggled with constantly, I think. At some level it was about the kids, and later, the grandkids, and maintaining the traditions of holidays and family. But there was also a bond between Denise and me that endured in spite of me.

Why she put up with this was for Denise to sort out. Why, for that matter, did Lisa? I needed time to get away, to think about my life and what worked and wasn't going to work. I was, as you can see, confused. The reality was I loved Lisa deeply. And I loved Denise very much. I knew it was time to get my family and my relationships in some order so that I could look forward to the rest of my life with more optimism than I was feeling, so that it wasn't all about just my career. That was an important transition, so that's why I left.

Listen, I don't want anyone to think I'm a saint, because I'm not. I don't want anyone to think that Lisa and I were casual buddies. It was more than that. It was a deep relationship. When you walk away from a job as CEO at sixty-two, there better be a damn good reason for doing so. And Lisa was a big part of that reason. I had two things in mind: that our connection was serious, and that in this type of office relationship, it shouldn't always be the woman who has to quit.

The more I considered retirement, the more reasonable the decision seemed. I'd made sure that Denise was financially secure for the rest of her life, and Nehama and Ari were striking out on their own. As for me, I had all the fuck-you money I would ever need. The multi-year refurbishment and decorating of Villa Splendid were coming along nicely, and my appreciation of the people, sights, and culture of the Dalmatian coast was intensifying with every visit. The prospect of a happily active life of inactivity there was growing, too.

Before that could happen, though, I wanted to see through some of my other big plans for MetLife, the biggest being the fulfillment of a goal of demutualization, expanding the company's horizons to make it as fit a competitor as possible for the other giants of the industry.

The breakthrough news came on January 31, 2005: the announcement of MetLife's acquisition of Travelers Insurance from Citigroup for $11.5 billion. The deal signaled the end of Citigroup's effort to invade our business, to become, in the media's terminology, a "financial services supermarket," and made MetLife the biggest provider of life insurance in North America.

Barely three months later, I had my own announcement: I would be retiring from MetLife in the spring of 2006. It was time. I would be turning sixty-two that May. I'd taken MetLife quite a ways, and I was fully ready to walk out of the corporate wrestling ring. The vineyards of Dubrovnik were looking a lot more inviting. I was thinking about buying a couple.

My send-off was a warm one. Among the parting gifts I received was quite a stunning one. An artist was commissioned to create a miniature model of MetLife's boardroom, a handsome wood-paneled interior that radiated solidity and wealth, attributes the company itself projected. The illuminated box sits in the den at Villa Splendid.

A few weeks after my retirement, we threw a party in honor of Paul Guenther, my old boss from my Paine Webber days, who was soon to step down as chairman of the New York Philharmonic. Guenther had recruited me as a member of the orchestra's board, and I was one of the chairmen of the gala.

I talked to a *New York Times* reporter who did a brief write-up of the event. We fell into a conversation about my own departure. I mused about the future for a minute. I mentioned the possibility of becoming a vinter, or that I might buy a store, or a small hotel. Maybe my childhood, all those days learning the motel business from Mom and Uncle Julie, were beckoning again.

Once an innkeeper, always an innkeeper.

"I'm looking to reinvent myself," I explained to the *Times*.

Famous last words.

# SEVEN

# NOTHING WAS HAPPENING

BEFORE I DELVE INTO WHAT we did to ensure that America got its money back and AIG found a path to the future, I have to dwell for a bit on AIG's past. For me, AIG was a competitor before it was my employer, and under Hank Greenberg's steely command it was a formidable rival, one I admired from my offices at MetLife for its willingness to expand its sphere of influence and stake out new businesses. Unfortunately, it ultimately did not manage the risks it was taking appropriately. Its management should have done a much better job of constraining its people.

As the meltdown played out in 2008, I found it excruciating to watch the company unravel. Because I knew the insurance business so well, I felt its pain more keenly. Certainly, I also could share the anxiety and frustration of millions of other Americans; my own financial security was being threatened, too, as I watched the value of my MetLife holdings drop and drop some more.

For a lot of the abuse heaped on AIG, the company could only blame itself, thanks to its terrible bets on the housing market. I wasn't there for the actions that laid the company low, or for the initial eleven months of public ugliness that followed. In retrospect, though, the shaming that followed the government's decision to rescue the company in September 2008 became so shrill, so hysterical, that it made the job we all ultimately had to focus on much more arduous. And nowhere was the hysteria more evident than in the behavior of Congress.

Early in October of 2008, the members of a House panel, the Committee on Oversight and Government Reform, called before them the two immediate ex-AIG CEOs, Martin Sullivan and Robert Willumstad, to account for the global financial liquidity crisis the company had a hand in creating.

The hearing's purpose was to examine AIG's mistakes and, in the words of one of its members, Representative Christopher Shays of Connecticut, "to understand what makes a private company like AIG 'too big to fail.'" But in reality, it was piñata time. With America casting about for villains, AIG was atop the most-eligible list.

"The committee has learned that a week after the bailout, executives from AIG's main U.S. life insurance subsidiary, American General, held this weeklong conference at an exclusive resort in California," Elijah E. Cummings, the Maryland Democrat, told the two CEOs seated before him. "Are you familiar with that at all?"

"I am not," said Willumstad. He took over at AIG in 2008 from Sullivan, who in 2005 had succeeded Maurice R. "Hank" Greenberg, who had been forced out in an accounting scandal. Sullivan departed in June 2008; the reign of Willumstad would last only three months before my predecessor, Ed Liddy, replaced him.

"All righty," Cummings replied, as he launched into a description of a lavish get-together at the St. Regis Monarch Beach resort in Dana Point, California. With the help of some photographs, the congressman recited the costs of the "swanky" September 24–28 conference: $200,000 for rooms, $150,000 for banquets, $23,000 spent in the spa. Sarcastically, he noted the $7,000 expenditure for "something very, very important: that is, green fees at the golf course." All told, the bill came to $440,000. To

Cummings, the event was proof of flagrant corporate greed. "It's a very bad thing," he said, "when you think about the fact that the United States taxpayer basically ended up paying for this."

The story was picked up everywhere and presented as emblematic of Wall Street arrogance. "Less than one week after the taxpayers rescued AIG, company executives could be found wining and dining at one of the most exclusive resorts in the nation," said Representative Henry Waxman, the committee's chairman. It was prime time for raking AIG over the coals, for reminding the American public what a bunch of cluelessly decadent fat cats were the people who ran this out-of-control insurance company. "While your retirement burns, these guys are getting rubdowns," read the headline the next day in a Georgia newspaper.

At this point, to me, AIG was damned if it did and damned if it didn't. I had an analogy for this type of situation, when someone was in an untenable position: "He was like a guy caught between a dog and a tree." And AIG was, at this time, that guy.

With this volume of static, no one could hear the company's explanation, its pointing out that the stories misrepresented the conference. This was not a retreat for AIG executives. It was a gathering sponsored by the American General unit for outside distributors, the kind of promotional event companies routinely organize to familiarize those who sell their wares with recent developments in services and products. To make money, you have to spend money. Only ten of the one hundred participants were employees of the insurance company. And the conference had been arranged and scheduled back in 2007, before there was a whiff of a crisis, and in a successful AIG division not even remotely involved in the practices that devastated the firm.

Still, the timing couldn't have been worse. Above all else, the company looked tone-deaf, inept. The forces lining up to vilify AIG were being handed ammunition on a silver platter. Any questionable dime AIG spent would now be seen as an affront to every decent hardworking American.

It was hard to imagine AIG sinking any lower.

The outrage over the St. Regis event underlined a level of anger that was making it impossible for outsiders to view the problems at AIG with any sense of proportion. Even in the impossible-to-defend case of AIG Financial Products, the Wilton, Connecticut–based unit that insured the toxic derivatives, the magnitude of public anger and recrimination was obscuring the facts. Though there were problems with investments in mortgage-backed securities in other parts of the company, FP was the biggest culprit. Still, out of FP's portfolio of 44,000 trade positions—the vast majority profitable—fewer than two hundred of its credit-default swaps were responsible for bringing the company to the brink of bankruptcy. That meant that only a handful of people in a unit of 420 employees—out of the more than 100,000 who worked for AIG worldwide—could be considered primarily responsible for blowing the company up.

The drama playing out was pitiful, and so counter to the history of the company, which for decades prided itself on the enviable figure it cut in the insurance industry for innovation, rigorous practices, and fiscal discipline. How had it become "too big to fail"? Not fundamentally because of its core business. It was a function of AIG's attempts to broaden its portfolio, to branch into side businesses that at one time looked limitlessly lucrative. It was a niche that turned into an all-consuming breach.

"Insurance is about keeping commitments," Liddy would write somberly in AIG's 2008 annual report. "AIG became a great company by keeping its commitments, and that has not changed. However, AIG strayed into businesses that were outside of its core competency, and shareholders have paid a heavy price as a result."

What a humbling admission. In the great beyond, you could imagine an apoplectic Cornelius Vander Starr, who out of a couple of offices in Shanghai, China, in 1919 started the string of insurance companies that decades later would come together under the banner of AIG. That anguish went double for Greenberg, the business savant who joined Starr's enterprise in 1960, and whom eight years later Starr tapped as his successor.

Tough, intimidating, and expansively gifted, Greenberg hatched the grand plan to integrate and grow Starr's disparate insurance companies under a corporate name he came up with, American International Group.

Greenberg ruled the company—there's no other verb for it—over the next thirty-seven years, turning it into the world's biggest insurance conglomerate, with a trillion dollars in assets and operations in 130 countries. In an industry typically painted in shades of grey, he functioned in living color. He pushed underwriting in new directions and explored new territories where he could sell his products. He was especially proud of the firm's AAA credit rating, what he called "a badge of capital strength that only a few American companies enjoyed."

"A global insurance fortress" is how he described his achievement in his 2013 book, *The AIG Story*.

He was a believer that sophisticated underwriting practices—and not money earned on investments—were the path to pre-eminence in the industry. "AIG's culture was characterized by a relentless quest to be first—first to develop and launch products, first to open and grow markets, first in performance from earnings to growth to assets," wrote Greenberg, who was never averse to tooting his own horn. "The culture spawned a commitment to innovation unlike the culture of any other insurance company."

A self-described "internationalist," Greenberg pursued opportunities around the world, in democracies and dictatorships alike. In the midst of the Cold War, he found business possibilities for AIG in the Soviet Union and China. Out of headline events—airline hijackings, industrialists' kidnappings—he pioneered new categories of insurance. During the Vietnam War, AIG insured U.S. supply ships on the Mekong River. It even insured secret government missions, as it did, according to Greenberg, after the CIA located a sunken Soviet nuclear submarine in the Pacific Ocean and a special ship was built to recover it.

From the headquarters of the holding company in New York, Greenberg was the utterly unique managerial glue holding together a geographically diverse empire with more than two hundred subsidiaries, many of them dominant players in their markets. American International Assurance (AIA), for example, was a Hong Kong–based insurance powerhouse; American Life Insurance Company (ALICO)'s business stretched from Japan to Brazil. The largest businesses Greenberg built were in the property and casualty and life, health, and retirement arenas. We recently consolidated these vast operations into two corporate units, AIG Property Casualty and AIG Life and Retirement.

The voracious—some would go further and say tyrannical—Greenberg also was on the lookout for potential profit centers outside the company's historic range of expertise. His acquisition in 1990 of the International Lease Finance Corp. (ILFC) was one such act of expansion. The firm owned commercial aircraft—one hundred of them at the time—that were leased to airlines around the world. Twenty years later, it was the largest such operation in the world, leasing out nearly one thousand aircraft and generating ample profits.

Three years earlier, in 1987, Greenberg had led AIG on its first steps into another field on the fringe of AIG's traditional business: financial services. As Greenberg recounted in his book, former U.S. Senator Abraham Ribicoff of Connecticut arranged for the AIG chairman to meet "a creative finance guy looking to develop new business in financial products." This finance whiz, Howard Sosin, was proposing a business that would "create customized products for large corporate clients wishing to hedge financial risks." He floated the idea of interest rate swaps, through which holders of loans could protect themselves against drops in floating interest rates. Borrowing money through the municipal reinvestment market, the group would invest in high-grade bonds. And with its pristine credit rating, AIG was a guarantor of stability. It had the unassailable standing to solidly back up the swaps. It was an attractive corporate parent for another reason: AIG would not come under the regulatory scrutiny of the federal Securities and Exchange Commission, viewed as the more exacting body overseeing Wall Street. Instead, AIG was monitored by the Office of Thrift Supervision, an agency of the Treasury

Department that regulated savings banks and savings and loans associations. It was regarded as a more relaxed policeman.

Sosin and AIG would part company in 1993, but not before AIGFP became a significant profit center for the company. Between 1994 and 2004, according to Greenberg, it earned $5 billion. Eventually, AIGFP would seek out other moneymaking opportunities in the derivatives markets, among them the instrument known as the credit default swap. Like an interest rate swap, it resembled insurance, but this one was for those who invested in what are known as collateralized debt obligations. CDOs are securities backed by assets such as home mortgages that have been assembled into large bundles, or "tranches." AIG and other assemblers of CDOs would then find buyers for stakes in these tranches, which are rated according to their level of risk. Investors receive payouts as the mortgages bundled in their tranches are paid down. The most secure of these bundles were rated AAA and received the premium designation "multi-sector super-senior" tranches. This was the level in which AIGFP specialized. Because these were deemed to carry the least risk, their rates of return were smaller than those in lower-rated tranches.

AIG and other firms developed the credit default swap to sell to CDO investors, or counterparties, as a hedge for them in the supposedly unlikely event of massive losses on the tranches. Written into these contracts was a proviso that if AIG's credit rating were downgraded, the counterparties could demand AIGFP post collateral to back up the CDOs and swap contracts. But AIG had been solidly AAA for so long and U.S. housing prices had been on such a steady upward path that the risk of the company facing some kind of liquidity crisis seemed, at least at the time, negligible.

The foolhardiness of this assumption would not immediately become apparent after the events of 2005, when Greenberg was toppled from his perch by then New York Attorney General Eliot Spitzer, who demanded the ouster of the longtime AIG chief following an investigation of AIG's accounting practices. One of the casualties of this period was AIG's coveted triple-A rating. Another, Greenberg asserts, was the rigorous polic-

ing of AIGFP's trades that he required, and that would have prev
the reckless deals by AIGFP under its president Joseph Cassano Jr., \
eventually brought the parent company to its knees.

Greenberg says in *The AIG Story* that the rogue trading started
FP after he left, that the division strayed disastrously from the sound
tices of old, such as the careful hedging of its positions in the cred
fault swap business. He alleges that after he was gone, "FP aban(
this hedging principle, committing to cover increasing volumes (
hedged risk, adding up to $80 billion." He and many others hav
served that FP began issuing more and more CDSs on less an
secure CDOs—tranches laden with billions in subprime mortgag
the shaky variety most vulnerable to default.

Before the crisis, Cassano and other FP executives were claiming,
ever, that even with the disruptions arising out of Greenberg's ex
the lowering of AIG's triple-A rating, the Financial Products unit wa
hedged for whatever happened.

"Credit risk is the biggest risk our group has," Cassano told fin
analysts at a presentation on May 31, 2007. "It's the single bigge;
that we manage. But with an AA plus/AA credit portfolio, there's
lot of risk sitting in there. And so while it is the largest risk, it's r
any stretch a risky business."

He also said: "My colleagues and myself have $500 million in'
in the company at risk to the activities of the business. And so
become very, very good caretakers of the value of the company."

Remind me, now: What was it that guy on the park bench said,
the dog not biting?

After FP's pronouncements were revealed to be woefully wron
Cassano was removed from his job, Gerry Pasciucco, a respected ai
complished Morgan Stanley hand, was brought in by Ed Liddy l
2008 to clean up FP, and ultimately to close it down. As Pasciucco \
discover, astoundingly reckless bets at AIG had been placed on mor
securities, based on the assumption that the AA rating AIG had held
2005 was in zero danger of downgrading; as long as an AA ratin

maintained, there were no collateral calls and no resulting threats to liquidity. As the problems in the securities lending program indicated, the bad mortgage bets went beyond FP. But it was indeed FP's multi-sector super-senior CDOs that caused the most damage, after Moody's and Standard & Poor's did in fact lower AIG's rating that September.

"AIGFP was itself doing things it shouldn't have been doing," Pasciucco would later say. (I relied on Pasciucco's analysis to a large degree and so I share many of his insights here.) The incentive was the extraordinary terms FP had with AIG: traders got to take home 30 percent of the money earned on a deal. When you looked at the vast amounts the group was dealing with, this added up to quite a chunk of change. "They went out and borrowed $30 billion on AIG's credit," Pasciucco says of work done on Cassano's watch. He added that with that money they bought $30 billion worth of securities, and thus were entitled to 30 percent of the spread between the cost of the loans and the return on the securities. "I mean, 30 basis points is tiny, but on $30 billion it's kind of a lot of money. And if I got to keep a third of it, what's my [personal] cost? I don't have a cost."

It was hubris on a titanic scale. Pasciucco said he found "enormous geopolitical risks" in FP contracts. In one instance, FP had entered into a deal to insure approximately $450 billion of bank deposits in Europe. In that contract, FP would be required to pay if a bank lost 10 percent of its value. Given historical trends, such an outcome was highly improbable.

Still, the magnitude of the exposure was breathtaking. "You think: Why would anyone do that?" Pasciucco says. "It's never happened where banks have lost 5 percent and they've stayed in business. But do you do $450 billion worth of it?" It seemed loony to Pasciucco, who explained that if AIG's rating at the time were to deteriorate further, the company would have had to come up with something like $60 billion worth of equity. He explained the mind-set that prevailed before he got there this way: "The thought was, 'We'll never not be "AA," so we're not going to worry about it.'"

As you probably know, the bottom fell out for AIG in September of 2008. A cascade of defaults by homeowners holding variable-rate mortgages, millions of which were due to have their interest rates reset upward, was erasing the value of AIG's CDOs. The financial markets were in free fall, with AIG in up to its neck in terrible risks and under relentless pressure. The final straw came after the rating agencies began putting AIG on "credit watch," and on the afternoon of September 15, 2008, when they lowered the ratings of AIG's long-term debt. The counterparties holding credit default swaps demanded AIG post the required collateral—billions and billions the company did not have. The housing market was wreaking simultaneous havoc on the company's securities lending program, by which AIG's life insurance companies loaned securities to third parties. AIG in turn invested that revenue in residential mortgage-backed securities (RMBs) that were loaded with subprime exposure. The margin calls the RMB shortfalls triggered added several billion dollars more to the company's immediate obligations.

As Geithner, head of the New York Fed at the time, would later put it in his book, *Stress Test*: "The company was bleeding to death."

None of this was happening in a vacuum, of course. From Fannie Mae to Citigroup, the subprime mortgage crisis was driving financial institutions to the edge. AIG's situation was as dire as any—and worse than most. I will tell you I was surprised at the size of the crisis; I had no idea how leveraged some of the other institutions had become. In the wake of the collapse of Bear Stearns and the bankruptcy of Lehman Brothers, AIG's stock price had dropped to less than $5 from a high of $150. Its access to a key market, commercial paper—a security that AIG, like other corporations, sells to meet short-term cash needs for payroll and other things—dried up. The commercial paper market was, in fact, completely paralyzed. Desperately on the hook, AIG turned as a last resort to the U.S. government, which had both deep enough pockets and the conviction that rescuing AIG was vital to preventing an even wider Wall Street collapse.

I had some thoughts about all of this, naturally; the first being that

Greenberg's removal from AIG indeed had devastating long-term effects on the company. He couldn't have done anything about the declines in the housing market, but I do believe AIGFP's management would have remained on a far tighter leash if he had been around, and as a result the company's writing of some of its riskiest contracts would never have occurred. Had Greenberg been at AIG in 2006, 2007, and 2008, he would have acted much more decisively. He would have recognized the problems as they began to surface and done something before they devolved into catastrophe. (At that congressional hearing in October 2008, neither Willumstad nor Sullivan acknowledged any oversight miscues on their parts. One committee member was compelled to wonder aloud who the heck *was* responsible.)

I also believe that in the hysteria of those initial weeks of the meltdown, the world lost sight of the fact that the bedrock of the economy remained strong, that a longer view would have recognized the country's essential fiscal soundness. Wasn't it true that in the midst of the "chaos," 93 percent of American homeowners remained current on their mortgage payments, and would remain so? Just as we were focusing that harsh spotlight on a few rogue traders at FP, we were looking so deeply at the cracks in the financial structure that we were neglecting to believe that the structure itself was solid.

The first time I was approached about the AIG job—when Liddy was eventually chosen—I had come up with the outlines of my own plan for rescuing AIG, one that did not involve a massive bailout. Bianco, my colleague from Paine Webber, can vouch for my having articulated the belief that the hugely expensive route that was taken, making AIG's counterparties whole for their swaps, was pursued too hastily. My plan called for a freeze on the billions of FP's toxic assets, holding off the counterparties from receiving their collateral payments. That would have eased the company's liquidity problems and permitted AIG to remain intact. Allowing time for the hysteria to die down, I thought, the markets would find their equilibrium and the value of the assets would slowly begin to recover.

Well, it was a thought. Looking back, I certainly can see that then Treasury Secretary Henry Paulson and Geithner were under ungodly pressure to reverse the river of bad tidings. So my idea will forever be consigned to the category of "what if?" Because in the frenzied atmosphere of that moment, the government did choose a different route, one that would turn proud, multinational AIG into a ward of the state, and prompt the *New York Times* to declare the action taken to be "the most radical intervention in private business in the central bank's history."

To the essential question—was the approach that Geithner and Paulson took ultimately the right one? Well, I believe that the actions were appropriate and decisive. Could we have done it differently? Could we have done it better? Sure. Were there better alternatives? Absolutely. But we needed to do something. There would indeed have been a worldwide depression today had we not acted. But—and here's the big but—instead of just acting, and moving forward and fixing, we started to play the blame game.

As I said to Ken Feinberg when we sat down to talk in June of 2012 for the taping of a podcast-type interview program he was developing, "That's where we failed. We failed by saying we're going to create laws, we're going to put people in jail, there should be a law against people who make bad judgments. If that happened the entire country would be in jail because all of us made mistakes in our lives."

That's the issue I have. It's not with the actions the nation took; it was the blaming and viciousness that went on after the actions were taken.

The intervention began on September 22, with the Fed's creation of an $85 billion "credit facility" for AIG, essentially a bridge loan for the company to pay off its massive margin calls and collateral obligations. Over the next six months, the magnitude of the rescue would essentially double in size. The Treasury Department would step in with its own infusion of capital, under the Troubled Asset Relief Program, in return for 79.9 percent stock ownership of the company. The Fed's loan would be revised during this period, with a less onerous interest rate and longer life of the loan, to give AIG "some financing breathing room," in Liddy's characterization to financial analysts. In the end, the government would extend to AIG an aid package worth $182.3 billion, with the Fed in the role of AIG's banker and Treasury as AIG's owner.

For the average person as well as the financial press, the layers of assistance would become increasingly difficult to track and decipher, as new "facilities" were added, designed to get the toxic assets off AIG's books. Anything as befuddling as the evolving structure of a complicated corporate bailout was sure to add to the public mistrust. Even more galling to people worried about making ends meet must have been the knowledge of just where the money borrowed by AIG was going: to all those banks and other counterparties that held AIG securities.

Some of them, in fact, were firms dealing with their own toxic exposures to subprime mortgages:

- Between September 16 and December 31, 2008, AIG made $22.4 billion in collateral payments to more than twenty institutions holding AIGFP credit default swaps, the largest of these going to French multinational bank Societe Generale, Deutsche Bank of Germany, and Goldman Sachs.
- Another $27.1 billion was paid to the counterparties to terminate the swaps.
- A further $43.7 billion went to counterparties in the securities lending program.
- In addition, more than twenty states were owed money via the investments they held with AIGFP; another $12.1 billion was paid out to them.

That meant an astonishing $105.3 billion was doled out to various banking and municipal customers. All told in this initial period, the biggest recipient, Goldman Sachs, got $12.9 billion; Societe Generale, $11.9 billion; Deutsche Bank, $11.8 billion; and Barclays, $8.5 billion. The financial crisis was, in this way, a shuttling of enormous amounts of treasure out of the pockets of ordinary Americans and into the accounts of companies that had a hand in the meltdown.

The saving grace was, we were going to find a way to give all that treasure back.

It turned out that I wasn't alone in thinking there might have been another way to go than paying the counterparties in full. In August of 2009 *Bloomberg Markets* ran a story quoting Janet Tavakoli, a Chicago-based author and financial consultant with a PhD from the University of Chicago's Booth School of Business, saying that strategy was a mistake. "We've run roughshod over the interests of the American taxpayer," she said. We've bailed out the Wall Street creditors; we've used AIG as a huge slush fund."

Later, Greenberg and Starr International would challenge the legality of the government's massive payments to these AIG trading partners. In a November 22, 2011, lawsuit against the Treasury Department and the New York Fed, Greenberg's lawyers alleged the United States had wrongfully taken control of AIG and "funneled" the bailout money to the company's counterparties, in violation of the Fifth Amendment. In seeking $25 billion on behalf of AIG's shareholders, they argued that the amendment applied because it bars the confiscating of private property without just compensation. (Greenberg asked AIG to join the suit after I got to the company, but we declined; more on that later.) The case went to trial in September 2014 in Washington before the U.S. Court of Federal Claims, which rules on lawsuits by plaintiffs asserting the government owes them money. [In June 2015, Federal Judge Thomas Wheeler ruled in Greenberg's favor, but awarded no damages.]

Some of the federal aid to AIG directly addressed the problem of resolving the very worst of the AIG Financial Products and securities lending issues. The Fed constructed a pair of vehicles late in 2008 designed to do just that, to allow AIG to remove the toxicity from its books. One of them, called "Maiden Lane II" (for the street on which the institution was located), involved the Fed purchasing $20.5 billion of residential mortgage-backed securities that AIG obtained via its securities lending program. The vehicle was financed by a $19.5 billion loan from the Fed and a $1 billion deferred payment agreement with AIG.

The other, "Maiden Lane III," was devised for a Fed purchase of $29.3 billion of those bundles of collateralized debt obligations handled by AIGFP. This would allow an eradication of credit-default swaps with a face value of some $62 billion. The purchase was financed by a $24.3 billion Fed loan, and $5 billion paid in by AIG.

It was up to AIG, however, to figure out how to close down the Financial Products unit and unwind the derivatives it still held. These had a notional worth—the total value of its leveraged assets—of $1.8 *trillion*. The job of unwinding all the contracts required FP to go through all of its trading positions and decide what to do with each of them: allow a trade to naturally expire under its original provision; negotiate a price with a counterparty to exit a contract; or find a new investor to assume AIG's responsibilities in the trade. Consultants from McKinsey & Company had begun trying to sort out the mess, dividing FP's business into twenty-two books of trades, many of them involving contracts that were still viable, and a few containing those toxic deals insuring the value of CDOs.

Liddy thought Pasciucco was just the man to fill the vacuum at FP caused by Cassano's exit. He'd spent his entire career at Morgan Stanley, most recently as head of the Capital Commitment Committee, which determined how much money the firm would invest in its corporate clients. That assignment entailed bringing together disparate groups of stakeholders within Morgan Stanley—from the more conservative credit department to the more hard-charging investment banking side—to a consensus on how to manage risk and enhance the balance sheet.

He needed him badly, in fact. "Listen, you come figure it out," Pasciucco recalls Liddy saying. "There's so much wood to chop at this place, I can't even begin to understand it." Financially secure after more than twenty-five years at Morgan, and intrigued by the challenge, Pasciucco agreed to come to FP for an initial six-month period. On November 11, 2008, his first day at the company in Connecticut, Pasciucco discovered that what he'd been told about the operation was true, that in the absence of the "big tree" leadership of a Greenberg or even a Cassano, the place was paralyzed. Or as Pasciucco observed: "Nothing was happening."

"I had heard that, literally, if you could just start making decisions you will be considered a hero," he said, adding that he walked into meetings that fruitlessly circled around the tasks at hand. "There were endless discussions about whether they should unwind an Italian swap," Pasciucco recalled, as a for-instance. "How to contextualize that, no one had any idea. So the meetings went on and on, and then the issue was tabled, and then it was pushed down the road."

Trying to get his head around what had gone on was one of his first jobs. "I had to think about whether we can figure out what the hole looks like, and how do you even think about this, what's the vocabulary we use?

"So I asked for a bunch of reports, and I said, 'What did Joe look at every Monday morning? Let's start there,'" he explained, referring to Cassano. He was given some Excel spreadsheets and the live feed from a Bloomberg terminal, and some other assorted bits and scraps. "And that really shocked me. Because one thing I did know was how enormous this thing was, even though I couldn't scope it out yet. But not to have any consolidated, verifiable [numbers]—not to say at the end of the day they weren't roughly okay, but it was very hard to have confidence in them because [the people at FP] kept misjudging what the prices were, what they should be. Which meant that your collateral positions were very difficult to figure out."

He quickly discovered that because there was such a dearth of communication among AIG's semi-autonomous businesses, no one had been aware of just how much exposure the company had to this one investment sector—the one that turned out to be fatally infected. "There was no measurement to say across the organization, 'Are we over-weighted in anything?'" Pasciucco recounted. "Because it would have shown immediately that you're over-weighted in domestic mortgages."

With representatives from the Fed and Treasury holding weekly progress meetings, Pasciucco had as a primary goal in those early months reducing the number of trades FP held, either by letting them expire on their prearranged date, or by negotiating a payment with the counterparty to exit the contract, or by finding buyers to take them over. He knew in the cases of the most volatile contracts, the deals could entail additional losses. But no alternative existed to wiping the books clean, because the deals all had to be wound down. He recalled telling the staff: "I'm going to assume that you're going to make 10 percent of the decisions and they're going to be wrong. We may lose money on some of them. It's not the end of the world anymore. We just can't *not* make decisions." Pasciucco was of course absolutely right.

Among the first he wanted to get rid of was an exotic brand of derivatives known as "power reverse duals," estimated by *Bloomberg Markets* to be a $7 billion business for FP. The instruments were what Pasciucco described as "long-dated bets on currencies" versus the dollar, in this case, the Japanese yen. Once the financial crisis hit, it became very difficult for AIG to find parties willing to hedge these bets. FP lost $50 million in 2008, engaging in an intricate set of daily transactions, trying to keep these thirty-year-or-more contracts hedged, and another $100 million in 2009. So Pasciucco was in a race to sell the positions to banks in Europe.

His competing worry was the declining financial health of AIG, which in the first quarter of 2009 reported the largest loss in its history. And if the beating that AIG's bottom line was taking led to another credit-rating downgrade, the resulting impact on the remaining contracts at FP would be calamitous.

The other huge problem was morale. As Pasciucco put it: "These people are the smartest people in the room. Suddenly, they're the most hated people in the world. They had no confidence in their decision-making ability anymore."

The people at FP were pariahs even within the company. "AIG had six PR firms under contract, and nobody wanted to touch us," Pasciucco recalled. "We ended up talking to PR people who were either like eighty years old or twenty years old and did party planning."

If the circumstances hadn't been so bleak, Pasciucco remarked, they would have been funny. "I told a friend of mine, who was one of the producers of *The Book of Mormon*, 'It should be a comedy on Broadway.'"

There was nothing amusing, though, about the isolation felt by him and the others trying to fix FP: "You felt so hopeless," he said. "Like there's no one that will help us, no one's going to throw us a lifeline."

Then, in the lifeboat, I showed up.

# EIGHT

# WE'RE NOT DOING
# ANY OF THIS

I WAS IN A DARK MOOD as I sat in my office on the eighteenth floor of 70 Pine Street, glowering at one of my secretaries, Betty Bell. She could see I was not happy and she looked terror-stricken as a result.

"Don't ever change my schedule again without consulting me!" I barked at her.

My blood was boiling, as it tends to when I suspect schemes are being cooked up behind my back. It was my first full week at AIG, the week of August 4, 2009, before I left on the trip to Croatia that was to cause such a hullabaloo. I knew Paula Reynolds was convening an "off-site" meeting that week, uptown on Park Avenue, in the offices of our real-estate group. She was the executive my predecessor Ed Liddy had placed in charge of AIG's restructuring. The gathering was organized to go over the progress of Project Destiny, the plan they had hatched to sell off AIG units quickly to try to pay back the government.

And I was left off the invitation list.

Actually, the meeting had been on my schedule and then, mysteriously, it was not. I asked Betty what was up.

"I was told you weren't needed there after all," she said.

"Oh, you were, were you?" I said, feeling the blood pounding in my ears.

Disinvited, huh? This was mighty fishy. First, because Betty, who I would discover was the most conscientious of executive assistants, had taken this action without informing me. And second, and more significantly, because I already was sensing that there were people at AIG, and in the banking world beyond, who harbored the belief that the company was already on a path and that they would be able to do an end run around me. Although on the day my appointment was announced, Reynolds disclosed that she would be leaving the company shortly, I suspected she wanted to stick around in some capacity. A longtime executive in the energy industry who came to AIG in October 2008 from Safeco, an auto insurance company, Reynolds retained her own public-relations guy at AIG, an arrangement I thought bizarre. Maybe she was hoping all along that "crazy Bob" would flame out and she'd get my job.

The investment bankers who would rake in additional hundreds of millions in commissions from a quick-and-dirty sell-off of AIG no doubt wouldn't have minded her staying on, too. I was already making noise about the outrageous amounts of money that our outside financial and legal advisers were making.

What planet were those people on? I wondered. Did they think AIG could be dismantled behind my back? A clear message was about to be sent to a conference room on Park Avenue.

And the deliveryman would be me.

Being an executive at a major brokerage and then leading a Fortune 500 insurance company had sharpened my skill at a business fundamental: understanding value; that is, how to place a value on things. As David Herzog, AIG's chief financial officer when I arrived, would later describe it, my ability was not "to put in an algorithm that's a foot and a half long." It was much more instinctive than that. "He just understands how to make money, and he understands value. And he understands growth," Herzog said.

Despite my abysmal college math grades, I was always good with numbers, as I had demonstrated in my stint as chief financial officer at Paine Webber; I had a talent for quickly digesting a balance sheet or a prospectus, analyzing its meaning, and forecasting a result with pretty good accuracy. (Much of my three-year retirement, from 2006 to 2009, was spent at my computer, managing my investments via Yahoo Finance.)

I don't think I can find an adequate clinical explanation for the source of my instincts about value, both in things and, more importantly, in people. I do know that it has something to do with paying attention to the subtle signals the world sends you, to which you have to remain vigilantly attuned. And that (surprise, surprise) reminds me again of the story of, "You said your dog doesn't bite!": Because sometimes, it's what people don't tell you that you have to be listening for. That day, the people on Park Avenue who decided I didn't really need to be at that meeting were conveying the message to me that I really, really did.

And I was going to make sure that if any teeth were going to be shown, they'd be mine.

Realizing the true value of AIG was destined to be one of the pillars of my strategy going forward. Making sure the people of AIG were rewarded for *their* value would be another. In many ways, the goals were intertwined. And neither seemed to have received adequate attention in the year that had passed since the Fed and Treasury began the rescue.

That said, I also realized that AIG was simply too damn big. Too big to fail, so they said—but also too big to be managed effectively. It wasn't one company; it was more than two hundred companies. A map of AIG's organizational chart made the periodic table of elements look like a child's board game. By itself, Chartis—the name with which our domestic property and casualty business was rechristened in 2009, to escape the AIG "taint"—had at least twice the value of the entirety of my former company, MetLife. So there were in effect three or four MetLifes sitting in AIG; that's how huge it was. It was unrealistic at this point to think we could adequately run all these businesses—from domestic life insurance and consumer finance to global leasing of aircraft and even selling auto insurance in Europe.

Many of the overseas businesses would indeed have to be sold. I saw that. It was all too massive considering the amount of money we owed. And it was too sprawling to be managed by one person—other than, perhaps, the man who had put this corporate jigsaw puzzle together in the first place. I said as much to Greenberg when I talked to him earlier that summer.

"I don't understand why that's true," Greenberg said. "I didn't think it was too big."

Greenberg, by the way, never thought anything was too big.

"Hank," I said, "you had thirty-five years to build AIG, thirty-five years to learn it. Nobody else is going to have those thirty-five years in training to do that."

When we could get the right prices, at the right moment, for the units it made sense to divest, and at the same time retained the right people and brought on others to help us, AIG would pay off its obligations to the government and return to its traditional profitability. I felt certain of it. At the right time. Not before.

Months before my arrival, Jim Millstein had put together his own rapid liquidation plan to show Geithner and the White House what that might look like, and to provide a sense of what kind of losses the government might be exposed to under such a scenario. Millstein described this approach as "an orderly sale of assets, a breakup of the company as fast as humanly possible, just to make AIG go away."

Millstein and his team estimated that in going forward with such a plan, the government stood to lose "somewhere between $60 billion and $90 billion."

Of course, even this was a guesstimate. " 'Look, we don't know, it depends,' " Millstein says he told his bosses. " 'There are a lot of big businesses here. There's a trillion dollars of financial assets on the insurance company's balance sheets. What is an insurance company but an investment fund and a claims-paying agent?

" 'A lot of this is going to depend on the recovery of the financial markets, and how fast and at what pace they recover. And the insurance franchises have been impaired as a result of the tarnishing of the name.' "

The assets AIG sold off in the year before I arrived were substantial by many measurements but minuscule in comparison to the amount of our debt: about $7.2 billion worth, representing about 4 percent of the money we owed the government. The largest of these thirteen transactions included the sale of the Otemachi building in Japan for $1.2 billion; AIG's 49 percent joint-venture stake in a Brazilian bank, Unibanco, for $820 million; a Connecticut-based specialty insurer, Hartford Steam Boiler Inspection and Insurance Co., for $739 million; and a Thai banking and credit card operation for $540 million.

A slew of banks and law firms were assisting AIG in the various deals. Investment advisers included Morgan Stanley, Goldman Sachs, Blackstone Group, and Bank of America. The heavy-hitting law firms included Weil, Gotshal & Manges; Cravath, Swaine & Moore; and Debevoise & Plimpton. The commissions being charged on the auctions were exorbitant, in the range of 2 to 2.5 percent. I wanted the numbers slashed in half.

"We're going to stop feeding that baby real quick," I said, at one of my town-hall meetings. "There's going to be a lot less bonus pool on Wall Street after I get done."

Even taking into account that the company was under enormous pressure to show progress, some of these deals seemed hasty. They certainly looked that way to an expert like Greenberg. Naturally, he was pained and incensed by the breakup of the AIG empire he had so meticulously assembled. Plus, the company he now headed, Starr International, had been AIG's biggest shareholder before the government's intervention all but wiped out its value.

Still, no one knew AIG as intimately as he did, so you had to listen when he spoke. And what he said was that these early transactions troubled him. As he noted in his book, *The AIG Story*, "Many of these sales were made at prices the buyers considered a steal." He pointed out, for example, that AIG had acquired Hartford Steam Boiler nine years earlier for $1.2 billion—and that price was actually deemed low at the time. This meant AIG was absorbing a nearly half-a-billion-dollar loss on that deal alone. What, someone might have wondered, did this portend for the sale of the bigger assets?

Within the company, too, there was some consternation about what was being sold, and for how much. Herzog says of the deals: "Some were more acceptable than others, and some were just downright offensive." The worst of the proposed deals in the pipeline, he reports, like Reynolds's plan to sell off the airplane-leasing unit ILFC for what amounted to a billion-dollar loss, he refused to sign off on. According to Herzog, he went to Liddy and told him he thought the premature sale was nuts.

"You're giving it away," he says he told Liddy. "I'm not signing a deal where we're going to write a check for a billion dollars to get rid of a company. I don't know what it's worth; it's not worth much at the moment. At some point it's going to be worth something. It's going to be worth more than a negative billion!"

If you consider the psychology of the early days after the crisis, the quick-sale mentality wasn't surprising. One of the mind-sets shared by many at this stage, even including the government to which we owed it, was that AIG was never going to be in a position to pay back that seemingly unscalable mountain of debt. So if there was scant expectation of recouping every dollar, why worry whether you were getting top dollar?

The sharks were circling for other bargains. For instance, Wilbur Ross, the billionaire investor in ailing businesses, made a play for United Guaranty, our North Carolina–based mortgage insurance unit, which behind Financial Products was our most troubled division as a result of its securities lending division. He was offering less than $100 million for it, and we weren't even going to be getting rid of our "back book"—policies for which we were still paying out premiums. We'd still be obligated for those. "Forget it, I'm not selling," I said.

My sense, too, was that there were many people at senior levels seeking to maximize their own positions at the expense of the corporation.

Many of those working in various AIG units wanted to have their own companies, I believed, to initiate IPOs and spin off their operations as independent businesses. If AIG sold more than 50 percent of the stock in any of these units through an IPO, the executives running them could take full control. Some of these people in our subsidiary units asked me for stock options—the right to buy stock at an agreed to, often advantageous price—in their own companies. "We can't have AIG stock anymore," they said. "It's dead." But if I didn't make the options in AIG stock, what incentive would they have to make sure that if we sold their unit, we got the best price for that part of AIG? None. They'd want the unit to go for the lowest price, so that their stock options started off at a low point. If they had a low starting point, they could make a lot of money and screw the rest of the AIG shareholders at the same time.

The strategic thinking I was picking up on amounted to: "I don't give a shit how much money is raised, as long as we get to do an IPO, and then we'll work out our executive compensation on our own, and nobody will be able to tell us what to do."

Even at this early stage, I'd concluded that many of AIG's subsidiaries would be in dire straits if we followed the executives' whims: our huge property and casualty business, for instance, was looking to have to add massive infusions of money to bolster its reserves—the amount the company holds aside in anticipation of future payouts. Without AIG to back it up, I believe the business would have collapsed. Both ILFC—our airplane leasing company—and American General Finance, a domestic commercial credit division, were also facing collapse if they were spun off. I was certain, too, that in a spin-off scenario, SunAmerica, a domestic branch selling life insurance and annuities, would have seen drastic cuts to its credit rating that would have made it impossible for it to be monetized at full value. The implications were not only potentially lethal to AIG; they posed a threat to the public coffers that had been opened to the company, and that taxpayers had every right to expect us to replenish.

This idea that an IPO was like a golden treasure map was absurd. As I explained in another of my town-hall meetings, this one with Sun-

America domestic retirement services division employees in a Marriott in Woodland Hills, California, on August 13, 2009, "You know, to just IPO your company, you just don't go to the stock market and say: 'Okay, here we are, take our stock, and we're going to get rich.'"

An initial public stock offering, I said, was far more complex and required a huge amount of consideration and preparation. Investors weren't simply going to line up. "You have to *sell* what your company is all about, *sell* why you're going to have a growth rate, *sell* where you are today," I said.

Of paramount importance, too, was showing an exemplary pattern of growth and organization, in ways that revealed why you'd make a good public company.

"And if you don't have a good story," I continued, "you're not going to get your stock issued at the right price. It just won't happen. And so we've got a lot more work to do here to get people really ready for prime time."

This was my philosophy in a nutshell. Nothing was going to be sold until I was satisfied that the sale was justified and I could determine the impact the sale would have on the remaining company. Millstein and I talked extensively about balancing my desire not to act rashly with the external pressures to repay.

He was always a voice of reason—even if I just took some of what he said under advisement. "You know, Bob, at the end of the day you've got an emergency loan from the Federal Reserve," he said to me, very early in this whole process. "They're not here to be a long-term lender, and the markets aren't there yet, to refinance [the debt]. You're likely going to have to deleverage the company by selling some assets." The good news, he added, was that some of the markets, especially in Asia, were already beginning to rally.

The reputation I was establishing as a scary, bombastic guy was helpful in my efforts to follow my own gut. Washington was in no hurry to hear from me, which seemed to provide me some additional maneuverability. AIG's hundred-thousand-plus employees were another vital interest group, and all the speculation about what might be jettisoned from the firm was raising anxieties all over the world. If there was any doubt that this rush to sell was the talk of the company, it was put to rest by the tenor of the questions at the town-hall meeting I organized in New York on August 4.

"We've heard basically about breaking up and selling and dismantling," one of the attendees who approached the microphones asked me. "What do you see left as the core that you would be building on?"

"I'm going to sit down over the next two to three weeks and begin to put together what that vision will be," I replied. "And what's important to me is that we have to think about the sum of the parts, and we have to understand, first of all, do these parts make sense together, or not? And then we have to think about whether they're greater than the whole, or less than the whole. . . . What's important is that at the end of the day, what's left is an organization big enough and diverse [enough] so that we have good 'business risk management.'"

What I meant by that, of course, was the sensible integration of risk across all parts of the company, in a way that protected and maximized the financial outcome. Much the same way as when you think about selling, say, life insurance, you consult the actuarial tables to consider mortality rates and so on, and make sure the risk is within the limits that help you realize an acceptable return.

As for Project Destiny: that was an elaborate set of blueprints developed by Reynolds and a team of consultants from McKinsey & Company over the first half of 2009 for remodeling and selling off the major operations of AIG. The ramifications for the company were monumental. A September 2009 report to Congress on the status of TARP by the U.S. Government Accountability Office hinted at the scope of Project Destiny: "According to AIG's former chief executive officer, AIG's plan is to sell businesses that constitute almost 65 percent of the company and employ approximately 70,000 people." This included a plan to relaunch the property and casualty business and sell it as part of a new entity called AIU Holdings. The divestiture plans for other major assets, like ALICO, our life insurance company with extensive ties to Japan, and Hong Kong–

based AIA, were also detailed in Project Destiny. Which really at its heart was a manual for taking the company out back and shooting it in the head.

The problem was, I didn't believe in it. As I'd told Millstein, I wanted to rebuild, not dismantle. If they wanted a guy simply to take the place apart, they could call 1-800-GOT-JUNK. It wasn't going to be me. If this was truly what was in store, I'd be buying the next one-way ticket for Villa Splendid.

So I took a car uptown and made my way that warm summer morning to the Project Destiny meeting in 277 Park Avenue, a fifty-story office building between 47th and 48th Streets. Crashing a gathering at the company I ran!

There was one seat left when I walked into the conference room, which was packed. Everyone was still settling in, and looked a bit surprised to see me. Next to me was seated a guy I hadn't met before. He introduced himself as Rob Gifford. "What do you do?" I asked. He said he was new, recruited to head up the global real estate platform. "I think there's a lot of work to do there," I said.

I listened quietly to Reynolds's presentation for a while. And then I couldn't listen anymore.

When I spoke up, the collar had definitely come off.

I jumped out of my seat, and exploded. "I don't know what the hell she's talking about," I shouted. "This is a terrible time to sell that business."

Silence. The tension was exquisite, everyone shifting uncomfortably in his or her seat. If anyone needed verification of the remark that I scared the hell out of people, well, this moment would certainly have served. I could tell I'd sucked the air out of the room.

"I need time to think our strategy over, but, you know, this makes absolutely no sense to me. I don't know what you have been doing here, but we're not doing any of this."

The meeting went on and on in this vein, for hours. Reynolds would offer up a part of the plan and I would shoot it down. Everyone seemed stunned. I looked over at one of my lieutenants, Brian Schreiber, who like me was no fan of the fire-sale approach. He was smiling. I took it as a good sign that he seemed to be liking this.

And that, as far as I was concerned, was the end of Project Destiny.

It didn't completely settle the matter, I'd soon discover. Those leaks that made it onto the Bloomberg wire and into other outlets while I was in Croatia affirmed for me that there were forces at AIG seeking to stop me in my tracks. Forget for a moment that as I've mentioned, some of the leaks actually worked in my favor, especially the stories concerning my disparaging remarks about Andrew Cuomo and Congress. Amazing how a little tough talk can lead to so many jumpy people.

And though in the past I'd faced down my share of corporate whispering campaigns and backstabbing, nothing in my dealings as a CEO at MetLife accustomed me to surreptitious undermining by members of my own board of directors. The MetLife board was a reliable partner, filled with extremely expert and consultative people, offering great advice and even at times useful challenges to accepted wisdom, as we mapped out the strategies to go public and buy Travelers Insurance from Citigroup.

This board, however, was something else again.

The eleven members of the board of directors included myself and CEOs and other senior executives from Wall Street investment banks and wealth-management firms, as well as from the fields of manufacturing (Boeing), airlines (Northwest), and retail (Sears, Roebuck). In the chairman's seat was Harvey Golub, the former chairman and CEO of American Express, an imperious fellow who was supposed to have been brought aboard to be our intermediary with Washington. Under the terms of the TARP rescue, Treasury had, in addition, three non-voting trustees on the board. They and officials of Treasury and the Fed, like Millstein and the Fed's Sarah Dahlgren, sat in on all our meetings—strange bedfellows for a Darwinian free-market advocate like me. (I wasn't an ardent fan of Ayn Rand's *Atlas Shrugged* for nothing.) Under these extreme circumstances, of course, the monitoring was completely understandable.

The board was made up of accomplished businesspeople, but only

Dennis Dammerman, the former head of GE Capital who helped to recruit me, did I consider at this point a reliable ally. Still, going into this, I could not have imagined the board of directors would actually become an impediment to my leadership. The last thing I wanted was "misalignment": the board and I being out of step—our thinking, in fact, in direct conflict.

I thought the board would be sympathetic. It didn't seem a ridiculous assumption. As an executive taking a new job, you have to do your due diligence. I not only spent a lot of time thinking about corporate politics and vision, and what was required to get the job done, I also met with and got support from key overseers, like Millstein and Dahlgren at the Fed. With all that groundwork laid, I was not concerned about being undercut by my own side. You have to think they want you; why else would they hire you?

Silly me.

The hit piece in the *Wall Street Journal* on September 3, 2009, spelled out for me in clear type what I was up against. "Will AIG Rein in its Brash CEO?" read the headline. "After uttering a string of incendiary remarks, the new CEO of American International Group Inc. may face harsh words from board members concerned that his tough talk has gone too far," it began.

> *Certain members of AIG's board, which put Robert Benmosche into the chief executive's role in August, have been taken aback by his comments at employee meetings, say people familiar with the matter. Mr. Benmosche said New York Attorney General Andrew Cuomo "doesn't deserve to be in government" and that Mr. Benmosche would leave dealing with "all those crazies in Washington" to the company's chairman, according to an account by Bloomberg News that was confirmed by Mr. Benmosche.*

The article did point out that some members of the board were "unfazed" by my manner and that many employees liked my "brashness." I can't say for certain who the "people familiar with the matter" were. But I had my suspicions. The first name of the triple byline on the story belonged to Joann S. Lublin, a *Journal* reporter of long service, with an enviable array of sources. (I didn't speak to her; I had been interviewed by another *Journal* reporter.) Golub was also for years a member of the board of Dow Jones Co., which published the *Wall Street Journal* until Rupert Murdoch bought it in 2007. I knew he and Lublin were friendly. Could I be wrong in putting two and two together?

The piece went on to say that "some AIG board members" were going to discuss how to "better manage" me, and that altering my "tone" might be a consideration in whether I held on to my job. And the piece threw Croatia in my face again, saying the board decided not to make it a bigger issue in the interest of keeping me focused on the payback.

A few things struck me about this article, aside from the fact that only two people were quoted by name. (One was Representative Elijah E. Cummings, who was given the opportunity to rake me over the coals about my comments once more. The other was . . . me.) I was forced to the conclusion that "certain members" of the board saw me as needing to be brought under control. The suggestions that my outbursts were childish and that Golub was going to be the "adult" who guided me to a more mature understanding of my role struck me as funny. (I also got a kick out of this line: "Another issue that has caught employees' attention: Mr. Benmosche's frequent use of four-letter curses during meetings." It seemed at future meetings I might have to distribute smelling salts for the faint-hearted.)

I also now concluded that Lublin was hostile to my plans for AIG. (She would later confirm this, going on a *Journal* television show and saying that I should resign.) I discerned that at least half the board was expressing doubts about me. It was also instructive to read that among my anonymous attackers, none of them thought to defend my trip to Croatia. The far more decent approach would have been for them to acknowledge our shared responsibility in the matter, in other words, to say to the press, "Look, we as a board gave him permission to go, we understood the conditions, we were pleased he was coming on board and if he could operate for a couple of weeks out of Croatia, fine."

Instead, they tried to make me look irresponsible. This convinced me that it would be futile to talk to Lublin; I'd have to look elsewhere at that influential paper for a fair hearing. And I had some evidence for my calculation that in the midst of everything else I had to deal with, AIG's board chairman was shaping up to be my biggest antagonist of all.

The strains resulting from this episode were so severe that my dealings with Golub would never recover.

To say that navigating these poisonous channels was frustrating was an understatement. And I had to put out other fires. Two of the executives who would be pivotal players in my plans, Herzog and Schreiber, the latter an expert in investments and the markets, were engaged in a bitter feud over past office grievances. I told them both that they had to find a way to work together, or they'd both be out. (They buried the hatchet, afterward becoming friends and allies.)

At the same time, I was growing leery of the corporate general counsel I'd inherited, Stasia Kelly. Reports were getting back to me about her complaints about my style. I suspected she might be a pipeline to Golub. So if I wanted some piece of information to get to him—we rarely spoke outside of board meetings—I would convey it to Kelly "in confidence." To my lack of surprise, I'd later hear some of those tidbits repeated by him and by other board members.

With a raft of distractions in this dysfunctional environment, I had major tasks awaiting me when I returned to work from Croatia on September 8, the day after Labor Day.

Some of the economic signs were encouraging. With market conditions improving, the company was performing better in some key parts of our business; we would in due course be announcing a profit of $455 million for the third quarter of 2009. It would be the second quarter in a row in which we had positive results, after a yearlong tsunami of losses. (In the comparable quarter in 2008, AIG's losses totaled $24.7 billion.)

Chartis, the property and casualty division, had a robust quarter, while our life insurance business continued to falter. This was due both to the hit our troubles delivered to our reputation, and to flagging consumer confidence in the economy: many people were cashing in their policies.

We were, of course, still perceived as a very sick patient, dependent on the government to keep us afloat. AIG had made only a minuscule dent in repaying our loans to the Fed. (Remember: the Fed was our lender; the Treasury our investor.) As a result we couldn't access the capital markets; commercial banks would not lend to us. A company of our size traditionally relied on issuing commercial paper—a short-term borrowing tool that allowed us to meet our obligations for inventory, payroll, and debt service on our other loans. Access to this kind of liquidity, however, was off the table. So when, for example, we had a scheduled payment of, say, $2.5 billion due on the fleet of planes we'd financed for our ILFC division, we had to rely on that line of credit we had with the Fed.

The irony of the rules the government now forced us to live by was that while on the one hand they kept us afloat, on the other they prevented us from fully pursuing the moneymaking opportunities that would help pay down our debt. Take, for instance, our American General Finance subsidiary, a unit acquired by AIG in 2001 that offered mortgage and personal loans and equity lines of credit to middle-range consumers, those with good rather than outstanding credit. Until the crisis, it was a solid performer, with lower default rates than those of our competitors. However, because AIG's debts were so huge, American General Finance was restricted from making more than $200 million in loans a month, at a time the consumer demand could easily have had us doing business on the order of $1 billion a month.

This was frustrating because our hands were tied at the very moment when the struggling U.S. economy needed the kinds of infusions of consumer spending that our loans helped make possible. The government's mixed message to us was: "We want you to lend, lend, lend so that you can pay us back, but we want you to pay us back before we let you lend, lend, lend."

The September 2009, progress report on us by the U.S. Government Accountability Office reflected the good-news, bad-news morass in which we were functioning. It pointed out that our credit ratings had been stable since May, that we were making progress in our efforts to unwind AIG Financial Products' credit-default swaps, and that our joint efforts with the government to restructure our federal debt had reduced our financial obligation and thereby helped to improve the equity positions of our shareholders.

But the report also noted that we were still deep in the weeds. The GAO was hedging its bets. "While federal assistance has helped stabilize AIG's financial condition, GAO-developed indicators suggest that AIG's ability to restructure its business and repay the government is unclear at this time," the report said. It also took up the Project Destiny issue:

> *Despite these efforts, the Federal Reserve and Treasury continue to carry significant exposure as a result of the assistance to AIG. Until the debt is repaid and the equity interests are repurchased or sold, the Federal Reserve and Treasury remain exposed to credit and investment risks. The ongoing potential of systemic risk remains a concern until AIG is restructured and market conditions improve. According to Treasury, "an orderly restructuring is essential to AIG's repayment of the support it has received from U.S. taxpayers and to preserving financial stability."*

"However," the report added, "an orderly restructuring depends heavily on AIG's ability to successfully divest assets."

The press's takeaway reflected the murky conclusion. "AIG Said to Be Stable, but Hurting for Cash," the *New York Times* said in its September 22, 2009, story about the report.

I have to say, I was still back and forth on the scope of the divestiture. That so many people were in a rush made me that much more resistant. Was Greenberg right? I wondered. During one of our weekly meetings, I bounced the idea off Millstein. Maybe, I said, we didn't have to sell anything.

"With enough time," I posited, "we could turn the operations around of the company as it currently stands, and maybe create enough operating income to be able to refinance everything."

Millstein clearly wanted to encourage me in my turnaround efforts even if I could tell this wasn't what he wanted to hear.

He listened patiently, then said: "We've left you a couple of [corporate] planes. Take one and go visit the major offices of the company. Go visit the outer edges of your empire. You need to do that anyway, see the people out in the field, introduce yourself. Then when you get back, call me, and let's have this conversation again."

I had in fact already started to visit the empire. Over the coming autumn weeks, I would travel even more widely as I tried to absorb, on multiple levels, the immensity of the enterprise.

Project Destiny was now in my rearview mirror. Reynolds left after that fateful meeting on Park Avenue, and in late September, McKinsey & Company would be gone, too. Its services, I said, would no longer be required.

Realizing optimal value was in the forefront of my mind. I saw this as an issue both across the spectrum of our holdings, and for me personally as well, because two months into my tenure, my compensation still had not been formally settled. And this really stuck in my craw. I was in essence working without a salary. And it wasn't even that I needed the money. That was not it at all. It was the question lingering in the air, in the hive-mind of the board and the company I was determined to save, of my value to it.

# NINE

# CLAWBACK

NO ISSUE IN MY TIME AT AIG was more emotional, or political, than pay. For the public, incensed at having its money go to private companies that brought the financial system to the edge of ruin, how much cash went into our executives' pockets was understandably of major interest. For our employees, on the other hand, the paycheck was a highly personal matter, the ultimate proof of their worth. Reducing the amount of their compensation would be viewed by them as such a punitive measure, such a kick in the teeth as well as the wallet, that some people would decide the job was no longer worth it, and leave.

Simply saying "good riddance" to them might have seemed a satisfying response for the public. But even from the taxpayers' point of view it was self-defeating. I—and they—needed these people to stay, and badly. At units like Financial Products, at the heart of the meltdown, the expertise of those who understood the deals was crucial to undoing the damage. My mantra of restoring company pride, too, was based on the idea that people would be rewarded appropriately, according to their contributions. At MetLife, I championed a model of personnel performance review that compelled managers to rank employees as a way of determining compensation. I liked to think I had a highly developed sense of how to assess value not only of financial instruments, but of people, too.

So the unprecedented controls over compensation that TARP had put into place by the time I arrived at AIG were a serious crimp in my plans—an impediment, of course, that I knew I had to live with. The subject consumed much of my time during my first six months at the company. Earlier in 2009, Congress, looking for additional ways to control the companies it bailed out, had passed the American Recovery and Reinvestment Act, which gave the Treasury the power to limit the amount of money paid to executives at the seven companies governed by TARP, including AIG. Specifically, the law mandated that the government itself set the compensation for the top twenty-five executives at each company, and establish guidelines by which the companies fixed the salaries of the next seventy-five highest-level employees.

There were rules set out on other items, like a $25,000 ceiling per executive on "perks" such as the use of corporate jets. All of these matters fell under the control of a "special master" appointed by Treasury, whose job it was to meet with the companies and hammer out the hard numbers. That person was Kenneth R. Feinberg, who took the job for no pay himself. A lawyer and skilled negotiator, he had previously assumed a delicate role after the terrorist attacks of September 11, 2001, as special master of the September 11th Victim Compensation Fund.

Feinberg and I had begun talking during the summer of 2009, shortly after both of us started our new jobs, when he waived the new guidelines and met my demands for my $10-million-plus AIG compensation package. In his lucid 2012 book, *Who Gets What: Fair Compensation After Tragedy and Financial Upheaval*, he noted that I was one of only three executives at the TARP companies to receive waivers of the $500,000 cap imposed on annual salary.

The special master and I met half a dozen times at Treasury's headquarters in D.C. in the fall of 2009 to try to come to terms on a variety of problems. One of our most intense struggles was over the $165 million in so-called "retention bonuses" to employees at FP that had become the focus of national outrage. As Feinberg described it in *Who Gets What*, our negotiation was "the most emotional battle" he faced. "It was not cordial or pretty," he wrote. "It was a heavyweight bout with the gloves off." I can vouch for that.

It was emotional partly because we understood the stakes. I knew Feinberg had a job to do, but so did I, and our interests did not naturally align. Having the government as a savior was of course something to be respectful of, but having it involved in something as fundamental as salary-setting was hard to get used to. The kind of tense relationship that existed between us and our taxpayer/shareholders was more fraught than anyone could ever have anticipated, especially around the pay issue. It was harder for free enterprise to thrive when decisions at the heart of employee motivation and performance were being decided in consultation with the government.

The my-way-or-the-highway stubbornness that was part of my nature made me uncomfortable with this close supervision. And I was also irritated by the grinding of the bureaucratic wheels. More than a month after my arrival at AIG—and even though Feinberg had signed off on my salary—the board had not formally authorized it and as a result I still had not been paid a dime. And then there was—to my mind—the ridiculous haggling over my using the corporate jets, an issue that almost drove me over the edge.

That particular issue came to a head on Friday, September 18, 2009, which fell on one of the most joyous days on the Jewish calendar. But I was in a less than joyous mood. That afternoon, just hours before the start of Rosh Hashanah, the Jewish New Year, I was sitting at Newark airport in New Jersey, waiting for a Continental flight to Tampa.

I was excited about the trip, actually. My daughter Nehama, finishing up her rabbinical training, would deliver her first sermon later that day before a congregation in Sarasota, a huge event in her life, and of course in mine and Denise's, too. I was looking forward to being there, to marking the occasion with her, to hearing the wisdom my daughter would impart. People often remarked on how alike Nehama and I were:

headstrong, outspoken, independent, intent on doing things our way. Few experiences in life could possibly have given me more pleasure than to be with her on this occasion, watching her conquer this meaningful summit.

My daughter, the rabbi. In the footsteps of her great-grandfather, Herman. The Yiddish word for pleasure, *naches,* expressed it perfectly. In completing another link in the Benmosche family chain, Nehama was spreading *naches.*

The means of getting there, I was not so pleased about. Not because I had an aversion to commercial travel. Far from it. Been shoehorning my six-foot, four-inch frame into narrow plane seats all my working life. But because less than two months into the job, how I traveled had become an issue at AIG, to a degree that was giving me second thoughts yet again about having taken it.

The folks at AIG were increasingly nervous about any use of AIG's corporate jets; a year earlier, the CEOs of the Big Three automakers came under withering public assault for using private planes to fly from Detroit to Washington to ask Congress for $25 billion in bailout money. But I wasn't flying on company jets to beg the government for money; they were a means to help me get the government's money back.

After selling some of its fleet, AIG kept two midsized planes at Teterboro Airport in northern New Jersey, along with a few smaller aircraft. And let me tell you: for the new CEO of a global concern, one who was expected to rapidly immerse himself in a complex constellation of businesses, make a multitude of informed decisions affecting thousands of employees, and work out the repayment of billions of dollars, the company plane was not a luxury. Oh, it's a luxurious way to fly, no doubt about it. For me, though, reliability and convenience were what mattered most, and I didn't have time to fret too much about how it "looked." The ability to get to all the places I had to, swiftly and without exposure to the chronic delays of the commercial carriers, was not a luxury at all.

There was mounting terror at AIG, however, about the remotest appearance of our thumbing our noses at the taxpayer. (Remember how the congressional committee ripped the company apart the previous year for a $440,000 promotional outing at a California resort?) The public relations problem of executive travel so worried Ed Liddy, my predecessor working for a $1 a year, that he would refuse a free upgrade to business class when he flew coach on his weekends home to Chicago. (The company did reimburse him for the economy-class commute.) God forbid someone freaked out over his taking advantage of extra legroom.

Hats off to Liddy for his cautious economizing. Far be it from me, a penny-pincher going way back, to look askance at cost savings. But the insecurity within AIG was extreme to the point of being self-defeating. And it went way beyond whether the CEO flew coach. The fear of a public backlash was such that employees felt they had to hide their association with AIG, as if it were something shameful. At its downtown Manhattan offices, the company had removed all the exterior AIG signage. Some of my direct reports told me that they had rummaged through their kids' drawers, stripping them of anything with the AIG insignia. AIG's initials even disappeared from employees' ID badges! And our huge property and casualty business was rechristened Chartis, under the assumption that American International Group was a name that lived in infamy.

Sad.

The scrubbing of the AIG brand went part and parcel with a rampant belief that the company itself would soon be a thing of the past—a mind-set I was challenging daily, in my determination to keep it as a going concern and find only the most strategic ways to raise capital through a measured divestiture. As I said, though, this fear of how things might look, of what might bring down the wrath of Congress and the regulators and the media upon us, had become ridiculously all consuming. And part of my job, I thought, was to eliminate this negative mind-set. I had to get this company to believe in itself again, and that meant not feeling anything but pride in saying that you worked for AIG.

The jet was essential in my mind to my completing the complex tasks on my agenda, and on a personal level, confirmation that I had the company and government's trust to do my job the way it needed to be done. That's how a GSD guy operates. And I had—I thought—negotiated an agreement with both Treasury and the company when I signed on at AIG for some latitude in my access to the corporate jet, including allowing Denise to accompany me on some trips. (Though just to be clear, I did fly commercially for that much-criticized Croatian trip.) Again, I thought I had obtained agreement on my salary, but in the waning weeks of September I still had no approved compensation. My patience was being sorely tested.

The board of directors was of no help. Golub explained to me that the directors were deadlocked on signing off on my terms for use of the jet.

"Harvey," I said. "You know I travel a lot. That's my way of conducting business. I don't sit in my office to find out what's going on. I go out and see what's happening."

"Well, the board is divided, five to five," he said.

In other words, he was letting me know that it would be up to me to break the tie. Well, with my salary and benefits still up in the air, this felt like one indignity too many. Were they actively seeking to piss me off, or were they just too cowed to act? These people were going to force me to be the bad guy, to vote myself a "perk" that would inevitably attract more ridicule, and right on the heels of the Croatian trip. Nope. No way would I walk into that trap.

Let me make clear my own attitude about the public's anger, because I don't wish to give the impression that I'm minimizing it. I'm not. Of course I recognized that it was real. I was made aware of it, virtually every day. But there is a difference between appreciating the outrage and becoming a captive of it. There was no way we were going to save this company if I dwelled on it. I had to set it aside, proceed without worrying about the scorn. I was not with AIG at the time these bad decisions were made, so I had no reason to feel guilt. My responsibility was to rebuild, not atone. I wanted people around me who shared that sense of mission. I needed partners who were going to help me, not thwart me. And that's why I believed that politicians and the government, rather than continually pounding us for our mistakes on social media and in the press, needed to stop, and instead step up and publicly support our efforts. Bad business practices got us into the mess, but the country had to be reassured that good practices could get us out of it again. Isn't that what leadership is about?

Well, sticking to my guns on the jet issue clearly was not going to win me friends. I got the bad press anyway. My good friends at Bloomberg ran a story the day before my Rosh Hashanah trip, another nasty little swipe, detailing a clash with the board over my travel. Citing "two people familiar with the matter," the news outlet reported that I was "rebuffed by the insurer's board" in my desire to use the planes for private travel.

So there I was on Rosh Hashanah, waiting to fly out of Newark. A morning meeting had compelled me to take a midafternoon flight and lo and behold, a shocking thing happened at one of the busiest airports in the nation on a peak-travel Friday: the flight was delayed. By the time I got to Florida, it was raining, the traffic to Sarasota was horrendous— and Nehama could not hold off on giving her debut speech any longer.

I arrived for the last ten minutes of her sermon. I was beside myself. Few things bring you lower than the feeling you've let your kid down, even your grown-up kid.

I approached her afterward and hugged her, proudly, but I wanted to cry. She said she understood and was happy I was there, which only made me feel worse. I tried not to show how much of a blind rage I was in, how out-of-my-mind fed up I was, how helpless I felt. All because of the damn AIG plane and the government and the board. "Fuck them and fuck everybody else," I muttered to myself, darkly. The pleasant life I'd been leading, I'd given up, *for this*? My daughter had to suffer: *for this*? I was angry at myself most of all. I had all the fuck-you money I could ever want, and here the biggest fuck-you was being aimed right at you know who.

The irony wasn't lost on me. Here I was, betting the future of this company on the belief that I could restore the employees' depleted morale— and my own morale was, for the moment, in the toilet. What was unclear to everyone at the time was that getting where I needed to be was not for me a negotiable perk: it was essential to my sense of well-being, to reinforcing a belief in my mission. It was, psychologically and practically speaking, a critical part of my compensation.

And my own compensation was just the start. There was Feinberg to grapple with, all through the fall of '09. Getting my pay right was only a very small component of what I had to do. And yet, seeing to it that I was appropriately paid would be symbolically crucial across this vast company, because that idea of being treated fairly had to start with me if it was going to be shared by everyone at AIG and we were ever going to restore the company to health and paying back the taxpayer.

Indeed, I viewed fixing employee compensation as the keystone of everything I was trying to do to rehabilitate AIG. The issue had become such a hot potato and so difficult to resolve that valuable time and energy were being drained away. And not just mine.

The fact was that the brain drain at the company was terrible for us, bordering on disastrous. Although some had been forced out, dozens of other pivotal people had left, twenty alone to join a Bermuda company called Ironshore, engaged in a joint venture with Hank Greenberg's C.V. Starr & Co. We'd lost senior officers in internal audit, tax, HR, even our chief operating officer. Many others, leery of the government controls on pay, were looking for an exit.

To put it simply: I needed people to stay. Especially, but not only, at Financial Products. And they needed to believe it was worth their while. We were making progress but we had a long way to go, especially at FP. Remember that these few hundred professionals were trying to work down incredibly complex derivatives, with a notional value of more than a trillion dollars. Without their active participation, we were sunk.

The daily nightmare I faced in those early months was contending with the public's belief that every dollar spent at AIG was an insult to their wallets, and a moral outrage to boot. And nothing was easier for everyone to condemn than the amounts of money we were paying our workers, especially those at Financial Products.

The controversy over the $165 million in "retention bonuses" paid to Financial Products employees for their work in 2008, the year the roof caved in, raged on all through my early months at the company, and was threatening to wreck everything I was trying to accomplish. The furor had bled into the fabric of AIG's story. We were no longer an insurance giant; we were simply the outlaw company that while on government life support further enriched ourselves with bonuses.

The term, however, was a misnomer. And the confusion, I think, had to do with more than language. "Bonus" is often defined as a reward for good work, and that's how the average person perceives it. But in our business, these "bonuses" are not rewards at all; they're part of one's normal compensation.

A more accurate term—as I've described it on several occasions—would have been "variable salary." This isn't just fiddling around with terminology. It describes a portion of one's annual prearranged compensation that is adjustable, depending on the level of performance. In the case of that $165 million: this wasn't an amount arrived at as a special inducement or reward. It was the amount those working at FP had been promised and were legally entitled to.

How it "looked" was another matter entirely, and one I had to take up with Feinberg, whose responsibilities concerned the seven companies that received what was considered "exceptional assistance" from TARP, of which AIG was one. The others were Citigroup, Bank of America, and four automotive concerns, aided in a separate bailout: General Motors and Chrysler and their consumer financing arms, GMAC and Chrysler Financial. When you thought about it, the mandate was a strange one—politically understandable, but with an odd socialistic odor: the U.S. was setting the pay and benefits for the top executives at each of the firms. The government's fear, certainly, was that in this treacherous environment, AIG and the other companies would be too generous, and the American people would ultimately place the onus for the salaries and bonuses on the regulators. But what constituted too generous? Since it would require the expertise of some of the very people who had, or appeared to have, a hand in creating the mess, how much was it worth to America to get its money back? And yes, it was hard for people to understand, or even swallow, the fact that these folks could indeed help return America's bailout money.

No one wanted to hear it, but senior officers at AIG were already paying astronomical penalties for the crisis. The idea that no pain was being felt there was simply wrong. As a result of AIG's losses, ten members of my executive group collectively lost $168 million in cash and future stock options, and five of the senior people at FP lost another $88 million. Yes, that's a hell of a lot of money. I also think it's a hell of a lot of punishment. And these folks were still with us, working extremely hard to help the company emerge from its troubles.

The government's control over compensation gave Feinberg huge power over us. And in a company as vast and unwieldy as AIG, there were other, logistical problems, in complying with the government strictures: I wasn't even sure how to figure out who our "top twenty-five" executives were!

Feinberg, a gregarious lawyer and professor with a Boston accent as thick as New England clam chowder, made his reputation in the aftermath of 9/11. He had ably served as the government's special master then, too, in the unenviable job of deciding who received money from the September 11th fund. Now, he was the point man on an issue that was eating up too much of my time at AIG. And with the strictures he was enforcing, he was driving us crazy. Even the government trustees on our board, appointed as a result of the taxpayers' 79.9 percent ownership, were chafing. One of them, Doug Foshee, had drafted a letter of resignation in exasperation, though he was persuaded to hold off.

When we'd first met over that summer to talk about my salary demands and a few other preliminaries, Feinberg made sure the setting was apt. Remembering me as a successful CEO at MetLife, he would later relate, he wanted an imposing backdrop for our meeting. "Environment means something," he said. (All these Washington fellows overestimated the impact of their offices on me.) So he had me meet him in a grand room at the Treasury Department dominated by a portrait of America's first Treasury secretary. Alexander Hamilton, the founding father of the country's monetary system, gazed down at us, expecting us to do our jobs, and well.

Impressive, but not as intimidating as he imagined. During that first sit-down, Feinberg had expressed shock at the size of my salary demands.

"Ten million!" he said. "Bob, that's like double what anyone else in the top twenty-five of these companies is getting."

"I'm worth it," I said.

His willingness to concede that I was worth it showed me that Feinberg was capable of seeing the light, though in the latter part of 2009 he made our lives hell.

Over a series of encounters all through the fall of 2009 I bargained, explained, and cajoled in the effort to hammer out a deal for the pay packages. In *Who Gets What*, Feinberg laid out the parameters: "We began the arduous task of negotiating individual pay packages for each AIG official. . . . How much cash? How much stock? How much of a discount in bottom-line dollars to account for past bonus compensation now overdue? What level of compensation would keep AIG personnel at their desks? How much would they be willing to discount their cash to avoid public and political criticism? Somehow I had to satisfy all my constituents—Benmosche, senior AIG executives, officials at both Treasury and the Federal Reserve, and my colleagues in the special master's office. It took months to hammer out the individual compensation packages."

Though the talks were tough, we developed a solid rapport and a mutual respect—despite media reports to the contrary. He told me that the other companies under his jurisdiction usually sent their heads of human resources, or some other executive on that level, to deal with him. I was the only CEO who regularly showed up as the representative of my company. Inside his office, Feinberg said, our meetings took on mythic proportions, with staffers vying for the right to sit in. (He joked that we should have booked the boxing ring at the MGM Grand for them.)

Hanging over our heads was the issue of those $165 million in Financial

Products retention payments. Of the $165 million, $45 million had been given to employees who were no longer with the company. The remaining $120 million did not require the returning of any cash, because that amount went to employees still with AIG; reducing their future pay packages could erase that figure.

The government was fixated on getting that money back, as Liddy, my predecessor, had promised. "After Liddy had testified in Congress, certain AIG officials who had received retention bonus payments had publicly promised to return this money, totaling $45 million, to the taxpayers," Feinberg wrote in his book. "They had not done so, and the public was watching." In fact, it was a public relations problem of a far greater complexity and magnitude than anything faced by any of the TARP companies.

After the "scandal" of the bonuses first broke, the condemnation spewed from across the political spectrum. Republicans and Democrats, free-market pundits and regulation-minded progressives were uniformly irate. They had a field day with us. Righteous indignation is easy to spew when an issue is portrayed as black and white. The public had no problem visualizing dollar bills being swiped from their pockets and being placed in AIG traders' wallets. When the president went on the record about it, the universal condemnation of AIG was as good as etched in concrete. "It's hard to understand how derivative traders at AIG warranted any bonuses, much less $165 million in extra pay," Obama said in March 2009. "How do they justify this outrage to the taxpayers who are keeping the company afloat?"

The battle over the retention payments—what I called variable salary—was having a terrible effect on morale at FP. The workers who had remained to try to clean up the mess made by a handful of employees were feeling abused and forsaken.

The employees' frustrations and anguish had been splashed in great detail on the op-ed page of the *New York Times* in March 2009, just after Liddy's testimony, when the paper published an open resignation letter to Liddy from Jake DeSantis, an executive vice president in FP's commodities and equity division who had been at the company for eleven years. Scathing in tone, and pointing out that most of the culpable employees "have left the company and have conspicuously escaped the public outrage," DeSantis's letter said he felt abandoned by the company. But he added that he couldn't bring himself to keep his retention payment, amounting to $742,006.40.

"After 12 months of hard work dismantling the company—during which AIG reassured us many times we would be rewarded in March 2009—we in the financial products unit have been betrayed by AIG and are being unfairly persecuted by elected officials. In response to this, I will now leave the company and donate my entire post-tax retention payment to those suffering from the global economic downturn."

Shortly after I arrived at AIG, during that initial flurry of August visits I made to AIG units in the Midwest and West Coast, where I talked about my commitment to protecting the workforce from the attacks being aimed at them from Congress and guys like Cuomo, I made a point of going to FP's offices in Wilton, Connecticut. Golub came, too. I was astonished to hear that I was the first AIG CEO to visit in years, and certainly since the crisis had begun.

Pasciucco was himself amazed at the scale of the hullabaloo over the bonuses. In comparison to the numbers he was dealing with, in the task of de-risking FP's securities, the figure was minuscule.

Just as daunting was the seriousness of the threats directed against FP employees. Politicians were demanding that AIG name names, the very definition of a witch hunt. Pasciucco would later recall it as a terrifying environment, in which schools were asking AIG parents to keep their kids out just in case "there was a nut job out there who would be only too happy to kill a kid from AIG, or a parent dropping them off." He went on: "People were being asked to resign from clubs, people were being followed, or thought they were being followed. Security at AIG said that there were people being picked up, parked near employees' homes, with guns in their cars."

Bricks were thrown through the windows of FP's office in London, too. Imagine trying to get a day's work done under such conditions. "The world was a little crazy then," Pasciucco would later recall.

As for me: I don't recall any threats being made against me personally. (Except maybe by some disgruntled politicos.) I had a driver but I traveled with no other security. I did, however, feel a great responsibility for the FP employees who were plugging away.

It should be noted that not everyone was of a mind to skewer the workers. In the *Washington Post*, for example, reporter Brady Dennis wrote in April 2009 about a fourth-grade teacher in Texas, who taught a daily unit on economics. One day she decided to focus on AIG and the bonuses. She "stood before her students," Dennis wrote,

> . . . *and stoked the populism in their young souls. Pretend you are taxpayers, she said. Now, think about AIG paying bonuses even after the government had committed $180 billion to bailing it out. "Can you believe it?" she asked.*
>
> *Then she turned the tables.*
>
> *"What if you were an AIG employee?" she asked.*

She wanted to know how the children would feel if they were not involved in making the bad decisions, and their families had received death threats. The kids decided to write letters of support to AIG, Dennis reported, including illustrating their letters with "peace symbols and smiley faces." One student wrote: "Hi AIG. Not all of USA hates you." Another said: "Keep working hard, dudes! Keep eating your vegatabos!"

I should have hired this teacher!

Some of the thirty cards drawn by the kids went up on the walls in FP's lunchrooms in Wilton and London and Paris. The workers were deeply touched—some wept. A decision was made, by the way for us not to identify publicly the school the cards came from, for fear that FP's harassers would turn their wrath on the teacher and her students.

This was the world we were dealing with when Feinberg and I sat down to talk about the retention payments.

I took the position with Feinberg that this $45 million was a ridiculous distraction. "Ken," Feinberg quoted me as saying in his book, during one of our sessions. "I am trying to rebuild this company. You are not making it easy. The dollars in dispute are nothing compared to what is at stake."

As for Feinberg's hands: I knew they were tied to some degree by events and people out of his control. Back on March 14, 2009—the day before an installment of the retention bonuses was to be distributed—Liddy had warned in a letter to Secretary Geithner that fiddling with salaries could make a bad situation worse for the company's credibility at a crucial moment. "I do not like these arrangements and find it distasteful and difficult to recommend to you that we proceed with them," Liddy wrote. "Honoring contractual commitments is at the heart of what we do in the insurance business."

Feinberg would later acknowledge knowing that the government would be on shaky ground if it had contemplated going to court on the matter. "Though I did not let on to Benmosche, I agreed with everybody at Treasury that it would be a huge public policy mistake to mount a court challenge to the validity of these retention contracts," he wrote in *Who Gets What*. "Sanctity of contract, enshrined in our Constitution, could not be lightly disregarded, especially by the Department of the Treasury and the Federal Reserve."

When I spoke in August 2009 to 150 FP workers assembled in Connecticut, I made it abundantly clear how I felt about the tactics that the politicians had used against them.

I also wanted them to know that the opportunity existed for them to redeem the company, and in a sense, themselves. Until then, the goals for unwinding the trades had been vague, built around Project Destiny's plans for a rapid sell-off of as much of the business as possible and a shutdown of the unit. The expectation had been that we'd end up losing money, even with the government's buying up of the toxic derivatives, and the losses would be in the range of $10 to $20 billion. So I told Pasciucco and his team: "Come up with a new plan. Set new targets. But if I'm going to commit to you, I want you guys to commit to me. I want everybody here who's committing to this plan to be here to execute it."

The people in that room, I felt confident, had been trying to do a job, but the world's rebukes were getting to them. Pasciucco himself was in a bit of a quandary. As he explained it, he was "asking these people to do transactions where they could make a difference of tens of millions of dollars," with no real incentive, other than their own integrity, their own sense of what was right.

Already, in fact, FP's twenty-five highest-paid contract employees, earning an average of about $270,000, had agreed to reduce their 2009 salary to $1 from March through the end of the year. Other officers of the unit had their 2009 salaries cut by 10 percent.

But that was entirely separate from the thornier point of contention lingering between Feinberg and me: how to resolve the $45 million that FP's former employees had and that the government wanted back. Until this matter was settled, compensation would be up in the air at AIG. Feinberg declared he would not approve pay packages of the AIG executives under his control.

The "clawback," as the process of compelling the return of the money was called, had to be accomplished first.

Feinberg told me he'd failed to resolve this issue before I showed up. A good 40 percent of the $45 million, around $19 million, had in fact been returned already by conscientious workers (the payments had ranged from thousands of dollars, to millions). And Feinberg was becoming impatient. He said that he told Kelly, our general counsel at the time, that if the money wasn't returned, he would have to recoup it by withholding the salaries of other executives at the company.

At FP, Pasciucco had determined that the traders' contracts had rock-solid guarantees regarding the money they received. He learned that if the employees in any way amended their agreements, their compensation would then fall under the provisions of TARP and could be legally altered by the government. It was highly unlikely anyone would agree to a change in the terms.

So it was up to me. "You're going to have to focus now on how we're going to get back the rest of that $45 million from the Financial Products people," Feinberg said to me, at one of our meetings. "And they've probably spent it already."

At the same time, I was getting an ever more bitter taste of the fix I was in, contending with hostilities inside the company and out. The fuss over my use of the jet, too, was getting to be ever more infuriating. In early October 2009, I was supposed to fly to St. Louis on the corporate jet to meet with officers of Edward Jones, the huge investment firm based there, about doing business with us again. On my way back I wanted to stop for a day in Chicago, where my son Ari was living, so that I could attend my granddaughter Aubrey's first birthday party, and then continue on from there to my next business appointment the next day, in Ojai, California.

"We have a problem with the plane," Jeff Hurd, an executive whose duties included running the fleet, told me.

"What's the problem with the plane, Jeff?"

"Since you're going to see your granddaughter and you're spending an extra day that's actually personal, there's a concern that you're going to violate the rules and have it for personal use," he explained. "So maybe what you should do is from St. Louis, fly back to New York, and then fly commercially to Chicago to see your granddaughter, and we can then have our plane pick you up or—well, we need to figure that out."

All the while the corporate jet would be sitting on the tarmac at Midway Airport in Chicago.

My last nerve was officially shot.

"Jeff, I've had enough," I said. I knew it wasn't Hurd's fault, but I felt the need to unload. "This place is chaos and the politics in this place are outrageous. You know what you can do? Take your company and all the planes and shove them up your fucking ass. Tell all the people in the fucking government to shove it up their ass, too, because I'm not doing this anymore. I missed my daughter's event in Florida, and there's no fucking way I'm not going to my granddaughter's first birthday. I told you that I'm not giving up my family for this fucking job."

After my outburst, the matter was taken up by AIG with Treasury and I was allowed to proceed with my original plans on the corporate jet. I was aware, of course, that in acting out I was using my leverage; I sensed that they needed me more than I needed them. I'm not saying I didn't enjoy some aspects of the job; just that I was more than willing, when things became untenable, to walk away.

By the end of October, and just after returning from a grueling fact-finding trip to our operations in China, Japan, Malaysia, and Singapore, I felt I had reached a point of no return on compensation. I saw firsthand the impressive pieces of the global business Greenberg had built, with so many deeply committed employees with a single question on their lips: How long was I going to stay?

My answer always was that I would be leaving sooner rather than later. And now, I was thinking it would be even sooner than that. Feinberg, Millstein, and their boss at TARP, Herb Allison, were scheduled to meet with me and the rest of the board for three hours on Tuesday, November 3. We were going to tell them that the displays of public anger toward the people at FP had to stop. But I had little faith that they were going to do anything about it.

"I am prepared to tell the board after they leave, and in an executive session, that I will send Harvey and Dennis [Dammerman] my letter of resignation next Friday after we announce earnings," I wrote on October 31, in an e-mail to a confidant whom I will not name. "I will say in the letter . . . that AIG is now stable and showing good results, that the people around the world are doing well and are energized, and thus my work is done. I will suggest the two senior guys for the US Life businesses and for the P&C Chartis businesses become co-CEOs. I will offer to help in the transition. This is getting too dangerous and I am sure they will cut my salary to under $500k next year to make a point that the President is the only one to make that amount. I could be wrong but I do not intend to take any more chances."

I never would send that letter. But I did complain to the directors, telling them of my weariness about the ongoing war over compensation. I also mentioned my desire to keep to a timetable I'd had in mind, of setting April 2010 as my departure date from AIG. "I'm done," I said at one point, although I really wasn't.

Like clockwork, the well-sourced *Wall Street Journal* went after the story big-time. "AIG's Benmosche Threatens to Jump Ship," shouted the *Journal* headline on November 11, 2009.

> *Robert Benmosche has told the board of American International Group Inc. that he is considering stepping down as chief executive of the government-controlled insurer, just three months after taking the job, according to people familiar with the matter.*
>
> *At a board meeting last week, the strong-willed industry executive told fellow AIG directors that he was "done" but agreed to think it over after other board members reacted with shock, according to the people.*

The article went on to report that I felt I was "in an impossible situation" regarding the controls placed on compensation by Feinberg. It said that my "frustrations hit a crescendo" at a three-hour meeting with him that I and other AIG board members attended in New York the week prior.

The subtext of this leak was that I was a prima donna capable of wild emotional swings. "AIG's Benmosche is a drama queen," complained the financial news outlet *The Deal*. "One of the things that has gotten lost in the mix of controversy over AIG is the fact that the original deal called for the insurer to disentangle itself from the financial system and to pay back the money taxpayers loaned it in two years—not to rebuild the company. This won't happen under Benmosche." (Actually, all these things eventually did happen under Benmosche.)

This crazy episode showed me that there was deep anxiety on the board about how reliable I was. "You resigned at that board meeting," Golub said to me, days later, referring to the November gathering. And I said, "Harvey, I didn't resign!"

"You absolutely resigned!" Golub replied.

"No, I absolutely said I was sick of waiting to announce that I would retire in April, and that I would like to announce it so that I can get control of the PR."

I hated to admit it, but I'd been boxed into a corner. The craziest result of the leak was that it guaranteed that I would *not* be leaving. I now had to counter the image of myself as a quitter. I would really have to see this thing through. The meeting erased some of my leverage: my ability to pull the trigger. I had a gun slipped under the door, I went to get it, and it was taken away from me.

Alarmed friends read the *Journal* article and contacted me, wondering what the heck was going on.

"Are you okay?" Tom Bianco e-mailed me the day the story appeared online.

"Doing fine," I e-mailed back. "When you have FU money and do something to help and they piss on you, I am free to say good-bye on my terms. Not the *WSJ* terms and time."

I wasn't going to let anyone think this all wasn't in my own plan. So now I had to focus again on moving forward, and that meant focusing on closing out this bonus issue. Until I did we'd be treading water, and all the while the pool would get deeper and murkier. I concluded that I had one option.

I would have to ask for the money back myself.

I said as much to Feinberg. "If you'll give me the compensation packages that we're looking for, I'll find a way to pay back the bonus money," I told him. "I'll go talk to each of the people who received it."

Feinberg was dubious. "How are you going to do that?" he asked.

"Just leave that to me."

And so began my personal clawback. An awful term for a crappy process. I had my own name for it: "dialing for dollars." Twenty-six million of them. It's one thing for a salesman to pick up a phone and convince someone they've never met to invest in a stock, or even buy a magazine subscription. It's quite another to ask people to hand back their earnings. People who no longer work for you, and are pretty angry to boot.

This, to say the least, was not going to be fun. I spent the better part of November on the phone. I had a list of names, some of former employees who lived in the U.S., others from Europe. I just got on the horn and explained the situation: "I need the money back." Some people were quite, er, resistant when I called. A few told me to go fuck myself.

Some wanted to strike bargains over the government's attacks. "Bob, I'll give back the $2 million under one condition," one of the former FP executives said to me. "That they stop criticizing us and creating fear for my family and how we live our lives."

The more he talked, the angrier he got. "You know what?" he said. "Fuck you and fuck the government. You're not getting my $2 million."

"Listen, I understand," I said, in my most soothing therapist's voice. "But we've got to all get past this. There'll be more money coming when this passes. You're going to get paid again. Let's have peace, because this is our chance at peace and maybe to do the right thing."

This guy eventually agreed to give back $300,000, well short of what I needed. Seven other holdouts wouldn't give up a penny.

Our backs against the wall, I told them that I would withhold a percentage of what they were still contractually owed. To get it, they'd have to take me to court.

"You've made a lot of money out of this company and you may have had nothing to do with the losses," I said. "But you know, this is the way it has to be. So you can have the money, but you'll have to sue me for it. You sue me, and then after you get done suing me, your lawyer will make the money, not you."

Some of them did sue, and some time after we did come to terms. Ultimately, active employees at FP came to the rescue, volunteering across the board to give up 20 percent of their bonus money. I rang up Feinberg.

"I got it all," I told him. "All of it. Don't ask me how."

In early December I flew to Washington and we worked out the details. On December 11, Feinberg announced the terms, which included pay packages for top executives. He also approved a $1.1 billion retention-payment program for 2009.

Of course, the stench of the bonuses never came off us. It would fade but never dissipate entirely. The good thing, though, was that we were starting to make money again. We'd earned almost half a billion dollars in the third quarter of 2009, the second quarter in a row that we were in the black. And the rating agency Moody's Investors Service had just issued a fairly positive report on us, reaffirming our A3 long-term rating, the seventh highest, and saying we showed "continued stabilization of the core insurance operations despite challenging market conditions."

The agency had a warning for us, too, about how a drop in the value of our assets could jeopardize our paying back our debts.

Overcoming that was my next big job.

# TEN

# OIL AND WATER

IF I HAD ANY HOPE of keeping AIG in the fight, I was going to need more help on the executive floor.

AIG was still deeply in the weeds as we rolled into 2010, a year that for a variety of reasons—including the state of my own health—would be the most challenging I ever faced. As for the company: even with two good quarters under its belt, it still had to prove it could sustain itself if it was going to regain the confidence of the markets. Some of our businesses were more hobbled than others; in fact, the farther you got from the political whirlwind in the U.S., the less affected our units were. In Asia, for instance, the PR hit on AIG barely registered, and our big insurance divisions there, ALICO and AIA, continued to perform well; AIA alone turned a profit of well over $1 billion in 2009. But in this country, the deep skepticism was going to continue to be a drag on our efforts to rebound. Some big retail brokerages like Edward Jones still wouldn't do business with us in key areas, such as the selling of our fixed and variable annuity plans. Why would a broker stick his or her neck out on a product that promised payments well into the future, if they didn't believe that for AIG there would be one?

Our earnings reports seesawed each quarter, swinging from promising to lousy. Though we'd seen profits in the second and third quarters of 2009, we dropped back into the red in the fourth quarter, to the tune of $8.9 billion. Many of our insurance units were actually turning profits; other factors depressed the balance sheets. The impact of our government debt was one major issue: we had to take a onetime accounting charge of about $5 billion, because we had to deduct from our assets a portion of our outstanding loan from the Fed. The numbers betrayed other problems, as in the $2.7 billion we'd had to pump into our reserves to cover higher claims than anticipated for one of our core businesses, Chartis, the giant property and casualty unit. Even if these were losses on policies written well before the crisis, they added to the impression of a potentially dismal future.

Overall for 2009, we lost $11 billion. By comparison with 2008, when AIG logged a $100 billion loss, this looked like progress. Although, as the *Wall Street Journal* noted, almost anything would. Remember, these results were separate from the money we had to pay back. I put the best possible spin on it when we announced the results: "While we are not out of the woods by any stretch, these numbers represent a substantial improvement," I said in our earnings announcement.

This calming language did not reflect the turmoil behind the scenes at the end of 2009, particularly among some of the people who reported directly to me. And at the root of the trouble was a belief that the government was going to bleed them all financially, take away what was rightfully theirs, leaving them with little to show for their loyalty to the company, for sticking with this battered enterprise.

On the night of December 4, it all came to a head. I had just finished up a grueling meeting in Washington with Feinberg and Millstein, finally putting an end to the retention-bonus controversy. I was on a conference call with several of my top executives. Anastasia Kelly, known as Stasia, our general counsel, led the call. She had come to AIG in 2006 after a stint at another embattled company, MCI WorldCom, which during her tenure had fought to emerge from bankruptcy. Among the executives were some senior executives, as well as another lawyer I'd never heard of.

The gist of the call: they were all ready to walk. Jesus H. Christ! This was a potential exodus with horrible implications, coming at a moment when we absolutely could not afford to lose people who understood the workings of this byzantine and far-flung company.

The issue was, of course, money. Compensation promised them— running into the millions of dollars—was now threatened. In response to the struggle over the retention bonuses, Feinberg had drastically cut the executives' salaries. Under the rules set down by Congress, senior executives who'd had their salaries reduced in this way were still entitled to large cash severance packages built up over the years, but only if they exercised this option by December 31, 2009. If they didn't, the cash payments would be off the table. The remaining alternative going forward would be to take the compensation in AIG stock, which didn't look at that moment like the most prudent investment.

It had been a long day, and I was having trouble grasping the legal strategy behind this call. Was this some sort of ambush? And who was this other law firm on the line? When had they been hired?

Hold on a minute, I said. Why, I wanted to know, were we using an outside lawyer at this point?

"We're not," Kelly replied.

"Well, there's an outside counsel on the phone."

"Oh," Kelly said. "They're *our* outside counsel."

"Who's *'our'*?" I asked, feeling the blood starting to pound against my temples.

"The other employees and I hired them as our outside counsel to discuss this matter with you."

"Wait," I said. "You're my general counsel! Who the fuck is *my* lawyer?"

"Well," Kelly said, "we'll have to work that out."

I could not believe what I was hearing. What were these people thinking, blindsiding me like this?

"Stasia," I said, "this call is over. You can't put me on the phone with my senior guys, and you're in the midst of negotiating a deal, and I'm unrepresented. And my general counsel is on the other side of the table!"

The call struck me as surreal. Surely, the government would not want virtually my entire senior staff to leave en masse, just as we were beginning to move forward with a recovery plan. In any event, we did work out an arrangement with Feinberg that averted disaster and allowed me to pay some of the compensation due them in cash. The rest they would have to take in AIG stock, and I persuaded them that in the long run this was a good deal. It will give you a sense of the gallows humor on the executive floor that the joke among my senior people was: "Bob is paying us in wampum." To which I replied, "One day, you're going to be very happy you had that wampum."

The confrontation was a reminder of the fires I constantly had to put out, and the many constituencies I daily had to be mindful of. One of them was the government.

Every Wednesday morning, we had a standing meeting unlike any in the history of American business: a session with the Fed and Treasury Department to go over everything we were doing. As our chief lender, the Fed had the responsibility to watch over its investment closely, to make sure the steps we took brought us closer to getting their money back. The deadlines set for the loans, the political environment, and the realities of doing business all amped up the sense of urgency for both them and for us in returning that $85 billion. So we had the Federal Reserve Bank of New York's full attention: a dozen staffers assigned to AIG that over time increased to twenty, with some assigned specifically to the de-risking process at AIG Financial Products, and others working on the mortgage securities issues at American General Finance.

Leading the Fed's monitoring efforts was Sarah Dahlgren, the Fed senior vice president in charge of monitoring AIG. After leaving graduate school with a degree in public policy, Dahlgren joined the New York City Department of Corrections as a budget policy analyst, working on Rikers Island before moving to the Fed in 1990. As she described it, our situation accorded her a magnitude of access to the inner workings of a company that no federal monitor ever in their wildest dreams expected to be granted. In addition to the regular Wednesday get-togethers, she sat in on every board meeting and most of my management team meetings. Not, however, to tell us what to do. She was clear that the understanding between AIG and the government was that I and the board remained the primary decision-makers. It wasn't quite that simple, of course. The U.S. had its three non-voting trustees on the board. And since the Fed and U.S. Treasury Department—our majority stockholder—were constantly looking over our shoulders, no big decisions could exactly be made *without* them, either.

The board, as I hoped both Dahlgren and Treasury's Millstein could see, was a fickle bunch. Although they both expressed the belief that the directors were an admirable and hardworking group—no board met more often than ours, I'd wager—I felt I could count on no more than half of them to support me. Admittedly, they made little attempt to get to know me, or I them. Several of them just considered me a loose cannon, including their leader, Golub, a former CEO himself.

As it turned out, after the "wampum" phone call, only Stasia Kelly left at the end of December, a departure that got some adverse media attention in our fishbowl environment because of the size of her severance package, which ran into the millions. I had no problem with her going, nor with the fact that she received the cash payment she was after. I thanked her publicly for her "tireless service" to the company.

Her exit gave me the chance to scout for another legal mind from the financial world who'd been in the thick of the crisis. I also wanted to bring aboard other people who could help us with building the AIG that would exist after we paid back our debts, with my vision of an AIG that would outlive this debacle. People who'd be valuable as we sought to stabilize our bottom line, streamline the company's businesses, reinvigorate our brand, and instill a new sense of purpose among the employees.

To that end, I was thinking about a guy named Peter Hancock. A sharp mind, people told me, when it came to the management of risk.

The Oxford-educated Hancock had worked for twenty years at JPMorgan, where he served as chief financial officer and where, in the early '90s, he led a unit that pioneered the selling of derivatives. The idea was to take some of the inherent risk out of loans by dividing them up into tranches and selling them to investors, or counterparties. The irony was that it was one of these innovative instruments, the collateralized debt obligation, or CDO, that two decades later took the industry to the brink—though it wasn't the concept that was at fault so much as a reckless overreliance on a particular type of loan, the subprime mortgage, that was used to back the CDOs.

Several people mentioned Hancock to me, including our auditors at PricewaterhouseCoopers, who at the time were threatening to deny us a designation as a going concern; as 2009 wound down, they still weren't convinced we would be around for much longer. That denial could have meant a further downgrade by the credit rating agencies, and that could very well have been a fatal blow. Hancock, I was told, could be instrumental in addressing this problem, and having acquired a reputation as the "father of derivatives," he had other specialized knowledge that applied uniquely to our needs. Plus, he was said to be motivated for a job change. He was on a grueling regimen, living in New York with his wife Maria and their children, but flying out every Sunday to Cleveland, where he was head of Key National Bank and an officer of its parent company, Keycorp, and then returning on Thursdays. We met on November 6, 2009, in my offices on Pine Street to explore a role for him at AIG.

It was one of those instant connections, even though you wouldn't have imagined that being the case. I was informal, he was cerebral; I was off the cuff, he more prone to contemplation. But in his intuitive knowledge and enthusiasm for getting a job done, I sensed a kindred spirit. So I knew right away I wanted him on my team. And he seemed open to being asked. Years later, at my AIG farewell party in Chicago, Hancock—who succeeded me as CEO—talked about his excited takeaway from that first meeting. "I felt Bob knew me better than my dad did," was the way he put it.

One of the reasons we had so urgently needed to resolve matters with Feinberg, the special master, was that as long as we couldn't set compensation for the top echelon of the company, we weren't going to attract the talent like Hancock that we needed. The impression was also still profoundly apparent that AIG might not be around for long. Hancock, for that reason, needed some reassurance that AIG was a mess worth diving into, that the government's involvement would not make the situation untenable, and that there was a reasonable possibility of success.

Hancock would later confide to me that my telling it like it was in standing up to the government was a huge factor in his coming aboard. My vow to pay back the loans figured in his decision, too. But, as he later said: "The more important promise to me was that there was going to be a company—whether it paid back the government in full or in part, there was going to be a company." The likelihood of this eventuality was affirmed for him after he went through the balance sheets with my lieutenants, David Herzog, our CEO, and Brian Schreiber, now our Global Treasurer, and talked about it with Millstein at Treasury and Dahlgren at the Fed. "They convinced me," Hancock later said, "that the government could be a constructive partner in what was a very complicated task."

So Hancock came aboard in early 2010 as executive vice president for finance, risk, and investments, a title that conferred a lot of responsibility and as a result immediately placed him on the short list to succeed me. When a successor might be chosen, though, was up in the air. In my frustrations over the retention bonuses in the fall, I'd sent out mixed signals about how long I intended to stay, but the idea of retiring in the spring of 2010 was looking increasingly unlikely. I wanted to bring in Hancock at an even higher level, with the title chief operating officer. But the board felt that the position would give too strong an indication that he was my heir apparent.

Hancock's appointment was mentioned by Golub in his "chairman's message" in AIG's 2009 annual report, which came out in early 2010. It also noted another key appointment: my hiring of Thomas Russo, a savvy, seasoned lawyer who as in-house counsel lived through the collapse of

Lehman Brothers after the government refused to bail it out. I met Russo through Denise; they had shared philanthropic interests. He joined AIG as executive vice president of legal, compliance, regulatory affairs, and government affairs.

Oddly, even as Golub noted these hires, he made other statements in his chairman's message about hiring that to me seemed unhelpful to AIG's cause. One paragraph in particular irritated the hell out of me, because it was completely out of sync with the state of our relations with the government, and with the special pay master in particular.

"The board has been intently focused on working with the [Fed] and the U.S. Department of the Treasury, as well as dealing with the pay guidelines and restrictions imposed by the special master, who has ultimate authority over a number of major compensation decisions," Golub wrote. "While we can pay the vast majority of people competitively, on occasion, these restrictions and his decisions have yielded outcomes that make little business sense. For example, in some cases, we are prevented from providing market-competitive compensation to retain some of our own most experienced and best executives. This hurts the business and makes it harder to repay the taxpayers."

Golub's sentiments weren't that different from things I'd been saying months earlier. And there was the rub. They no longer needed to be said. We had settled this issue; bringing it up again, publicly, sent all the wrong, disruptive signals. Feinberg and I had found common ground, and Golub made it sound as if we hadn't. Here in a nutshell was the problem between Golub and me. The CEO and the chairman were not speaking with one voice. To my mind, our chairman was sticking his nose where it wasn't needed, and didn't belong.

Even worse: his statement seemed to be the opposite of what we wanted to convey to those auditors who were looking us over, examining whether we were a safe bet to stay in business. Golub's assertion that we weren't able to hire the talent we needed risked playing into the skepticism about AIG's viability, and the possibility that we would be found to have a "material weakness" in our ability to function—the worst outcome possible in an assessment of a company's prospects for the future.

"Harvey, you can't say that," I told him. "We're now facing a material weakness in our accounting. We're busy trying to recruit and retain very talented people—and I think we have very talented people."

"Well, I don't see any," Golub said, restating the low opinion of our team that I had heard him express at other times.

I explained that though Feinberg continued to take a hard line with us publicly, it was a bit of theater. "He has to beat the shit out of me in the press because the country and the government want blood," I said. Demonizing me was fine, because in our face-to-face meetings we brought our authentic selves: no bullshit, no grin-fucking. I told Golub, "I got what I needed from Feinberg in December."

Unfortunately, I had more luck getting through to Feinberg than I did Golub. Golub was a smart, experienced corporate hand, for sure, but I could see that his view of his role at AIG was far too interfering. I wasn't going to share the job with him. No way. If he continued down this road, we were bound for bumpier times.

"Oil and water," was how people who knew us described our relationship. Feinberg observed the friction at that November board meeting, later remarking that it seemed as if Golub was "second-guessing" a lot of my decisions and later saying of what he saw: "I sensed two very large personalities, and Harvey taking Bob to the woodshed." Millstein saw it, too. Oil and water. I knew this tension couldn't go on indefinitely. But worrying about him was not worth it; as long as my senior staff had my back, and at least some of the board was supportive, I wasn't going to dwell on it. I also didn't want to waste political capital on internal upheaval. My solution was to have as little to do with him as possible.

I was elated that Hancock and Russo joined us. Not only would hires of this caliber send a signal to our critics and overseers, who wondered if we could attract the kinds of people we needed to unravel our knotty problems, but also, practically speaking, they would enhance our strategic planning. We could focus more confidently on the steps needed to ramp up the payback and recovery.

One of those complex problems was the roadblock our government obligations threw in front of our efforts to re-enter the capital markets, to be able to raise money from the private sector—a fundamental vital sign. The obstacle was twofold: on the one hand, there was the Fed, which as our foremost secured creditor was entitled to be repaid before we dealt with anyone else. For other lenders, we remained radioactive. On the other was Treasury, which owned the vast majority of the company in preferred shares. This left little incentive for investment by the common shareholders we wanted to entice back.

As I discussed with Hancock, Herzog, Schreiber, and the others at senior levels, our other imperative was communicating firmly, both to employees and the world, about what the composition of AIG would be after the dust settled. It would be a trimmed-down behemoth, to be sure. We had to make clear, though, which divisions would continue to be our core businesses and which we were interested in selling.

We were first and foremost and for all time an insurance company. With that basic premise, the path became clear. We would hold on to our insurance core: domestic annuities and life insurance, mortgage insurance, and our property and casualty business. My goal, in other words, was an AIG that would be the world's biggest property and casualty insurer. It would have a robust life insurance and annuity presence in the U.S., with some other select operations revolving around that nucleus.

An assortment of other entities around the world, brought in or created under the AIG flag by Greenberg, now would have to be sold. Not until the price was right, of course. But they were all candidates for divestiture. Among the biggest was ALICO, the Japan-based life insurance company that operated in Asia, Latin America, and Europe. Three other Asian insurance units were also likely candidates: AIG Star Life Insurance and AIG Edison Life Insurance, also in Japan and Nan Shan in Taiwan. Consumer finance and credit card operations from Peru to Poland to the Philippines were also on the list. And so were ILFC, the aircraft-leasing division, and American General Finance, our U.S.-based credit card subsidiary.

The biggest of the big kahunas, however, was AIA, our largest foreign insurance entity. In fact, our strategy of paying back the Fed in full hinged on the success of this one sale. We owed the Fed a total of $83 billion; as the senior creditor, it had to be paid first. Once we had decided on which of our insurance units would define AIG for the future, AIA was by far the most valuable entity we had to sell. So getting top dollar for it was the prize I had my hungry eye on. Not that this was going to be an easy breakup to accomplish, psychologically: Hong Kong–based American International Assurance Company, or AIA, was embedded deeply in the DNA of AIG. It cemented our identity as a global company. China was where it had all begun, under Cornelius Vander Starr, in 1919. He was forced to take the business out of the country in 1945 when Mao and the Communist regime assumed power. And then in 1992, under Greenberg, AIA returned to China, becoming an Asian life insurance powerhouse.

Now, however, we could ill afford to feel nostalgic about it. Ever since the bailout, a sale of AIA had been under discussion. My predecessors at AIG had a sale of AIA in mind as part of Project Destiny, but the sale price I'd heard being considered at the time, $20 billion, was a laughable undervaluing of the company. A public offering of AIA stock on the Hong Kong Stock Exchange had been mulled, but a sale with a hefty cash payout would put us on a faster track.

In February of 2010, I authorized our bankers and consultants at Goldman Sachs and Blackstone to make the introductions to our potential buyer for AIA. Prudential PLC, a midsized British life insurance and asset management company, headed by Tidjane Thiam, was interested. Thiam was looking to expand the reach of his company—a wholly separate company from the U.S. insurance giant of the same name—in Asia. Acquiring AIA, with 23 million policyholders in the region, would make Thiam's Prudential the dominant insurance force everywhere from China to India to Vietnam to South Korea.

The $35.5 billion deal we hammered out met my price expectations.

Under the agreement I worked out with Thiam, we'd receive $25 billion in cash, which would go quite a substantial way to pay off the AIA-backed credit facility that had been set up by the Fed. The remainder would be paid to us in Prudential PLC stock that we would eventually sell off. In the interim, we would own an 11 percent stake in Prudential.

I was ecstatic. But the joy would soon be drained away by Golub. When I laid out the deal for him, he was furious. "How dare you have a conversation without telling me!" he said.

I believed that there was no possibility of keeping these sensitive negotiations secret—remember, AIG's fate hinged on our getting top dollar for this "crown jewel"—if I had confided them to Golub as they were being carried out. I had no reason to be trusting—of Prudential, either, for that matter. Thiam was enthusiastic, but I needed to be certain the interest was genuine and the financials were achievable.

Golub told me he didn't like the deal: he wanted more cash up front. Now I was the angry one. "Harvey, you were ready to accept $20 billion for it last year," I said incredulously. "You guys were going to go for $20 billion, and you were thinking about maybe going to $18. I'm getting you more cash than you would have gotten by selling all of it, and you still have more to go, because you're going to get a percentage ownership of the combined company!"

Well, Golub insisted, he wanted better terms. A more secure guarantee that we'd get the cash. As I needed solid backing by the board to press ahead, I worked with our bankers at Credit Suisse and JPMorgan Chase, who agreed to underwrite the whole thing. That should have been enough.

But there was more pushback to come.

At our board meeting on Saturday, February 27, we brought in Thiam and the bankers. The board was being advised by Blackstone Group, which was making a fortune off of us in fees. Stephen Schwarzman, the CEO of Blackstone, spoke up: he didn't think we should approve the sale to Prudential. He thought AIG would do better with a public offering of AIA stock. An IPO was also what some of the senior people at AIA, led by Mark Wilson, the AIG executive vice president who ran AIA, were after. My suspicion was that what Wilson really wanted was to run AIA outright; the price we got for it was immaterial to him.

I argued strenuously against this alternative, which seemed far riskier. "I can't imagine you'd want to play the market right now," I said. "We're getting a really good price and we're getting clarity. Because right now nobody thinks we can do anything." I reminded the room that we only had a few years to pay off our debts. "We have no right to play with the government's money," I added. "We ought to do this in an expeditious way."

Was I getting through to them? I pressed my case about the positive impression the deal would leave. "This would be a big boost for us: '$35 billion for AIA? Holy shit! It looks like they could actually make it!'" Think, I said, about the message it sends to our institutional clients around the country. "It brings us to a whole new level of possibility!"

After the bankers and consultants were gone, the eleven members of our board of directors were left to discuss and decide. I had one vote. The remainder belonged to these other leaders from the fields of transportation, manufacturing, finance, and media. Some were lawyers. Several had Harvard degrees. And as I would shortly realize, after Golub called for a straw vote, I was not in firm control here.

One of the directors, George L. Miles Jr., the former CEO of a PBS television station in Pittsburgh, had to leave to give a speech. He would call in his vote later. So ten directors remained in the conference room in 70 Pine Street.

Robert S. "Steve" Miller, former chief executive of Delphi Corp., spoke first: "I can go either way," I remember him saying. "But if the CEO tells us that it's really critical that we do this, I'm going to vote with the CEO."

Hallelujah. One-zip.

Arthur C. Martinez, chairman of the Home Shopping Network, spoke next and in the same vein. We needed to do the deal, he said. "It's real, it's demonstrative. I vote yes."

A third yes followed from Dennis Dammerman, my most trusted ally on the board. Wow, this is going well, I thought. Maybe I really was being overly paranoid.

Then dissent raced into the room. Three no votes in a row, from Christopher S. Lynch, formerly a partner at the accounting firm KPMG; Morris Offit, who had his own capital management firm; and Suzanne Nora Johnson, a lawyer and former vice chair at Goldman Sachs. All of them thought it would be a horrible idea, allowing a competitor in the global insurance marketplace to buy AIA.

I voted next, making it 4–3, and then Laurette Koellner, a senior executive at Boeing, voted yes, too. It was 5–3 for going ahead. Douglas Steenland, head of Northwest Airlines before its merger with Delta, countered with a no vote.

We were now 5–4 in favor, with two votes to go. Golub and Miles, the latter to vote by phone, still had to weigh in. If they were both yeses, I had a 7 to 4 majority. Not the unanimous consent I was after, but at least a clear majority.

And then, disaster. It was Golub's turn to speak. Despite our differences, I expected he would back me on this deal. Well, he didn't. After giving the Prudential offer careful consideration, he said, he had to vote no.

It was now 5 to 5. I couldn't believe it.

And I thought my head would explode. I was beyond livid, but mainly at myself. How could I be sitting here, watching this happen? Had I set myself up for this? The biggest decision in the history of this company—the first big step toward the potential salvation of AIG, for the more than 100,000 people who worked for it—and we were split down the middle. Terrible. At this point, I thought, we couldn't move forward unless we were all prepared to take the leap together.

We sat there for a while, waiting for George Miles to finish his outside speaking engagement and get back to us. Finally he called in and asked how the vote had gone. We told him we were waiting for his vote.

"I vote yes," he said. That made it 6 to 5 for the deal. But I wasn't elated. Far from it. This wasn't the Supreme Court, where bare majorities hold sway. Justices are not bound by their colleagues' opinions for their institution to survive. A company in deep trouble, on the other hand,

A portrait of me, around the age of 17, outside the family business, the Patio Motel in Monticello, New York. (Courtesy of the Benmosche family)

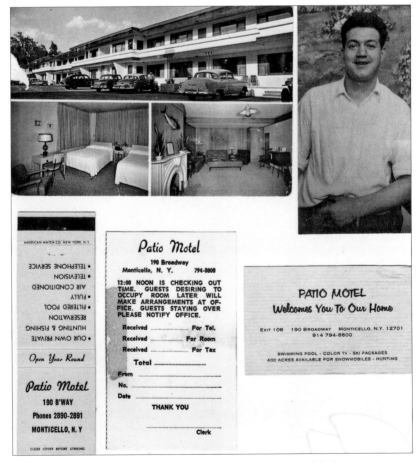

I received valuable business lessons at The Patio, the second lodgings we ran in Monticello. A postcard from the motel is pictured here, along with a Patio matchbook, receipt stub, and business card. And that's my father, Daniel. (Courtesy of the Benmosche family)

My mother, Lillian, and I, dancing at my brother Mike's Bar Mitzvah in the fall of 1964. (Courtesy of the Benmosche family)

In uniform in 1961, my junior year at the New York Military Academy in Cornwall-on-Hudson. I'm with my mother and a girl I was seeing at the time, Judith Ann Soloway. (Courtesy of the Benmosche family)

Denise and I in May 1976, in the shot that became our wedding photo by default. For the actual wedding, my father-in-law had loaded the camera incorrectly! (Courtesy of the Benmosche family)

My young brood, at my nephew's Bar
Mitzvah in Boston in 1982. Denise
and I and little Nehama and Ari.
(Courtesy of the Benmosche family)

Posing with our mascot, Snoopy,
on April 5, 2000 at the New York
Stock Exchange, as we marked the
launch of MetLife's IPO. From left,
exchange chairman Dick Grasso
and former MetLife CEOs Harry
Kamen, John Creedon, and Bob
Schwartz. (Courtesy of the NYSE)

Maurice "Hank" Greenberg, the former AIG chairman and CEO and a business legend, photographed in his office in New York on September 22, 2004. (Credit: Diane Bondareff/Bloomberg News)

The AIG hotel "junket" at the St. Regis in California that raised hackles in Congress was also a boon to editorial cartoonists, as this pointed jab in October 2008 indicates. (Credit: Darkow/caglecartoons.com)

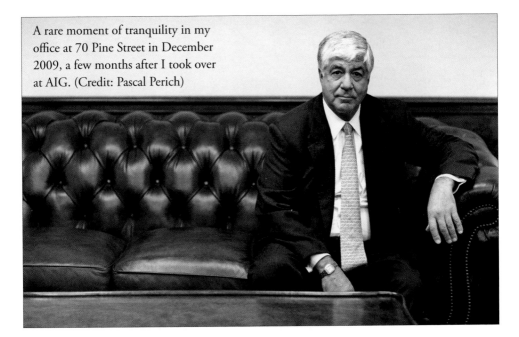

A rare moment of tranquility in my office at 70 Pine Street in December 2009, a few months after I took over at AIG. (Credit: Pascal Perich)

Another of the cartoons that lampooned AIG, this one a takeoff on March Madness. (Credit: Matson/caglecartoons.com)

AIG was the butt of Jon Stewart's jokes on *The Daily Show.* It won't surprise you to learn I didn't think he was funny. (Credit: Comedy Central)

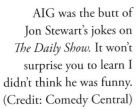

President Obama, speaking to reporters about AIG outside the White House on March 18, 2009. Flanked by Treasury Secretary Timothy Geithner, left, and director of the National Economics Council Larry Summers, Obama called the $165 million in retention bonuses to employees of AIG Financial Products "outrageous." (Credit: Jonathan Ernst/Reuters/Corbis)

That same day, my beleaguered predecessor as CEO, Ed Liddy, suffered through congressional tongue lashings over the bonuses as he testified before a subcommittee of the House Financial Services Committee. (Credit: Susan Walsh/AP)

Rep. Elijah Cummings (D-Md.) listens to testimony at the subcommittee hearing on March 18, 2009. At first a vocal AIG critic, he later became a friend and ally as the payback unfolded. (Credit: J. Scott Applewhite/AP)

Jim Millstein, the restructuring mastermind at Treasury who became one of my closest allies, testifying at a hearing regarding the bailout of the auto industry before a congressional oversight panel in Washington, in February 2010. (Credit: Ann Heisenfelt/Getty)

Another sharp shiv to our gut from an editorial cartoonist. (Credit: Mike Keefe/caglecartoons.com)

The image of this protester, outside AIG's offices in Washington on March 19, 2009, gives you some sense of the intensity of the anger AIG's bailout provoked. (Credit: Pablo Martinez Monsivais/AP)

Another day, another protest. This one on March 21, 2009, organized by a group calling itself the Connecticut Working Families Party, was a bus tour that went to AIG executives' homes. (Credit: Stan Honda/AFP/Getty)

At Villa Splendid in Dubrovnik, Croatia, on August 26, 2009, amid the hubbub over my trip to my Adriatic retreat just weeks after taking the top job at AIG. I'd cleared this trip with the government ahead of time, but I still got grief for it. Here I sat down with a Reuters reporter in an effort to counter some of the negative press stateside. (Credit: Nikola Solic/Reuters/Landov)

Examining our ripening grapes in our small vineyard in Viganj, on Croatia's Peljesac peninsula, two hours north of Dubrovnik. The location proved excellent for my goal of importing Zinfandel vines from California to reintroduce that variety to the country. (Courtesy of Lyn Hughes, copyright 2013)

Kenneth R. Feinberg, the "pay czar," appointed to oversee executive compensation at seven corporations, including AIG, that were bailed out by the Troubled Asset Relief Program. A tough negotiator, he's giving a progress report here to the House Oversight and Government Reform Committee on October 28, 2009. (Credit: Andrew Harrer/Bloomberg/Getty)

Houston, April 21, 2010: One of the numerous appearances I made at "town hall" meetings for AIG employees, at which I answered questions off the cuff. They were effective morale-building tools. (Credit: Ted Nevins/AIG)

Then-AIG Chairman Harvey Golub, right, onstage with me at the May 2010 annual shareholders' meeting in New York. I'm speaking and he's listening, which was my preferred arrangement. As a result of our increasingly intense standoff, he left the board two months later. (Credit: Joe Vericker/Photo Bureau)

Sarah Dahlgren, center, an executive vice president at the Fed and another key ally of mine, at a congressional hearing in May 2010. On her right is Thomas Baxter Jr., general counsel at the Fed. (Credit: Mark Wilson/Getty)

Projecting my customary optimism about the fate of AIG, on this occasion at a congressional oversight panel hearing on TARP on May 26, 2010. (Credit: Yuri Gripas/Reuters/Corbis)

A favorite photo of mine: My granddaughter, Aubrey, perched in front of the TV, watching yours truly testifying before Congress on May 26, 2010. (Courtesy of the Benmosche family)

Tom Russo, AIG's general counsel, and I, speaking to Elizabeth Warren, chair of the TARP Congressional Oversight Panel on Capitol Hill on May 26, 2010. (Credit: Yuri Gripas/Reuters/Corbis)

Joseph Cassano, former chief executive officer of AIG Financial Products, at a federal hearing on the role of derivatives in the financial crisis, in Washington on June 30, 2010. (Credit: Andrew Harrer/ Bloomberg/Getty)

My one-on-one with President Obama in the Oval Office on January 14, 2011. (Official White House photo by Pete Souza)

My superb oncologist, Dr. Abraham Chachoua, and I, on October 2, 2011, exactly one year after he diagnosed my cancer. (Courtesy of NYU Langone Medical Center)

Filmmaker Michael Moore—to my mind, a cheap-shot artist—directing a scene in front of AIG's offices on Water Street on August 20, 2009 for his anti–Wall Street screed, *Capitalism: A Love Story*. (Credit: Youtube.com)

One of my favorite views: The Adriatic, from a terrace of Villa Splendid, the house I lovingly restored over a period of six years in the 2000s in Dubrovnik, Croatia. (Credit: Gianluca Colla/Bloomberg/Getty)

A sign of progress: On October 16, 2012, a banner displaying our updated logo was unfurled at the New York Stock Exchange. In fulfilling the vow to pay back the American taxpayers, my efforts to restore AIG's good name were paying off, too. (Credit: Joe Vericker/PhotoBureau)

That same day, as part of the branding rollout, my team and I rang the NYSE's opening bell. From left, Bill Dooley, Jeff Hurd, Sid Sankaran, Tom Russo, Peter Hancock, myself, Jeff Hayman, Jay Wintrob, Brian Schreiber, John Doyle, and David Herzog. (Partially obscured on left: Duncan Niederauer, then the exchange's CEO.) (Courtesy of NYSE)

$205 billion
paid to America from AIG

A shot from our "Thank You, America" ad campaign, in which AIG employees expressed the company's gratitude on the occasion of our paying back the taxpayers in full. (Courtesy of AIG)

Arriving at the White House on October. 2, 2013, for a meeting of the Financial Services Forum with President Obama. With me, from left: Lloyd Blankfein, CEO of Goldman Sachs; Keith Sherin, chairman and CEO of GE Capital; and Douglas Flint, group chairman of HSBC Holdings. (Credit: Saul Loeb/AFP/Getty)

I'm with my family as I accept the 2013 Insurance Leader of the Year award from St. John's University. Clockwise from bottom left: Denise; my daughter-in-law Clair; my son, Ari, my sister Jayne, and my daughter, Nehama. (Credit Joe Rosen/PhotoBureau)

The changing of the guard: with Peter Hancock, my successor as CEO, as we announced his appointment, on June 11, 2014. (Credit: Joe Vericker/PhotoBureau)

One of the retirement events for me, this one at the Water Club in Manhattan on November 13, 2014. (Credit: Joe Vericker/PhotoBureau)

needed coherent alignment. AIA was only one of dozens of significant decisions we'd have to make about where to take AIG, and if this vote was any indication, every move was going to be divisive, energy-draining. And this board was too torn to be an effective partner.

Golub turned to me and said, "I guess you won."

It didn't feel like a victory. "Wait a minute," I said. "I didn't win anything. This was a chance for us to move this company forward in a transaction the likes of which nobody's seen before. I feel that if you're in that much doubt and we're divided, we shouldn't do the deal. So as far as I'm concerned, I'll switch my vote to no. Because you don't have the stomach for this."

I wasn't interested in an argument. As a CEO, I didn't operate that way. For better or worse, we were going to have to do it my way, or I wasn't going to do it at all. I wanted the board to back me. If they didn't, they could take it and shove it. This wasn't a democracy. Fuck-you money, remember? "I'm not going to get into a big debate," I said. "'Should we or shouldn't we sell?' I don't want to do that. You guys want to be divided on how we go forth—I'd just as soon change the plan."

"Bullshit," Golub said. He was having none of this. Maybe he saw my behavior as petulant. Or maybe he felt he had lost fair and square. "You got your vote," he added. "Now do it."

He asked for the official vote, and now it was unanimous, in favor of the Pru deal. But I knew the real sentiment in the room, and even though we went ahead, the taste that stayed with me was bittersweet.

We announced the deal with Prudential PLC on March 1. Wall Street was impressed. "This diminishes the wrath directed at AIG from Americans angry at the bailout," Clark Tory, a senior analyst at Aite Group, a financial research and consulting firm, told Bloomberg News. "Benmosche's not entirely out of the woods, but . . . as the pressure on him backs off, people will say this management team is doing a decent job."

A week later, another major announcement: we were selling our second largest foreign insurance unit, American Life Insurance Co.—ALICO—to my former company, MetLife, for $15.5 billion. In this deal, we'd receive $6.8 billion in cash and $8.7 billion in MetLife stock and securities. (Oddly enough, as a result, AIG would now have a 20 percent stake in a company I'd taken public ten years before. Because I remained a MetLife shareholder, I had to recuse myself entirely from this deal.)

Through the sales of ALICO and AIA, which were expected to be finalized by the end of 2010, AIG stood to collect $51 billion. Which was huge. It would allow us to pay back a substantial portion of the $83 billion we owed the Fed, going in a major way to deleveraging our balance sheet and paving the way for us to being able to re-enter the capital markets.

After the AIA announcement, I went to Asia for talks with regulators and our own people at AIA, some of whom were expressing skepticism that the deal would ever get done. The whispers bothered me, but I kept an optimistic public face, even after I began to hear rumbles out of London. Reports in the British press said some of Prudential PLC's large shareholders were balking at the price. Too high, they said. Could the firm even raise that kind of money? The deal was subject to the approval of British authorities and Pru's own stockholders, so this was worrisome, even as Prudential sent out some reassuring signals.

Amid all of the globe-trotting, one of the most important appointments I had coming up was closer to home, in my least favorite city, Washington. I was being invited to testify before the Congressional TARP Oversight Panel, chaired by Elizabeth Warren, an Obama administration official, soon to be U.S. Senator from Massachusetts and a persistent critic of Wall Street. I knew I'd be facing questions about our timetable for returning our bailout money, and how much we expected to be able to repay. The pessimistic guesses within the government were all over the place. The Congressional Budget Office predicted that the country would lose $36 billion on its AIG loans; the Office of Management and Budget said around $50 billion. So much faith they had in us.

Buoyed by the AIA and ALICO agreements, I was prepared to paint a far rosier picture. I planned to reiterate for the panel my belief that the taxpayers would be made whole, and then some.

I still had plenty on my plate, but I was feeling pretty good. Things were beginning to click. I'd advised holding on to our properties until the market conditions improved, and that was indeed what was happening. I even got to spend a week in Croatia that May, looking over the grapes in my vineyards.

And then the bottom dropped out. Little was I aware of the bitter fruit I was about to be served.

# ELEVEN

# "ONLY ONE OF US CAN BE HERE TOMORROW"

"YOU ARE BEING ASKED TO testify before Congress later this month. What do you plan to say?"

The employee's question was on an index card handed to me during my latest town-hall meeting in lower Manhattan. I had an answer at the ready.

"'I'm so happy to be here!'" I said, with good-natured sarcasm. The room erupted in laughter. "And I really mean it, too!"

It was the afternoon of May 10, 2010, and I actually was in a fine mood—good enough that I wasn't dreading that upcoming hearing of the Congressional TARP Oversight Committee, headed by Elizabeth Warren, and pleased enough to be able to kid about what we were all going through. "It's hard to believe I've been here for nine months," I said. "It only feels like nine years."

The recent news had been highly encouraging: along with the pending sales of AIA and ALICO, we'd had a very positive first quarter of 2010. Our profits in the first three months amounted to $1.5 billion, a complete turnaround from the previous quarter. Other signs of renewed strength could be seen in developments in our aircraft leasing company, International Lease Finance Corp. or ILFC. Though we were still looking to get out of that particular business, the unit scored a breakthrough early in the year, as it was able to re-enter the capital markets. This was absolutely major. No business can credibly attest to future survival without showing it has access to private credit. In this instance, we defied a prediction by Moody's that we were not healthy enough to obtain secured financing—the kind backed by an asset deemed to have positive value. A total of $4 billion was loaned to us, money we would use largely to pay down other debts. And it even included a sale of $750 million in senior notes after the recent departure of both ILFC's founding CEO Steven Udvar-Hazy and his interim successor, John Plueger.

This was an important milestone, and I wanted everyone to understand that. "It says that people are willing to invest in ILFC, which is part of AIG. And it's about all of you. It's about 'We have confidence in the people, in the process and in the business, and that one or two individuals is not what we're buying here. We're buying the company and the stability and the trajectory of this company, as it pulls itself out.'"

That we could turn profits was a validation, too, of my belief that AIG was, indeed, a going concern. I wanted this faith absorbed into AIG's culture as if it were our religion. The employees had to believe it, too; I made myself the chief conduit for that message. And maintaining the trust I'd established with the employees was vital to my spreading it. I told the workforce very little that I did not also say in private. This open relationship was the backbone of my strength at AIG. You might say that my philosophy in running the company was as a populist—although one, of course, who got the last word.

In the informal report card I delivered that day, I noted some other high points, such as the work at unwinding the toxic swaps at FP. That we were able to hold on to many key people, under the guidance of Gerry Pasciucco and now Peter Hancock, too, was paying off, in the saving of billions in the value of the remaining contracts there. I mentioned continuing problems, too: the American General Finance division was still bleeding money. And while the businesses poised for sell-off were admired by the bond-rating agencies, other units like SunAmerica, our domestic life and annuity franchise, and Chartis, our property and casualty unit, still needed to improve performance and raise their ratings. Chartis was having some of the ups and downs endemic to insuring against weather events and other disasters. As you learn quickly in the property and casualty business, disasters do happen—like the 8.8 magnitude earthquake in Chile that occurred on February 27, for which we had major claims to pay out. We were also projecting some significant losses in the second quarter due to our exposure in a massive oil spill in April in the Gulf of Mexico, emanating from an offshore drilling platform we insured for British Petroleum. That catastrophe, the Deepwater Horizon spill, required BP to clean up large stretches of waterway and Gulf Coast shoreline.

Another concern raised at that town-hall meeting was about the state of the AIA deal. Though I remained cautiously optimistic, its prospects became increasingly murky in the weeks after the announcement. Skepticism about Prudential PLC's ability to finance the purchase was rising, not only among analysts but also among regulators, such as Britain's Financial Services Authority, which required additional assurances that Pru's capital structure could support the purchase.

If you had any doubts about the dramatic impact of globalization, look no further than the problems that were mounting halfway around the world for the AIA deal. They started in Thailand, where AIA was a dominant insurance force. Violent political unrest broke out in April, threatening the stability of our investments there: Thailand's financial regulations did not allow us to take profits out of the country, so we put them in government bonds. In light of the violence, a financial domino effect took hold. Interest rates on bonds began to plummet, and that, in turn, put tremendous pressure on the life insurance products we sold. An end result was a realization by regulators that we needed to pump more capital into AIA, and that determination got the attention of the FSA in London.

"We've given them a few minor concessions to make it easier for them to move forward," I told the employees. "My expectation is by the end of this week they'll probably get permission and be able to start issuing their prospectus."

Man, was I off.

We miscalculated on both the level of shareholder opposition and CEO Tidjane Thiam's ability to deliver. But as late as May 26, when I traveled to D.C. for the hearing before Elizabeth Warren's committee, I still thought a deal was possible.

As for AIG's day, and by extension, mine, under the oversight committee's microscope: I knew the company was in a much stronger position than it had been fourteen months earlier, when Ed Liddy was given that abusive dressing down by Barney Frank's panel. But judging by Warren's opening remarks that day, it did feel as if time had stood still. We were going to fixate, yet again it seemed, on the outrageousness of the AIG bailout and whether it should have happened at all.

"The company," she said in her introductory remarks, "was a corporate Frankenstein, a conglomeration of banking and insurance and investment interests that defied regulatory oversight and that would not have fit easily into the existing bankruptcy structure. Its complexity, its systemic significance, and the fragile state of the economy may all arguably have been reasons for unique treatment. But no matter the justification, the fact remains that AIG's rescue broke all the rules and each rule that was broken poses a question that must be answered."

Regardless of whether these were valid issues, I really wasn't the person to debate them. The damage had been done. I was the guy hired to repair it.

Being before Congress reminded me of all the times I was disappointed by its members, on both sides of the aisle—even people I supported, like Hillary Clinton, whose Senate campaigns I contributed to. (She let me down when she failed to cast the deciding vote on an issue related to asbestos that was vital to MetLife.) Later, I was equally chagrined by the shabby treatment I received from Senator Mitch McConnell, the Kentucky Republican who would become majority leader: I was solicited by his campaign in the run-up to his 2014 run for re-election. After all the schmoozing, I agreed to make a contribution—only to be informed that the senator in the end decided he didn't want our money. Even at that late date, AIG was still too radioactive.

Warren's hearing was nevertheless a prime opportunity to demonstrate that we were indeed fixing things. And so I knew that this wouldn't be a good occasion for "crazy Bob" to show up. The panelists no doubt had read some of my colorful remarks about Washington early in my tenure. Today they would meet cool and collected Bob, Bob the guy AIG and the country were counting on. I wasn't going to say in so many words, "Happy to be here!," but I was taking the platform and the committee seriously.

As I waited to testify, I did have a moment to reflect on the strangeness of life, how I ended up in this singular position. What would my mother, Lillian, have made of all this? Let that committee know you've got things under control, she'd say. My ultra-practical mother: *Just give them the pen!"*

Outside experts were called in to testify, to repeat the tired mantra of AIG gloom and doom: the taxpayers would be left holding a $36 billion bag; no, actually it was $50 billion they stood to lose. I must say I found some solace in what came out that day from the committee, which was required to inform Congress every month on TARP's progress. (Its largest report, at 350 pages, was the one about AIG.) J. Mark McWatters, a Texas lawyer and vocal critic of the bailout, at least acknowledged the inequity of AIG's counterparties being made whole: "It is ironic that although the bailout of AIG may have rescued many of its counterparties, none of these institutions are willing to share the pain of the bailout with the taxpayers and accept a discount on their termination payments," he said. "Instead, they left the American taxpayers with the full burden of the bailout.

"It is likewise intriguing that these too-big-to-fail institutions were paid at par, that is, 100 cents on the dollar, at the same time the average American's 401(k) and IRA accounts were in free fall, unemployment rates are skyrocketing, and home values were plummeting."

Couldn't have agreed more.

Later in the day, Millstein, my ally in Treasury, would be subjected to some tough questioning from Warren, who found it very hard to believe that we might possibly be on the right track. Her view was no doubt still the majority opinion in this country—a sad commentary, really, on how little faith the public had in American business. Millstein tried to explain something that was perhaps difficult for this committee investigating TARP to hear: that the bailout was money well spent to avoid something that would have been far worse.

"Are we just supposed to take your word for it that it's all going to work out fine?" Warren asked, referring to AIG's prognosis.

"Well," Millstein replied, "the question I think you need to ask yourself today is, as a result of the government's actions, is the company today stable? The answer is yes. Is it improving? Yes. Is it executing against the restructuring plan? Yes. Is it moving to a position where it can give up on its government support and stand alone? Yes. Are there risks? Certainly. A company of this size and scope can't help but have risks to its outcomes and financial performance. But in terms of, you know, where it was and where it's going, it's making progress."

When it was my turn, I led with an expression of AIG's gratitude. "Were it not for the commitment of the U.S. government at a time of great uncertainty," I said, "AIG would not be on the path it is today. I want to thank the government and the American taxpayer." I truly had come to believe that public intervention was working. But the committee remained fixated on the testimony of experts it brought in who had far more pessimistic viewpoints. A research analyst from Keefe, Bruyette and Woods, Cliff Gallant, told the panel AIG stock was enormously overvalued and predicted the company would fail without ongoing U.S. support. An official of Standard & Poor's testified that the company—which currently assigned us a BB, a grade lower than what it considered investment-worthy—would continue to have a "negative outlook" on AIG's future. Along with the government estimates of the losses taxpayers would shoulder on the AIG rescue, the mountain of naysaying evidence looked pretty steep.

So when the committee's deputy chairman, Damon Silvers, associate general counsel of the AFL-CIO, asked me about the discrepancies in these prognostications and mine, I got a little testy.

"I can't comment on Mr. Gallant," I said, referring to the Keefe, Bruyette analyst. "You'll have to get him to figure it out. I know what I'm running. I know the company I'm running. And I have confidence in this company. And I know what I'm talking about. So you'll have to see whether he understands the company as well as I do."

"Mr. Benmosche, I just—that's not an acceptable answer," Silvers replied. "If—you know, we represent your majority stockholder, or at least we kind of do. We're trying to look out for your majority stockholder. I'm frankly frightened by what Mr. Gallant said on behalf of the American public. And I would like you to explain specifically, with reference to numbers, why he's wrong."

We did go through some of the numbers detailing AIG's performance—an exercise that didn't result in a meeting of the minds, because we were looking at them from such different perspectives. But Silvers did acknowledge that he was "sympathetic" to my approach of selling parts of the company far more slowly than the government would have liked.

"I think selling assets prematurely is a certain way to realize losses," he said. "But I'd appreciate to hear it from you, in your own words, why you've taken that view and what the benefit has been for the public as an investor in AIG?"

"I think so far, you have seen prices improve," I replied. "I think at one point, they were thinking of selling AIA for the high teens. And so we got a very aggressive price. And other properties that are out there, we are finding people who are willing to come to the table and talk to us about more value. Because you cannot buy a business that is in trouble, number one.

"And number two, you have to sell when the time is right."

I thought we'd gotten the timing perfect on the AIA deal. But in actuality it was coming apart at the seams. Prudential was having trouble convincing some vitally interested players that it had the resources to pull this off. On the day I was testifying in Washington, RiskMetrics, a London-based investment advisory group, came out publicly against the sale, warning that "the profit targets for the deal to work are on the high side." Asked about the situation after he testified, Millstein told reporters the government could envision AIG going back to an IPO for AIA if Prudential fell through. (I understood why he said it. His first concern had to be the protection of the taxpayers.) This all came on the heels of a report in the *Financial Times* that AIA's chief executive, Mark Wilson, was confiding that he'd quit if the deal went through.

Thiam let us know the terms had to be altered if he was going to get the deal approved; the shareholders were to vote on June 7, and he needed 75 percent in favor to proceed. So after reassuring Warren and the oversight committee of how swimmingly things were going at AIG, I and my staff were trying to figure out how to save this sinking deal.

The sense—and hope—was the shareholders were far more likely to say yes to Thiam if we cut the price. He was asking for a reduction from $35.5 billion to $30.4 billion, with the up-front cash portion cut from $25 billion to $22 billion. It would still represent a huge infusion of money and give us momentum for exiting our obligations to the Fed, which would be entitled to the first $16 billion from the sale. But our board of directors would have to reapprove the purchase agreement under these new terms. So we made plans for a board conference call over Memorial Day weekend, even though I was deeply worried by this point that the directors were divided and in the end might have cold feet.

Some of the investment banks we did business with also were talking down our prospects for Prudential shareholder support—banks that, it should be noted, stood not to earn a dime from a Prudential sale. Goldman Sachs and Blackstone were in on an AIA deal only in the event we went the IPO route. In fact, when Goldman Sachs was asked by the board what it thought of the probability Pru shareholders would endorse the sale, Goldman's trading desk in London said only about 60 percent.

And so that weekend, the board, led by Golub, imposed its will. Directors expressed their concern about lowering the price, and, that in any event, if the Pru vote failed, we would in effect be irreparably devaluing AIA. The whole venture, they seemed to feel, would seriously hurt our chances for a decent return once we moved to the other alternative, the IPO. This, remember, after the board the previous year had been ready to sell AIA for less than $20 billion! We had only ten of the eleven directors available for the meeting; the eleventh, Arthur Martinez, was on vacation in Italy. Unfortunately, Martinez's views were never conveyed to his fellow directors.

Millstein, alarmed by where the board, encouraged by its investment bankers, was heading, spoke up on behalf of Treasury. "I want to stress that your management team is telling you that this is essential," he said of the sale, and then asked if my senior officers would each speak about why this deal was important to pursue. In turn, David Herzog, Brian Schreiber, and Thomas Russo all made cases for letting the sale proceed at the reduced price. Then Peter Hancock took a crack at it, explaining, essentially, the huge financial risk in not going ahead.

Dahlgren was on the call for the Fed. I hoped she might speak, too, because it was repayment of the Fed's loan that hung in the balance. But she remained silent.

The vote wasn't even close. Martinez and I were recorded as being in favor of going forward at a reduced price. Every other director was against.

And that was that. The deal was dead. We announced that we would not accept the new offer. And Prudential PLC said on June 3 that as a result, it was canceling the purchase. Golub got his wish. The board of directors was now leading us in a new direction: backward.

"AIG's Declaration of Independence," read the headline on a long article in *Business Week* that week about the collapse of the AIA deal. Good God. How in the hell was that the conclusion the magazine drew from this fiasco? Well, our esteemed board chairman was the source for this ludicrous assertion. "Golub, the former chairman of American Express, said in an interview that the company was setting its own agenda, not letting the government set it," *Business Week* explained. The article was illustrated by a picture of Golub's head on Thomas Jefferson's body. "We're a Delaware corporation, we operate under Delaware law and our responsibility is to all shareholders," the piece quoted Golub as saying. "We'll come up with the best restructuring plan we can, one that makes sense for all shareholders. The plan has to be acceptable to all constituents."

The press saw the outcome, naturally, as a blow; the only question seemed to be, how big of one? "Big Setback for AIG in Repaying Taxpayers," said the *New York Times*. Many took pains to point out that it was *my* setback. That was true, but this was more than merely my problem. Golub and the board were now operating in an alternate reality, one in which this was a company that had already taken back control of its destiny. We still had miles and miles to go before that would be the case, and in the meantime, it was imperative for us to seize the kind of prime opportunity the AIA sale represented. Arranging an IPO would take months—and who knew what the conditions of the market would be then? Standard & Poor's said as much. "We believe the sale of AIA will now take longer than AIG previously anticipated and poses increased execution risk because of the volatile conditions in the capital and equity markets," it declared. The situation, in sum, was far more fluid—and from the government's point of view, far more urgent—than the board's position indicated.

Our public position was that we had other encouraging options to explore. Even Geithner tried to put a good face on the collapse, telling reporters he was confident we would yet secure a better deal. Privately, though, we were in disarray. And if I was disgusted, the Fed was livid. It was waiting for clear signs that its money would be returned, and here, the board was acting as if we had all the time in the world to make good on the loans. That Wednesday, June 3, during our regular weekly session, Dahlgren let me know the board's vote was not the result the Fed had hoped for. "We're very upset with what happened," she said.

"I appreciate your being upset," I said. "Why didn't you say something over the weekend?"

"We've been instructed not to tell the board what to do," she replied. "The board has to do what the board has to do."

"I understand that. But you know, Sarah, we have a big exposure, and you're sitting with a special-purpose vehicle"—one of the lending mechanisms the Fed set up for us—"which includes shares of AIA and AL-ICO, and you're at risk for that money."

Well, the Fed did decide to speak, or rather, act. They threatened to put a hold on spending waivers for us, and since we could barely lay out a nickel without Fed approval, this would amount to a severe turning of the vise. We were subjected to another squeeze: they immediately called in their $4 billion loan to our ILFC division.

And I was at the end of my rope. In rejecting my plan for AIA, the board made a huge statement. It publicly thwarted me. It complicated our relations with the Fed. Its chairman not only wanted a say in how I led the company, he also made it clear he would openly challenge my authority. As you may have gleaned, I don't govern by committee. An organizing principle of my career was that if the obstacles to achieving my goals grew to the point that my effectiveness was being curtailed, I was out of there.

Fuck-you money gave me the courage of my convictions.

Among some people I respect, Golub was also respected. "A brilliant man and very hands-on and very intrusive," was how one close friend and colleague of mine at AIG described him. The friend added: "He felt that he had an obligation to look into things, not to micromanage them, but to look into them. I think from his point of view his definition of a chairman or a board member was very expansive, but it may be taking the role to an extreme."

Of me, this friend added: "I just think if you give the ball to Bob, he will run with it and not have any excuses if he fumbles. [But] he's got to know he has the ball. The problem is when you have two people who think they have the ball. It's an accident waiting to happen. . . . You had two very strong people in extraordinarily powerful positions who had different visions. And the question was, 'Who was running the show?' "

That *was* the question. Intellectually, I knew some level of adversarial friction in a boardroom is not a bad thing. When dealing with big numbers and a lot of uncertainty, a rigorous challenging of assumptions can be helpful in establishing the best possible plan of action. I think the government, too, was not unhappy that we had some fiercely smart minds in that room, battling it out.

The problem, though, was that with the weight of responsibility, the boldness of the steps required, and the unrelenting pressures of the process, the board to my mind had become dysfunctional. Maybe—and it's a long shot—if Golub and I were both less headstrong we could have forged some kind of authentic partnership; we both liked to spend leisure time in Florida, and perhaps, if we'd gotten together over golf . . . nah. I don't even play golf. Ultimately, our visions were in such serious conflict that I concluded it was pointless to continue down this path.

I needed to do something drastic.

And so I did.

In the annals of corporate showdowns, the one that ensued was kind of wild. It put knots in the stomachs of hard-nosed people with stern constitutions tested over years of tough business and fiscal decisions.

"We had the most dramatic board meeting of my career," Millstein would say of it later. "I've never seen anything like it."

July 14, 2010. Bastille Day. Weirdly apt for the meeting to occur on a holiday celebrating liberation. Because one way or the other, it was going to end in freedom for me. "Either he goes, or I go" may be a cliché, but it perfectly suited this particular day at the office.

The board met on the eighteenth floor of 70 Pine Street, where I was going to make my case for an escape from our current dysfunction. The directors were all there, and Millstein, Dahlgren, and the TARP trustees. Millstein was not planning to stay for the entire meeting; he was supposed to be heading out of town early to visit his daughter at sleepaway camp. He certainly couldn't have anticipated what I had in store, and what a day of reckoning this would turn out to be. I motioned to him to come over and talk to me.

"I won't be here when you get back," I confided.

"What are you talking about?" Millstein asked, looking perplexed.

"They haven't resolved this," I said, referring to the difficulties with Golub.

"Really?" Millstein said. "George told me they resolved this," he added, referring to George Miles, the director in charge of the board's governance committee.

"No, they just think we should get along. That's how they resolved it. So I'm going to tender my resignation at the end of this meeting, and you'll have to figure out who's running AIG."

"That's not going to happen," he said.

"Okay, well, I'm telling you, that's how it is."

I intended to use the meeting as a recap for where we stood. To go forward, I first had to go back, to remind everyone how far we'd come since I'd started nearly a year earlier. "When I arrived, it was every person for themselves—abandon ship," I explained. A plan had been in place, I reminded everyone, to unwind the entire corporate center of AIG, to sell off the subsidiaries fast. FP was to be shut down the previous November, at a loss of somewhere between $10 and $20 billion. Morale within the company had hit rock bottom; our client and employee retention rates were low, and our auditors were on the verge of declaring our financials so questionable they would declare that we had a material weakness.

I went point by point through the changes I'd made, beginning with my efforts to get the workforce believing in AIG again, the battles with Feinberg over compensation, the clawback of the bonus money, the improving situation with FP, the subsequent hiring of new executive talent, and the sale of ALICO. And then I launched into a discussion of future plans: the rejiggered proposal for an AIA IPO in the fall; the sales of other units, such as the Star and Edison insurance companies in Japan and Nan Shan in Taiwan; the need for our investment department to make improvements; to proceed with efforts to buy back the assets in Maiden II and Maiden III and continue rebuilding AIG's central corporate entity. The talk of things to come led to another question, one I posed for the board. Would I be allowed to find a new management team for AIA, one that I could work with to steer the company through the IPO?

The board, though, had a question for me, one that, of course, I figured was coming.

How, they wanted to know, was I getting along with Harvey Golub?

"I don't get along with Harvey," I said. Golub was sitting right there. It could not have come as a shock to him; as recently as the day before, some of my senior people had been in conversation with him about how untenable the situation was. I explained that it was about more than getting along, that the conflicts between us were serious. "Look," I added. "We really need to think about leadership and vision because we've really come through a terrible time. We can't continue to have these battles. It's not working well."

By this point, lawyers had been summoned to the room, attorneys from powerhouse firms: Simpson, Thacher for the board and Davis, Polk for the Fed. I was asked to make it clear right then and there that I was not going to submit my resignation.

"I don't know that I'm not going to resign," I said. "But we'll figure that out today."

The room tensed up. Was I in or out? What was crazy Bob up to? I glanced over at Millstein and at Dahlgren, who were both trying not to look my way. The fact was I was not up to anything. I didn't *want* to resign, but I would if I had to. Croatia in the summertime was looking mighty tempting.

"You can't have a company without a CEO, without it being announced," one of the lawyers said.

And with that, the board asked both Golub and me to leave the room. They were going to meet without us in executive session and try to figure out what the hell to do.

It turned out that at least two people close to me, one of my senior direct reports and Millstein, had been advising Golub privately in the days before the meeting that the only course for the company that made sense was for him to step down. I learned later that in the executive session, Millstein spoke up after Golub and I departed for our respective offices on eighteen and had a frank discussion with the board.

"We told you this for the last month and a half, but you didn't believe it, and so he's going to resign at the end of the day today unless you make a choice," Millstein later recalled explaining to the board.

"Well, what do you think?" he was asked.

"I'm not going to tell you what to think. You guys have to figure this out," Millstein said. "We're going to script this process in a way that is beyond reproach, so you sit with your lawyers and figure out what you are doing as a board to resolve this, and Sarah and I are going to sit with Davis, Polk and we're going to figure out what we should or shouldn't say as your lender and shareholder; and the lawyers are going to meet and come up with a process that works for everyone, and we'll figure this out before the end of the day."

It was a cliff-hanger moment. A process was indeed worked out: the board would converse by themselves, and then they were going to ask Dahlgren and Millstein back in to get the government's input. Next they would talk separately to Golub and to me, and then make a decision. But what decision, exactly?

Back in my office, I really wasn't sure what would happen next—whether this really was my last day at AIG. As the board met behind closed doors, Golub walked through my open one.

"You know," Golub said, "I think I need to work on my relationship with you."

What the fuck.

"Harvey, we don't have a relationship," I said. "We're not going to have one. All I can tell you is that the board needs to make a decision today where we're going. But I think only one of us can be here tomorrow."

The conversation was without rancor. Golub seemed alternately to want to mollify me and keep me on the ropes.

I added, "So if you want to be the CEO . . ."

"No, look," he said. "The fact is I know it's easier to get a chairman than a CEO. There's no contest here. But I really feel that we should work together. It's going to take time—the next three or four months—to do that."

But we were out of time, and I saw no advantage in prolonging this agony. "It's just not going to work, Harvey. And so if the board wants you to stay on, that's great. Then I'm going to leave at the end of the day and go to Croatia, and you're running the company. It's yours. I'm done."

What I was thinking was: I've got to get the hell out of here. I could no longer see any upside in staying. Here I was trying to save this company, and I was being treated as if I was the problem. Fuck it, life's too short, I said to myself. I considered all the money I had coming to me, a lot of it, from my tenure at MetLife: a $100,000-a-month pension after taxes for the next twenty years; I had close to $20 million in deferred compensation and 401(k)s. I had $1.7 million in MetLife stock options and I owned almost half a million shares.

"What am I doing to myself?" I thought. The feelings I wrestled with weren't pleasant: if I did leave, I would go out as someone who tried to save AIG but couldn't get the job done on his watch. "That's my legacy?" I asked myself. "How terrible." But rather that than stick around; prolonging this turmoil and letting AIG go down as a result was no option at all.

With that, Golub left my office. Where he was headed I did not know. I stayed put, waiting for word of an outcome. White smoke, or black? Meantime, Dahlgren and Millstein were called back into the session, and just as Millstein was about to speak, the doors of the conference room swung open.

Millstein would later fill me in on the events that followed, which he described as "like the third act of Shakespeare, when everybody goes crazy. Eventually order is restored, but in the third act, shit happens that you just can't believe."

Golub entered, "looking like King Lear on the heath, a little disheveled and unkempt, and clearly troubled," Millstein would recount.

"I want to talk to my board," he said.

"That's great, Harvey," Millstein said. "Sarah and I will get up and you can talk to your board."

"No, no, what I have to say, you can hear as well," Golub responded, and sat down next to Millstein.

Golub's misgivings about me spilled out. "I'm not sure if leaving Bob in charge of the firm is the right thing to do," he said, according to those present. "You know, after all, he's threatened to resign a couple of times, and I'm really uncertain, and I think if I do it, I'm just leaving you guys open to this again, being held hostage. He's very unpredictable, he's very volatile, and I'm not sure he's really fit to run the company, and I feel like it would be dereliction of my duty as a director and as a fiduciary officer to allow this to go on."

The strained silence in the room was broken by an unlikely voice addressing Golub directly: that of Morris Offit, a director who had never been a big fan of mine.

"I've got to say, for the good of the firm and the future of the company, I think you have to resign," Offit told Golub. "We can't go through another CEO change. We've had five in five years. Bob has got the loyalty of his team, he's gotten the company to stand up and fly right, and despite the fact that he and I have disagreed on important matters, as have you, he's the right leader for this firm."

Other directors spoke up, echoing Offit, telling Golub that the only way for him to lead now would be to leave.

And at last, he did.

While Shakespeare was happening in the conference room on the other side of the eighteenth floor, I was still cooling my heels in my office. An hour or so passed, and no one had come to get me. So finally I wandered over to the conference room to see if I could get an update on my fate.

To my astonishment, everyone had left.

"Where's the board?" I asked someone.

"The meeting's over," they said.

Little did I know that Harvey was out and a new chairman installed: Steve Miller. Nobody called me in, nobody discussed it with me. I did find a draft of Golub's resignation letter on a desk, so I knew I still had a job. But it's a fact that no one on the board, on that day or ever, spoke to me about Golub's departure.

I did speak after the meeting to Millstein, who was in his car on the way to his daughter's camp when he picked up his phone and told me the news.

So many things rushed through my head. Golub was out. They'd seen the light. We could all move on.

And still: Holy shit. A thought passed through my mind:

"This place is fucking unbelievable."

TWELVE

# AN UNFINISHED SYMPHONY

OCTOBER 21, 2010. The most difficult day I've ever faced.

A car took me to Peter Cooper Village, the massive apartment complex in Manhattan's East 20s, developed, as you may remember, by my former company, MetLife. My son Ari was now living there, having moved from Chicago with his wife Clair and their daughter Aubrey. Ari thought I was coming over to talk over the progress of the AIA IPO, which looked as if it was going to be oversubscribed and on track to bring in more than $20 billion.

I wasn't.

I'd always considered Ari an extension of my right arm. He'd gone through some growing pains of various sorts—all kids do. But he'd matured into a man I was deeply proud of, someone I could confide in 100 percent, who understood the trials I faced and for whom I always tried to be there. The father I never had, I wanted to be to Ari. To Nehama, too, without a doubt. With Ari, though, there was an extra level of worry on my part—a special concern I like to imagine that my father had for me, as his eldest son. My dad was simply gone too soon, long before we had a chance to seal that sort of bond.

On my way over after a meeting, I called Ari and asked if he would meet me in the lobby of his building on East 20th Street. I greeted him with a big smile and said, "How's my sonny boy?" When I asked him to walk outside with me, I could tell from his knitted brow that he sensed this was no ordinary greeting.

"Son, I have to talk to you about something," I said.

Now a look of real worry crossed his dark features. "Is it about Oma?" he asked, our name for Denise's mother.

"No. It's about me."

"Oh, no, Dad, it's not . . . ?"

We sat down on a bench.

"Son, give your dad a hug."

We embraced and I revealed what I knew. I had lung cancer. In fact, I had undergone my first rounds of chemotherapy earlier that day. My doctor, a pulmonary oncologist at NYU's Perlmutter Cancer Center on East 34th Street, Abraham Chachoua (pronounced Sha-SHOE-ah), had laid out the prognosis.

A year to live. Probably. Maybe.

The cough had started a couple of months earlier and had become more persistent. I returned from my morning jogs and couldn't stop hacking. My family was growing concerned, and when I couldn't ignore it any longer, I made an appointment with my cardiologist, Nieca Goldberg. I was due for a checkup, anyway, as a result of other ongoing issues, including the stent that had been inserted into my heart.

Early October was a hectic time, and finding an hour to follow up on health problems was a pain in the ass. I was trying to manage the preparations for the sale of AIA, I had to be in D.C. for a financial services forum, and I was fighting with Lisa—again. I really had no time to be dealing with doctors. But I relented and scheduled the appointment at NYU Langone Medical Center with Dr. Goldberg, for Friday, October 1—an especially significant day because it was the eighth anniversary of my mother's death. That night, I got a call from her office: "You need a CAT scan immediately. Come in to NYU tomorrow."

"I'm not doing it tomorrow," I said, "because it's my granddaughter's birthday. I am not missing that. You'll have to do it on Monday."

The CAT scan led to a biopsy of a growth on one of my ribs. I then flew down to a financial services forum we'd organized in D.C., and on Wednesday the sixth got a sobering phone call there from Chachoua.

I don't recall every word, but several phrases stood out. "Stage 4 metastatic lung cancer." "Spread to the lymph nodes." "Highest stage of presentation." And: "Survival could be in the vicinity of a year."

It was a lot to process, but I took it all in pretty calmly. I hadn't had a cigarette since I went cold turkey thirty years earlier. Before that, I'd been a heavy smoker going back to the 1950s. Now, at this late date, it seemed to have caught up with me. I was paying the price.

Chachoua wanted me to come in immediately to talk about options. "It's very deadly," he explained. "And we need you to meet with a surgeon right away to decide whether there's any surgery possible."

"That's fine, but I can't," I said. "I'm in Washington and then I want to go to Florida for the weekend." This didn't sit well with Chachoua. An Egyptian-born Jew who settled in New York after medical training in Australia, he was an engaging, highly skilled guy with an aggressive approach to treatment. The shelves of his eighth-floor office were lined with hundreds of elephant figurines, a collection that grew over the years. They were gifts from grateful patients who appreciated his personal touch as well as his dedication.

There was nothing Chachoua could say to change my plans. From D.C., I was heading to a speaking engagement in Orlando, and then on for the weekend to Boca Raton, where I had a condo. I decided to go by myself. I needed to be alone—completely alone—to think.

I didn't lapse into "Why me? Why now?" self-pity, though. I was upset, of course. Who wouldn't be? For your loved ones, there's no good time for news of this kind. But it was potentially devastating for my plans at AIG as well. All the work I'd done, the battles I'd fought, were starting to make believers of people who just months before were positive AIG would never meet its obligations, or survive. And now it was my survival that was on the line. I could be gone before I had the chance to prove the doubters wrong.

Terror wasn't what I felt. Worry, or anxiousness, maybe, for Nehama and Ari, mostly. I dwelled a lot on my father's early death, and the plans he left incomplete. I'd only recently received a letter, in fact, from a lawyer in Monticello who'd handled my father's real-estate dealings. He revealed to me for the first time that my dad had bigger plans for a string of motels in the Catskills. "It's a shame your dad never got to finish," he'd said.

I didn't want my plans sidetracked. I was even haunted by visions of the return of my nemesis, Harvey Golub, waiting outside the boardroom doors, saying, "Let me back in!"

For the moment, I told no one, not my sister Jayne the doctor, or Denise or Lisa or Ari or Nehama. I was by temperament and habit the strong one, the adviser, the decision-maker, the consoler. I wasn't quite ready for the tables to be turned.

One person did suspect something: my secretary, Maria Escobar, a smart and fiercely loyal assistant who had been with me almost continually since my Paine Webber days. As the keeper of my calendar, she couldn't help but notice the multiple entries for doctors. I shared my confidences with her and considered her a friend.

"Bobby, are you OK???" she e-mailed me on October 1. So, confronted, I did confide to her my news after I got the diagnosis that next week. But for the moment I didn't inform anyone else at AIG or in the government. I had to be careful about how I parceled out the information. The state of my health not only had personal consequences, but at this point carried heavy financial implications as well. Anything that could weaken faith in the company's management was dangerous.

My schedule for the rest of October was punishing: Chicago for a meeting of the Business Council; then Frankfurt, Germany, for discussions with clients and brokers; then Dubrovnik, for a weekend break at Villa Splendid; then Zurich, for the board of Credit Suisse First Boston, of which I was a director; then back to New York and finally Florida. I felt fine, so I made no attempt to slow down. Now, though, I'd have to add time for the treatment of my illness—not to mention for a series of disclosures to my family that were going to take patience and cause grief. I had to figure out exactly how I would inform each of them.

And, of course, this reminds me of a story. There are two adult brothers, Jack and Fred. Jack is going on vacation, and he asks Fred if while he is away he'll take care of his cat. A week later, the vacation over, Jack arrives at Fred's house to pick up his pet.

"I don't have the cat," Fred says. "The cat is dead."

"What do you mean 'the cat is dead'?" says the outraged Jack. "What the hell happened? You can't just shock me with news like that. You have to prepare me for this terrible blow. You're supposed to build up to it slowly, with a story, something like: 'Well, you see, the cat saw a bird and before I could stop him he dashed out of the house to chase it. He climbed a tree and then he jumped onto the roof. Then he jumped off the roof and landed in the street, and he was hit by a car. Unfortunately, he didn't make it.' That kind of story. So I can steel myself for bad news."

"Okay, fair enough. I see your point," says Fred. "I'm sorry."

Some time later, Jack goes away again, and asks Fred to look in on their frail mother while he's gone. When he returns, Jack asks Fred how their mom is getting on.

"Well, you see," Fred replies. "Mom was up on the roof . . ."

So now, I had to explain to people, somehow, that it looked like I might be the one up there on the roof.

Denise was first. She was in Europe in mid-October; I asked if she wanted to meet me at Villa Splendid over the weekend of the sixteenth. I didn't say anything just yet. She sounded so pleased just to be getting together for a few days in this spot we both loved.

"We have something to talk about," I said, after we both had settled in.

"What do we have to talk about?" she asked.

"We need to talk about me."

This was far from the way I normally opened a conversation. People you've been with for a long time sometimes know when upsetting information is coming, just by your intonation and the words you use. I didn't have to lay out a mom's-on-the-roof scenario for Denise. The introduction was all Denise needed before she broke down.

I explained the situation. We both had a good cry. "Listen," I said. "This could have happened in 2005, before I retired from MetLife and we had a chance to enjoy this beautiful house. Or it could have occurred in July, when I was fighting with Harvey and the questions would have arisen about whether I'd have time to really get AIG on a proper footing.

"So we have to be happy for what we've had, and what we have now," I added. Denise, who had gone through her own hell with cancer—three times—listened quietly. She was devastated.

And still, life had to go on. That Monday, the eighteenth, I flew to Zurich for the board meeting of Credit Suisse, and then on Wednesday the twentieth to New York.

The next day, the twenty-first, was huge: the pricing meeting for the IPO of AIA, the biggest chunk of AIG we were planning to sell. And on top of that, it was day one of my adventures in the world of cancer treatment. The start of my chemotherapy.

Surgery, it had been determined, was not an option. One alternative was the use of molecular profiling to see if there was a mutation in the cancer that was "targetable," as Chachoua put it, with a special oral medication. Obtaining the profiling results, however, would take weeks. A faster approach was possible with conventional chemotherapy. Ultimately, we opted for chemo. Two drugs administered intravenously—Alimta and Cisplatin—were the cocktail Chachoua recommended. Overnighting near the offices AIG maintained in Jersey City, I made my way Thursday morning to NYU's cancer center. Denise came with me. The medical staff assumed this would be the first of several days of chemo, as was the norm. I had other ideas.

I wanted the entire three-dose regimen administered all at once.

"You can't do it in one day," they said.

"It has to be done in one day," I replied.

The drugs, I was told, were designed for a treatment that continued over a series of visits. This schedule wasn't going to work for me. I simply didn't have time to keep coming back, I said. Plus, I wanted to see quickly what kind of effect the chemo would have on my body.

"I need to know if I'm going to look like a freak," I said to Chachoua. "Is my hair going to fall out completely? How fast will it fall out, how obvious will it be?" Paramount in my mind was how people would react to my appearance. If I looked sickly, not myself, it would affect how they dealt with me. At work, it might erode their confidence that I could carry out the plans I had laid out so forcefully. Morale might quickly swandive if they saw me and thought: not long for this world.

Chachoua explained that while multiple doses of the medications could be given at once, NYU's practice was not to do so. His expression told me I was not his ideal patient. And he could see, too, that I wasn't going to compromise on this point.

So for the next eight hours, I was in a hospital room, hooked up to the IV, getting drugs pumped into me in a relentless cycle of medication, hydration, medication, hydration, medication, hydration.

Back at AIG's offices on Pine Street in Lower Manhattan that afternoon, the details of the deal for the first stock offering for AIA—our giant Asian insurance division—were being hammered out. This was the most important day so far, in AIG's complex campaign back to solvency and independence. As we were planning to sell half of AIA's total shares in this first go-round, this would amount to nothing less than one of the largest IPOs in history. I'd left the day-to-day prep for this event to my capable senior officer for investments, Brian Schreiber. But I wanted to be in on this meeting, at which the share price we were seeking would be set, and we'd be confirming for our banking partners the allotments they were to sell.

At this hour, though, I was in a reclining chair at NYU, cell phone in hand, tubes in my arm. On the AIA conference call, I gave no indication where I was, though I wondered if the hubbub of nurses and technicians around me was audible. (As it turned out, it was; Schreiber later confided that he deduced I was calling from a hospital or doctor's office. To his credit, he never mentioned this in any of our interactions while I was CEO.)

After the call ended, I decided that I had to bite the bullet and begin disclosing my condition. But first came my kids. Ari was nearby, Nehama a bit farther away, in Philadelphia, so our face-to-face conversation would not occur that day. As Ari and I walked around the courtyard of his apartment building and Ari tried to absorb the magnitude of what I was telling him, I asked him if he might take time off from his job and travel with me to Croatia to help me figure out my own transitional alternatives in the event I became incapacitated. It was a lot to ask of him, so soon. All I can say is that I was thinking out loud, and not all that logically. And most of all, with my heart.

He immediately said that of course he would. That's my boy, I thought, but ultimately I realized mine was an impractical request. He had a young family and, as he revealed to me that night, blessing of blessings, Clair was pregnant with their second child. I was impressed by his composure, and even more so after we went back upstairs and he took Clair into their bedroom to explain to her what was happening. The day grew longer, we all cried some more, and I asked if he and Clair would stop by the next day, in Suffern, where I was going for the weekend to rest.

The weekend turned out to be not so restful, because there was so much planning and talking to do. Denise wanted to fortify me, so on Friday she made a matzo-ball soup with sweet potatoes for me and Ari and Clair. It was delicious, and I said so. I also said it didn't need the potatoes—which everyone thought was funny, because that's just the kind of thing I *would* say. No holding back, even on the subject of matzo-ball soup. I guess they laughed out of a sense of relief that, with the unknown looming, I would continue to be *me*.

We watched some home videos on Saturday, shot in Europe, of my mother's brother, Uncle Julie, and others of my family; he'd been diagnosed with cancer before the footage was shot. I was fixated on his appearance and expressed my frustration that he'd been told his life expectancy was four years—which suddenly sounded to me like such a luxurious amount of time. I called Nehama that morning and asked if she might drive up for an event we were hosting that night in Suffern, a dinner for a bunch of friends, and then the showing of a movie at our restored gem, the Lafayette Theater. The film was a documentary Denise had produced, *Ahead of Time: The Extraordinary Journey of Ruth Gruber*, the story of an intrepid Brooklyn-born woman who received her PhD at twenty, became a New York newspaper reporter at twenty-four, and eventually went on secret missions for FDR. Nehama said she couldn't make it. I sighed. I wasn't going to do this on the phone. Soon enough, I'd be on the road, heading to Philly.

First, though, I made the half-hour trip to Lisa's house in Bergen County, New Jersey. We weren't speaking at the time. Because I wouldn't divorce Denise—the status quo suited me just fine, I explained—Lisa had broken off with me. At least that is how I perceived things to be. But this was news I had to deliver in person to someone who remained very special to me. Lisa took it very hard, was immobilized by it, in fact. The relationship was too important to both of us to just say good-bye. Actually, my condition would spur us to a reconciliation.

Back in Suffern, the family went ahead with the dinner Saturday night at Marcello's, an Italian restaurant down the street from the movie house. It so happened that among our guests was Serena Ng, a *Wall Street Journal* reporter I'd known for a long time and had come to like, and her husband. Bad timing. We didn't say a word to her about my health, which she naturally would have been duty-bound to report. I felt okay, but the first predicted side effects of the chemo were kicking in—an annoying case of the hiccups. Ari went to the drugstore for the remedy Chachoua had prescribed.

On Sunday, as I prepared to drive to Philadelphia with Ari, more people had to be told. I called Steve Miller, who had taken over as board chairman after Golub's departure. Keeping the details to a minimum, and not mentioning the advanced stage or kind of cancer, I tried to sound matter-of-fact about the illness. The effect on people of not telling them what kind of cancer you have varies greatly: some are happy not to have too many details; others assume the absolute worst. Miller sounded stricken; he told me how much he admired my dedication to AIG and my desire to press on. Amid the calls to my brother and sisters, I spoke to our general counsel, Tom Russo. We agreed it would also be prudent to get in touch with our lawyers at Simpson Thacher to discuss our responsibilities and how best to release the news to the company, the press, and the public.

Nehama wasn't home when we arrived. Ari and I sat and waited for her with the babysitter, Brenda, and my grandson, Eliashu, the beautiful boy she had adopted with her then-partner Jacob. When after about ninety minutes Nehama returned from her quilting class, Ari took Eliashu into the backyard so that I could tell my daughter in private. She took it as hard as everyone else had, maybe even harder, but she brightened a bit when I said that we would spend time together soon, as a family, hopefully at the condo in Florida. In any case, somewhere.

Life is strange: if the diagnosis had come down sixteen months earlier, all the people who needed to know this deeply personal information would already have been brought into the loop. Now, my loop was the entire world.

And, of course, I understood. I was the CEO of a publicly traded corporation, one beholden to the taxpayers under extraordinary circumstances, and working under the intense glare of the media. If the company's leader was sick, people had a right to know. I could not avoid this reality. Under federal law, a public company must reveal information it deems essential to investors' decision-making. My health fell into this category. But how much specific information were they entitled to? I was adamant that the type of cancer not be disclosed. I did not believe the world was entitled to my detailed medical records. Who agreed or disagreed, I did not care.

The government had to be informed ahead of the general public, too, so I placed a call to Millstein, the Treasury's point man on AIG, with whom by now I shared a solid, mutual admiration.

He sounded truly sad. He extended his sympathies, but he also indicated, as I well knew, that there was still a lot of work to do. If the AIA IPO worked, we'd be able to pay off our debts to the Fed, entirely, and then have only TARP left to resolve.

"How long can you be here?" he asked, gingerly.

I really didn't know, and I said so. "It's not good. It's very serious. But I think I can make it through May." I told him that we remained hopeful that we'd find a therapy that worked. After May, though, "If nothing helps, I'm going to get really sick."

We decided to go wide with the news that Monday, October 25. With my savvy legal ally, Russo, in attendance, I called Christina Pretto, our senior executive in public and internal relations, into my office on Pine Street so that she could prepare the communiqués.

"What kind of cancer do you have?" Pretto asked, right off the bat.

"I'm not going to tell you," I said. "Because then when the press asked you that same question, you would be in an impossible position. This way, you won't have to lie."

And that was the posture I maintained. I gave no significant details to my staff or to the board.

"Dear Colleagues," began the letter we sent that day to AIG employees around the world.

*It's with great regret that I must share with you some unsettling news: I have been diagnosed with cancer, and last week I began an aggressive round of chemotherapy. That's the bad news. The good news is that I feel fine, and I continue to work according to my normal schedule. As for my long-term prognosis—I will have a better idea over the next couple of months of what that will look like as I continue to undergo treatment and my doctors refine their diagnosis.*

*. . . Because of all of you, we as a team have made extraordinary progress toward repaying taxpayers and cementing a clear path for AIG to emerge as a sound, independent company. As I have said before, I have every intention of staying at AIG and seeing that path completed. From the day I arrived here, you have given me tremendous energy*

*and strength, and frankly, learning that I have cancer makes me even more committed to working with all of you to turn AIG into the success story we all envision. It's a turnaround I want to complete.*

The words were sincere—and were just a few of the thousands that would be spilled that day on the subject of my illness. "We're getting news into our operations here that American International Group president and chief executive officer Robert Benmosche has been diagnosed with cancer," Neil Cavuto announced a few hours later on his Fox Business News program. "It doesn't say what type of cancer this is, but it is going to require aggressive chemotherapy. Anytime they put 'aggressive chemotherapy'— as someone who has had cancer—that is a pretty big deal."

The subtext was: "How long has he got?" Again, human nature. To reassure all of the interested parties, we put out a statement that week that if for some reason I could not perform my duties, Miller, the board chair, would step in as a temporary replacement. Miller and I had talked about other possibilities but I shared my belief with him that he was the best choice. This led to some speculative articles about what should be AIG's course. The *Wall Street Journal* pointed out, "If directors force an exit unnecessarily, they risk losing a valued leader. But an executive distracted by cancer treatment may not be fully effective, harming investors."

It was a fair enough observation, though I didn't think it applied in my case. At no point did the treatment instructions include "stop doing what you normally do."

Some of the other passages of this October 29 *Journal* article, by Joann Lublin, suggested that AIG was misguided in sticking with me. (For reasons noted above, I'd long believed Lublin wanted me out; the diagnosis was another opportunity to help me to the exit.) "Critics contend," she went on to say, that "corporate boards often fail to intervene fast enough when cancer strikes a CEO. . . . 'Their personal relationship clouds their judgment,' says Robert Robins, a retired Tulane University political-science professor and an authority on disabled leaders."

Modern oncology offers a rebuttal: Neither then nor in the ensuing years did I ever miss a day of work due to cancer. Not a one. Still, at this early stage, I knew there was the possibility of inviting more uncertainty by not disclosing everything about my condition. I thought about how Apple took heat over the years for not answering all the questions about Steve Jobs's terminal illness—even though it had gone so far as to reveal in 2004 the type of cancer its founder faced. Until Jobs's death in 2011, the speculation about his health was continual.

I could see, in my case, that the media would, by reflex, try to fill the vacuum of available information.

"AIG didn't say what type of cancer Benmosche has," Bloomberg News reported on October 26. The article hinted at the reporter's effort to uncover my condition: "There are more than 100 different types of chemotherapy drugs, many given every two to three weeks, said Otis Brawley, chief medical officer of the American Cancer Society. Without knowing the type of cancer or the specific treatment, it's impossible to predict the severity of side effects, Brawley said."

For the most part, the press took a respectful posture; if the announcement had any positive effect, it was in giving reporters an opportunity to stop and take the measure of what had been accomplished at AIG; Bloomberg noted, for instance, that AIG's stock price had risen 37 percent since the start of 2010. And though my illness would continue to come up in news stories, attempts to uncover more of the details were mercifully few. As a matter of fact, we managed to keep the nature of my cancer out of the media until after I retired from AIG. Chalk that up to a display of some common decency on the press's part, combined with my willingness to describe generally the state of my health, whenever I was asked. Which was often.

I'll tell you, though, what was really at the heart of my reticence: that a focus on lung cancer would be all the world needed to stop us dead in our tracks. That the severity of my illness would be used to curtail our progress and allow the vultures to rush back in. That I'd be marginalized and my legacy quashed.

That I would be compelled to leave behind an unfinished symphony.

This possibility became ever more apparent to me in the weeks after my all-in-one chemotherapy day. The expressions of sympathy and encouragement poured in from every corner of my life. I was particularly touched by the heartfelt e-mails I received from other AIG employees who were undergoing cancer treatment and, like me, were just getting on with their work. And I heard from many of the people I'd worked with over the years.

"Bob, OMG, I am so sorry," read the e-mail on October 25 from Tom Bianco, my colleague from Paine Webber and Chase. "What is the diagnosis? What kind are we talking about? When did you know? How long have you been doing the therapy? . . . I hope you know that you have always been one of my lifelong touch points and I cherish our relationship. You are in our prayers."

I had to be as closemouthed with Tom as with the rest of the world. "We will talk but for now, the less said the better," I e-mailed back.

My family, meanwhile, was feeling the burden of having to explain to people without giving details—a challenge that, Ari said, "I learned to deal with better every day."

I was learning, too, in navigating my daily life, that illness ties friends and family and colleagues up in etiquette knots. People think you expect to be asked about your health, and so they ask and ask and ask. "How do you feel?" they want to know. "I feel with my hands," I always wanted to reply, sarcastically. Those closest to you have the biggest problem with this, because they are the most invested in your answer. Their anxieties can be catching, and sometimes, my frustration with all of this got the best of me. "Are you okay today?" Denise would ask, in the most well-meaning way. "If I'm not okay, I'll tell you," I'd snap in reply. What I always wanted to add—and occasionally did, at such moments—was, "Leave me the fuck alone! I've got cancer. Believe me, I haven't forgotten!"

The cancer did have a deeper effect on my outlook: It took away some of my ability to think long-term. I suddenly was spending more time considering how much pleasure other people would derive from what we were accomplishing, rather than how much enjoyment I would get. I became very aware, too, of the frequency with which we all speak of our regrets, about the people we neglected or didn't spend enough time with; the things we meant to say, but never did. I planned to work as hard as possible to erase regret from my vocabulary.

So high on my list had been an early phone call to Beth, my first child, the daughter conceived when I was too young for the responsibilities of fatherhood, to tell her of my condition before she heard it on the news, and that I wanted to see her again, soon. My mind wandered back, too, to my father's premature death and his unfinished symphonies. The knowledge that he had left a host of real-estate projects brewing in Sullivan County, plans that died with him, bolstered me in my determination to see my big project through.

Physically, I really did feel pretty good. Hiccups and a bit of fatigue were the only minor bothers. My schedule remained as hectic as ever, as the momentum built over our major divestitures and the plans moved ahead to pay off our Fed credit lines. I did not yet share all my thoughts regarding who would eventually replace me, but I knew it was an issue that had to be addressed; I was determined that down the line my successor would inherit an organization far more disciplined than the one I joined. The timetable for my departure remained fairly blurry, with a tentative retirement now set for 2012—depending, of course, on how well my body held up. If my body held up. Everyone seemed to be following my lead on this, and I wanted to be as optimistic as possible.

By early November, as we waited to learn if the chemo I'd received on October 21 was having any effect—it can take weeks to know—the tension over my diagnosis and treatment was beginning to wear on the family. Denise, Nehama, Lisa, and even Ari were showing signs of their anxieties in spite of their efforts to mask them. Our nervousness was well founded: The chemo wasn't working. We'd soon be informed that the first round of chemo and a follow-up barrage of the drugs a few weeks later failed to produce any effect. Somehow, I think we'd all suspected as much.

Then, eureka. In the midst of our worrying came some extraordinary news. An e-mail from Chachoua spelled it out. I forwarded a copy of it to Ari on November 2. In the subject line, I typed, "Rib."

"Hello there," Chachoua wrote. "We have, as you may recall, sent out the tumor tissue for molecular profiling. The results show that you have a mutation in the EGFR receptor. This makes you a candidate for targeted therapy with a drug called Tarceva. People with this mutation have as high as a 70–80 percent response to Tarceva. We need to discuss this on your next appointment, or if you want to come in sooner I would be happy to do it."

According to the makers of Tarceva, about one in seven patients with lung cancers such as mine test positive for EGFR, which is short for epidermal growth factor receptor. A protein located on the surfaces of cells, EGFR can become overactive through mutation. As a result, cancer can develop. I had the mutation that responds to the drug, which is taken orally once a day.

I'm not the type who spends hours online absorbing every iota of detail about health issues. My response to Chachoua indicated as much.

"So this is good news?" I e-mailed back.

"Very good news," he replied.

Normally, patients develop a resistance to the pill after about a year or so. But its value could last longer—as it would in my case. This was the first really encouraging news since the diagnosis. I felt some relief. And so did everyone around me.

"Very good news is exactly what we want to hear. :) Even if we don't understand it," wrote Nehama.

"HALLELUJAH!" was Denise's one-word response.

It so happened I was just digesting this information as I was headed with Ari to Napa Valley for a CEO event hosted by JPMorgan Chase. In the time before the conference, Ari and I indulged our love of wine by visiting a few vineyards for tastings. Lisa joined us there and the three of us got to spend a memorable day together. Along with some excellent Napa Valley reds, we had, for the first time in a while, the taste of hope on our lips.

Around this time, I had a conversation with Serena Ng. I wasn't doing a lot of press right then, but I made an exception for Ng. We sat down for a Q&A for the *Journal*, and naturally, the talk veered into the territory of my health. She asked specifically about AIG's leadership plans, post-Benmosche. I was as frank as I could be. "If I thought I would die in three weeks, I would have said to Steve [Miller]: 'Look, I need to be out of here in three weeks,'" I said. Then I added:

> *I don't know what my life span will be yet, or what the full signs will be, but what I do know is that I'm not sitting here with just a couple of months.*
>
> *Sometime in the first quarter, I'd like to reach a fork and tell Steve what I'm finding out from the doctors. If the prognosis is good, and I've got enough horizon and good health, then I would like to see the government get [bought] out. But if at that point we find maybe it's a little too tenuous and there's still concern, then I will ask the board to start a more serious discussion on how they will deal with succession.*
>
> *If anything has significantly deteriorated, I am going to obviously have to disclose it because if we do a stock offering in March, I have to feel compelled to do it. Steve Jobs and Apple were severely criticized for the secrecy that went on in his case, and Steve Jobs is a huge contributor to Apple. Not to say I'm not a contributor, but my role in AIG today is clearly not the same as his. We chose to disclose early and say this is how we're going to deal with the succession plan.*

Ng followed up. "How much does the board know about your condition since you haven't told them what form of cancer you have?"

I knew what information I'd kept from the board, but I wasn't sure if the board was actively seeking to learn more. As I explained to Ng, AIG's medical staff was in touch with Chachoua. It was entirely possible some additional details had been related, simply because the AIG doctors had the task of monitoring me, especially at times my schedule didn't allow me to be immediately available for follow-up visits at NYU.

"It's important that for a company that gets this close to the finish line, I don't screw it up," I told Ng. "I don't want my cancer or my health to screw it up."

I felt I was in extremely good hands with Chachoua. I'll tell you why I had such confidence: He went at my cancer with a ferocity I recognized. It was the same focus and energy I used in the daily task of pulling AIG out of the miserable circumstances in which I'd found it. At an NYU benefit, I'd heard him say something that struck me deeply. He was with a group of oncologists in some advisory meeting and a question came up about how they approached their jobs. Several of them talked about how they hoped to make their patients comfortable, give them a good quality of life for the time they had left.

Chachoua thought of this as aiming too low. Frustrated with what he was hearing, he spoke up. "The first thing I think is, can I cure them? Because that, after all, is what the patient wants from us."

A cure, a solution. Yes. Exactly. That's what I wanted. What the workforce at AIG wanted. What the taxpayers wanted.

Chachoua had persuaded me to do a second round of chemo in mid-November, just to see if I showed any improvement. I didn't. And so on November 22, the next phase of my adventures in cancer land began: I started taking Tarceva.

Tarceva. Three weeks earlier, the name meant nothing to me. Now it sounded like the most beautiful word I'd ever heard.

# THIRTEEN

# "I HAVE GIVEN UP ALL HOPE OF A BETTER PAST"

LIFE COULD BE DIVIDED FOR me now into two phases: BC and AC. Before Cancer and After Cancer. The latter was the reality I'd now be living in for the rest of my days—however many I would get.

And at the start of 2011, I was increasingly optimistic that I'd get more of them than I'd thought when I first learned I had the disease. Dr. Chachoua told me that the Tarceva was working. The tumors remained, but their metabolic activity was receding toward a measurement of zero. In other words, they were becoming inactive. Dr. Chachoua was clearly encouraged. But if I asked, "How long is it going to be this way?" he'd answer something like: "Enjoy your wine and have a good time. Each year, we'll see."

Well, "year" sounded a lot better than "week" or "month," even with the side effects the pills caused. I broke out in severe acne on my face, for one thing. I didn't lose my hair, but shaving became an ordeal. For the first time in my life, I grew a full beard. On other parts of my body, rashes and sores developed; some mornings I woke up with blood on my pillow from the blisters on my scalp. And changing my blood-pocked shirts several times a day was part of the new normal.

But my outlook remained upbeat and my energy on most days was good. I tired out some, but generally I felt vigorous. Some people even thought the beard made me look more dapper. I retained both my sense of humor and my normally hectic schedule. And I tried to build in as much down time as possible. Vacationing at Villa Splendid in Croatia over the Christmas holidays of 2010, I ran with my daughter Nehama every day along the hilly paths and streets of Dubrovnik, clocking between 2.8 and 3.8 miles on each run. Being with family in my beautiful stone house, on the terraced property with a path leading down to the rocky shore of the smooth-as-glass Adriatic, recharged my batteries every time I stayed.

Everywhere I went, my illness continued to be a subject of intense curiosity, especially for the media. That I remained adamant about with-holding the specifics of the diagnosis only made them more curious. I understood of course that the questions would keep coming. Nothing I could do about that. My concern was that if I uttered the words "lung cancer," they would dominate every conversation from then on, and doing my job would become even more difficult. I said as much to Neil Cavuto on the January 14, 2011, edition of his Fox Business program.

"So allow me: What kind of cancer do you have?" he asked me, as he had a few months earlier.

"I'm not going to discuss that, Neil," I said, "because I think it is some-thing that will give reporters an opportunity to call every expert in the world and decide when I'm going to die. . . . So I feel that telling what my disease is just opens the door for more speculation." I explained that my doctors would keep AIG's board of directors informed in terms of my prognosis. "And knowing the specific disease, unless you're my doctor, you can't really know much more than that," I added.

Happily, the conjecture about my cancer—and there were news out-lets opining on it far more callously than the thoroughly decent Cavuto—was accompanied by increasingly promising reports about AIG's own health. January 2011 represented a watershed for us. That month we would announce that our loans from the Fed had been completely paid back, and that Treasury's stake in AIG had been converted to com-mon stock—the formal start of the government's eventual exit from the company. Cavuto led off his interview with me that day by describing AIG's ever-more-plausible reversal of fortune as "a comeback that is nothing short of breathtaking."

On a Bloomberg News program around the same time, *In Business* with Margaret Brennan, praise emanated from none other than Hank Greenberg: "I think Bob has been the best leader they've had since I left the company," he said. And still more positive words were expressed by Andrew Ross Sorkin, the *New York Times*'s young ace on the finance beat, in a kickoff column for 2011 in which he named me "Executive of the Year":

> *The tough-talking, sometimes foul-mouthed CEO took over what had to be the most reviled company in the country. . . . Mr. Benmosche, who was recently found to have cancer, fought bitterly with the government to run the company his way—and for the most part, he and taxpayers have won. . . . The bailout of AIG will never be popular. But if Mr. Benmosche can keep the insurer on the same path, he should be.*

The news tide was turning for several reasons, but to understand why, I have to retrace some of the events of the latter half of 2010. One major change was that AIG could now speak with one voice. After Harvey Golub departed in July 2010, I was no longer hampered by second-guessing from within the company. Steve Miller, the new chairman, was fully engaged and asked all the right questions, but ultimately left vision and management to me. And though the collapse of the sale of AIA to Prudential PLC in June 2010 put a disastrous brake on our momentum, we did have a fallback strategy—a stock offering for AIA. It was to take place in Hong Kong in October.

Importantly, as I'd long suspected they would, the markets were recovering, and the projections for the businesses we had identified as our core units looked to be on track. At the same time, I was now freer to fill positions with the people I needed. Immediately after Golub's resignation in July, I flew to Hong Kong to fire Mark Wilson, who'd been CEO of AIA since 2009.

I'd grown disenchanted with Wilson when he began to advocate vociferously for a plan I didn't favor: selling more than 50 percent of AIA through an IPO, at the time when I was trying to sell AIA to Prudential PLC. Why more than 50 percent? Because, I suspected, he wanted to be the head of an AIA that was independent of AIG. That told me he was the kind of ego-driven executive I didn't want.

The person I wanted at the helm of AIA was Mark Tucker, a fifty-two-year-old Brit who himself had been a CEO of Prudential PLC and had also been Prudential's chief in Asia. An avid footballer, both as a fan and player, he was tough-minded and knowledgeable, just the fellow to get AIA ready for the IPO. I put the wheels of Tucker's hiring in motion in the weeks before that tumultuous July board meeting. I arranged to fly him in early July to Zurich, where I had a Credit Suisse directors' meeting, from South Africa, where he was attending the World Cup. I had also arranged for him to talk individually to the members of the AIG board to get their consent. Afterward, Tucker—who had a mouth like mine—was furious. He reported that Golub, still chairman at the time, told him they might stick with Wilson.

"You dumb fuck!" the outraged Tucker shouted at me, his salty language totally justifiable in this case. "You fucking get me to come all the way from South Africa. And then Harvey tells me that maybe Mark Wilson's good enough? Are you fucking kidding me?"

I tried to calm him down; I'd get to the bottom of it. Of course, I was beyond furious myself.

I learned that our advisers from Morgan Stanley—who I suspected had been lobbying to kill the Prudential PLC deal because the bank would earn no money from it—were making it extremely clear to the board that we could not change leadership at AIA three months before an IPO. With Golub gone, however, the board reluctantly agreed to go along with me. I sat down with Wilson in Hong Kong right after that fateful board meeting in July to tell him I was making some changes, and that I needed him to leave immediately.

"Isn't it a shame it's come to this?" I said to him. "I tried to work with you, but you seem to have had your own view of what we're going to do. You think you're going to be here for the IPO, and that isn't in the cards."

Wilson, to his credit, conceded a judgment error. "You know," he said, "I guess I picked the wrong side."

I really do try to avoid seeming paranoid whenever possible. But I took his statement as confirmation that within the top echelons of this still-tribal company, there actually were sides. I had perceived him as an ally of Golub and he now acknowledged as much.

Tucker's experience in building an insurance brand in Asia would prove to be a valuable commodity as we amped up for selling a chunk of AIA. His time at Prudential PLC included a prior attempt to buy AIA, so he was intimately familiar with the unit. We announced his appointment on the nineteenth, months in advance of our plan B for AIA—selling shares in the company in a stock offering in Hong Kong.

It was at this point in late summer 2010 that we were ready to implement the strategy for the huge financial coup we were trying to pull off: an exit, favorable to the taxpayer, from all of our government obligations. Millstein and I, of course, had critical expertise, input, and support from top people in both of our organizations: Hancock, Schreiber, and Herzog for AIG; from Treasury, TARP administrator Herb Allison and his eventual successor, Tim Massad.

The Fed, you will recall, was in essence our banker, having extended us loans in the midst of the crisis when no commercial bank would, and the Treasury was our owner, via the majority stockholding position it bought to help stabilize the company. First, we'd had to resolve all of our remaining loans from the Fed, our first-in-line creditor, which at this point totaled about $47 billion. This would be the initial move in an intricate and ambitious series of steps to facilitate the recapitalization of AIG— the process that would bring us, with useful new regulatory restrictions in place, back to the equity markets, to new fiscal health and independence.

For the Fed payback to be completed, we projected the need to earn at least $20 billion or more from an IPO for AIA. The second piece was a cash payment by us of about $6 billion. The third part was a more complex transaction, involving our borrowing from TARP the remaining $20.3 billion of what we owed the Fed. So in effect Treasury was lending us additional money to complete the Fed payback, and then taking an even bigger stake in AIG stock in return. This was a crucial step, because we could not start to exit our financial obligations with Treasury until the Fed was out of the lending picture.

Once paying the Fed was complete, the other major facet of the "recap" could begin. This involved taking Treasury's preferred shares in AIG—valued at $49.1 billion—and converting them into 1.655 billion shares of common stock, which would be sold over time to the public. To accommodate the additional money being drawn down from TARP to pay back the Fed, Treasury's ownership of the company shot up from 79.9 percent to 92.1 percent.

The sale of Treasury's common stock meant AIG did not have to lay out $49.1 billion directly. Instead, the value the public now placed on the company through the buying of the shares at a satisfactory price would make whole the taxpayers' generous rescue of the company. In the eleventh hour of negotiations over the shape of this deal, we granted existing shareholders—now owning only 8 percent of AIG's common stock—special warrants. These were coupons that could be redeemed to buy AIG stock for a "strike price" of $45. For every two shares owned, a stockholder got one warrant, good for ten years. During that time, if AIG's stock rose above $45, the warrants would become a valuable commodity.

We announced the recap plan on September 30, 2010. It was an insanely busy moment for me, as you will remember that I was just about to undergo tests that would reveal my cancer. I can't help but think of the irony of the new phases both AIG and I were entering simultaneously.

"Today, we're glimpsing a lot of sunlight, an awful lot of sunlight," I said, in revealing the financial details to the press and public. "This plan accomplishes several goals. First, it vastly simplifies current government support of AIG. It then sets forth a clear path for AIG to repay the Fed in full; it sets in motion the steps for the U.S. Treasury to exit its ownership in AIG over time."

It would be several months before the first of the sales took place, but the shares would be sold, in phases, to the public with the intention that the share price would meet Treasury's goal for full repayment of our TARP obligations. That share price, it was determined, was $28.75. I was holding out hope that the price would end up being slightly higher than that, $29 or thereabouts, so that we could make good on the vow to return the money at a profit to taxpayers.

The announcement of the recapitalization plan was greeted with both enthusiasm and skepticism. Geithner issued his rosiest statement to date, saying the recap plan "dramatically accelerates the timeline for AIG's repayment and puts taxpayers in a considerably stronger position to recoup our investment in the company." Not everyone was buying this line of thinking, however. The dire predictions only months before by government analysts, who said that in the end the AIG bailout would cost the country anywhere from $36 billion to $50 billion, still hung in the air in the fall of 2010. "It's early yet for taxpayers to declare victory, given persistent questions about AIG's health and official estimates made this year that the bailout will end up costing taxpayers," *Forbes* magazine observed on September 30. The government-appointed auditor of TARP, Neil Barofsky, expressed concerns about Treasury's lack of "transparency" in its methodology for calculating the conversion of the preferred to common shares. But we felt differently, believing that the conversion was the clearest way to compensate the American taxpayer.

Some major investors, like Greenberg—whose Starr International was AIG's largest shareholder at the time of the 2008 rescue—remained bitterly angry over the way their stake in the company had been all but wiped out by the government takeover. I do think they had some valid points to their grievance, in that AIG was treated differently from other companies enmeshed in the crisis: the government's appropriation of 79 percent of the company in exchange for a large credit line was quite a heavy penalty, especially when you looked at how other institutions were treated. They got the liquidity without paying such a massive price.

Still, we had to decline Greenberg's request to sign on to the litigation he filed later in 2011, when he sued the government for $25 billion over its handling of the AIG rescue. (This was the suit he would win, in June 2015.) Claiming Treasury had used AIG as a vehicle to give "backdoor bailouts" to the banks and other counterparties in AIG's securities transactions—firms that were reimbursed 100 cents on the dollar for their contracts with AIG—Greenberg accused the government of seizing AIG's private property in violation of the Constitution. (Although Greenberg became a target for derision over the optics of the suit, most notably in a scathing piece by Jon Stewart on *The Daily Show*, the litigation was by no means frivolous.)

The question of fairness, of course, goes to the heart of an even more difficult one, a question I've been asked constantly, and that is, whether the government should have swooped in and rescued Wall Street in the first place. I've pointed out earlier in the book my belief that there were alternatives—as through, in the case of AIG, a freezing at the outset of the toxic contracts at FP. But even that would have required some form of intervention by the regulators. So my answer in hindsight is that the government made a pragmatic choice, in the midst of a crisis. And let's remember that shareholders in some other companies embroiled in the chaos were left with nothing—a total loss. AIG's stockholders had at least some small fraction of their investment spared.

Or as I explained to a dissatisfied AIG stockholder at our annual shareholders' meeting in 2010: "A deal is a deal. We can't renegotiate what was done. We're looking forward, not backward, because we can't redo the deal. The fact is we're here, we've survived, we're strong and we're vibrant. That's the good news. We can't fix the past."

And then I quoted for him the words of wisdom I'd heard spoken by my rabbi daughter, Nehama: "I have given up all hope of a better past."

What I was banking on now was a better future, which was feeling more and more achievable. At the end of October, the IPO conducted in Hong Kong for AIA exceeded our expectations. The 7 billion shares, or 58 percent of the unit, that we sold generated $20.5 billion, an amount that went a long way toward erasing doubts over what we'd been saying about the company's future. On the New York Stock Exchange, AIG shares were up 40 percent for the year to about $40 a share. Adding the proceeds of the IPO to our other deals—the impending closing of the sale of ALICO to MetLife, and the sale of much of American General Finance to Fortress Investment Group—anyone could see that we were about to clear a momentous hurdle: paying back in full our senior creditor, the Fed. (You'll remember that our financial obligations to the Fed, our lender, were different from those to the U.S. Treasury, our majority stockholder.)

Some other financial transactions had to occur in the complexities of resolving the payback: we had to, for instance, borrow that additional $22 billion from TARP to pay off the two "special purpose" lending vehicles the Fed had set up in 2008 that used AIA and ALICO as collateral. But we now would have the cash on hand to pay off the entirety of our debt to the Fed.

So with the wheels of the payback turning, we entered 2011 with a little bit of a wind at our backs. This was reflected in the growing chorus of approval we were hearing from regulators, analysts, and business journalists.

The completion of the recapitalization plan was announced on January 14, 2011, the day I talked with Cavuto. The Fed had its billions back and Treasury's shares were converted to common stock. Geithner—with whom I'd been dealing over the preceding sixteen months through an intermediary, Millstein—was now publicly patting us on the back. To describe our efforts, he even resorted to the "T word."

Turnaround.

Music to my ears.

"I would especially like to thank Bob Benmosche and the entire leadership of AIG who transformed this institution in less than two years under very trying circumstances," Geithner said in a press release that day. "Our extraordinary and hardworking staff here at Treasury and the great team at the Federal Reserve also deserve high praise for helping make this day a reality."

If you listened very carefully to those diplomatically crafted remarks, you could almost hear his sigh of relief. I thought the acknowledgment was late in coming: Where was this kind of statement when the pitch-forks were out for the workers at AIG Financial Products? Still, Geithner and Hank Paulson and Ben Bernanke had taken a lot of heat them-selves for the AIG rescue, had put their reputations on the line, and so even a belated expression of support by them had meaning. No one, after all, was ever going to throw any of us a ticker-tape parade for this unpopular rescue. Yet the country needed to be reminded that the limb AIG and Treasury and the Fed had all climbed out on was proving to be a sturdy one.

We had a lot of persuasion still to accomplish ourselves, because the nation remained in far from a forgiving mood where AIG was concerned. Although some people in the press had begun to believe in the prospect of a complete turnaround, the average consumer remained angry that we had to be turned around at all. How much confidence people would have in us going forward, and how they would perceive the company once the mess was behind us, were things everyone on my executive team had to be worried about.

Because with the company's recapitalization, we were placing our big-gest bet yet on the belief that the world saw a future for AIG.

I have to admit that I was skeptical at first that the hatred of AIG went very deep. Maybe I was blinded a bit by my own outrage: I remained an-gry at the degree to which the company had been scapegoated. Yes, that is how I felt—that it wasn't ordinary people who despised us, it was that the newspapers unfairly whipped up a frenzy against us. And it bugged me that we'd had to come up with brand identities for our biggest units, like Chartis, that hid the association with AIG itself. Hardly anyone in the public even knew there was a connection. I didn't see that as particularly advantageous, going forward. But I had no data on which to draw conclusions.

So at my behest, we embarked on a multi-year study of the attitudes about the company held by various groups: the general public, the investment community, and the distributors and brokers who sold our products. The "reputation research" project by Ipsos, a global market-research firm, soon was reporting back on the serious challenges we faced. And some of the results—showing how extreme were the views about the company—surprised me.

In a telephone sampling in September 2010 of 1,001 American adults, we learned, for example, that three out of five of them held AIG responsible for the crisis. They blamed AIG more than any other company! To make matters worse, a majority of respondents had no idea that we'd made any progress in our recovery efforts. That we were in the process of paying them back was not getting through to the taxpayers.

This drove me crazy. As a corporate brand, AIG advertised very little; on television not at all. So given how relatively little awareness there was of AIG before the crisis, I probably shouldn't have been taken aback as much as I was by how deeply our name had been blackened by the bailout. (As it turned out, the survey confirmed that most of the country was unaware that we were the parent entity for subsidiaries like SunAmerica, Chartis, and American General.) The survey found that among investors and brokers, our image was far more solid. These groups reported being appreciative of the scope of AIG's reach and resources and the quality of its employees. So it seemed that the more informed people were about who we were and what we did, the more favorable their impression was. This at least was an encouraging sign.

The early results from Ipsos persuaded me that it was too soon to deal with the identity issues, to have Chartis, for example, revert to the AIG name. But I wasn't going to give up on that. The sermon I was preaching inside the company was all about restoring pride; I remained determined that after the psychological beating we'd taken and the shaming our employees had been subjected to, we were going to reunify all the parts of the company under the AIG brand. This philosophy later became part of a campaign that we would call "One AIG."

That would have to wait until we finished job one: making the taxpayers whole. And by the first quarter of 2011, as Cavuto and Sorkin and others were beginning to articulate, we were well on our way to doing so. It was no longer accurate to think of us as a charity case. We were on the path to becoming an independent company again—with one very unusual, very big shareholder. We were at a place where we could start to talk about the company's stability, and start rethinking how we wanted to do business. Still, until we resolved the government payback, there would be lingering doubts about the truth of our optimistic forecast. And the people we did business with would remain concerned about whether, in the end, AIG would make it.

At least we had solid arguments now to temper some of that anxiety. We were a leaner company than before, certainly: the selling off of major subsidiaries and some other trimming meant we were down to about 65,000 employees, from more than 100,000 before the crisis. Leaner also meant simpler, and more narrowly focused, on a smaller number of businesses. The narrowing allowed us to provide greater transparency about the risks we took; unwinding our exposure in businesses requiring billions of dollars of debt to support—such as Financial Products and American General Finance's consumer credit card operations—amounted to a dramatic lowering of risk overall.

By other measures, the indicators of AIG as a going concern were good; our client retention rate, for example. Year to year, 85 percent of our clients stayed with us, even through the worst of the last few years. And contrary to what might have been predicted, the statistics showed we also were strong when it came to employee retention: 31 percent of those 65,000 workers had been with the company for more than ten years—an impressive figure in the high-turnover insurance industry. And of the two thousand employees in AIG's top leadership positions, an astonishing 57 percent remained at AIG for ten years; one out of five had been with the company for twenty years. This was no minor matter. One of my biggest worries when I took over was whether there would be a mass exodus of talent from the company, which would have been utterly disastrous. My strategy focused on motivating the troops, instilling a new belief in themselves and our rebuilding effort. The numbers indicated that all that time I spent traveling (yes, in the corporate jets!) and talking to our people face-to-face paid off.

But with TARP's money still on the table, little else about us would stick in anyone's mind than that we were a leech on the American economy. So, in the spring of 2011, our continuing job was to dispel that perception. And the absolute best way to do that was to make a lot of money for the American people!

In addition, we had to reinforce the idea that AIG was going to have a life after the payback. To accomplish that, we needed to issue and sell some new shares in the firm ourselves to prove to the capital markets that we could raise money for future operations. These goals required us to sell the hell out of the first stock issue of the recapitalization, or what some of us were calling AIG's "re-IPO."

This entailed putting on a show of sorts, and taking it on the road. A show for potential buyers—hedge funds, mutual funds, pension funds, a whole range of institutional investors—with the goals of selling them on the stability of AIG and its growth potential, and securing as high a price for the stock as possible. We were doing it, mind you, on behalf of our major shareholder, the government. I'm not making a case here for AIG's altruism. This was a matter of survival. It was simply an imperative that we do this. Not only were we fighting to pay back America. We were also fighting for our professional livelihoods and reputations.

And the "road show" was the fight as a ground war. Our mission was the corporate equivalent of door-to-door combat. To promote the recapitalization plan and convince investors that the stock was good for their portfolios, we divided our senior people into teams that in May 2011 would spread the gospel of our comeback around the world. I led one team, with Brian Schreiber; Mary Jane Fortin, CFO of SunAmerica; and

John Doyle, our chief executive officer of global commercial insurance. Peter Hancock led another with David Herzog; Rob Schimek, a senior vice president; and Jay Wintrob, executive vice president for domestic life and retirement services. The re-IPO road show began on May 10 with a rehearsal of our pitch in a hotel conference room on Wall Street. And then we went out to tell our story to key people around the world.

Much of it is a blur now, of jets and Marriotts and offices in gleaming towers. All told, we pitched before seventy-seven separate meetings and met with 530 individual investors in Europe, Asia, and North America. Our aim was to convince them all that we could access the unsecured market; that we could finish the successful de-risking of our contracts at Financial Products; that we could go to the banks for the commercial credit to replace the Federal Reserve credit, and then go to the equity market to raise additional capital.

There was a downside possibility: that we would establish a price for the Treasury stock and fail to achieve it. In my mind, a $29 share price was absolutely essential to our recovery. As I said many times, we were not going to sell these shares unless the American taxpayer got back all of their money plus a profit. Wall Street did not agree. As I told a town-hall meeting in New York that spring, Wall Street thought we had time enough down the road to make that happen. We should sell the stock for less, they believed, "'because people want to buy it for less.' And that's the way Wall Street thinks," I said.

"What I believe, for everyone here at this company, we would never want to see a headline that says: 'This time the American taxpayer *almost* got back everything they were promised. Maybe they'll get more in the future.'

"I just don't think that's what we stand for."

And so we made it clear—and we had the support of the Treasury, from the top down—that come pricing night, if we had to go below $29, we were going to pull the deal.

The stock price seemed a pretty clear choice to me, even if it was hard for some investors and others to immediately understand. It caused some confusion, because the value of AIG, a company living on government life support for nearly three years, was something of a mystery. How much was the stock really worth? Just five months earlier, when we announced the completion of the recapitalization plan, the stock was selling for more than $60 a share. But it was a very odd stock, because very little of it was actually being traded and so it didn't take much volume to move it. Nobody quite understood at that point what the re-IPO would mean, and so the price was being driven by speculators, many of whom were looking to make money by shorting the stock.

Over the following months, as the significance of the recapitalization came into better focus, the stock price came down and began to perform in what I considered a more reasonable representation of its true value; by May, in anticipation of Treasury selling the first 200 million of its 1.65 billion shares, the price was in the more realistic $30 range. (The number of shares in the first offering was to be kept fairly modest, because the stock market was in a downturn and we wanted to create conditions in which the offering would sell out.) In the meantime, our road-show teams developed our pitch to investors. It was crucial we come up with a strategy that made accessible and believable the robust path we saw for AIG that only a few outside the company could at this point envision. We were, after all, selling stakes in an idea that many people still couldn't get their heads around—that AIG would actually, truly, viably continue to exist.

What evolved as our selling strategy makes for an interesting case study in tailoring a message to extraordinary circumstances. Because if the natural impulse for us in going around was to paint a glowing portrait of AIG's prospects for the future, to talk in a formulaic way about the company's accomplishments, we quickly realized that this approach was insufficient. We found in the early road-show meetings that when we couched our presentation in terms of what we had achieved, eyes would glaze over and minds shut down. Those we were reaching out to thought they already knew where AIG stood. What stuck in their heads was a picture of AIG as filled with besieged employees, all looking for a way out. And boy, is selling into that kind of perception an uphill struggle.

The lightbulb-over-the-head moment came when Christina Pretto, my head of communications, spoke up in my office one afternoon. "Let's not talk about AIG in terms of accomplishments," she said. "You've got to talk first about the myths about AIG. Frame it as a discussion of what people think they know about the company. And then knock the myths down."

It was an object lesson in the absolutely vital importance of how a business tells its story. In each visit, we had a very finite amount of time in which to speak—an hour, tops. And as we learned, not every office we traveled to was going to be receptive. In some rooms, in fact, we faced outright hostility. We'd walk in and instantly see that we'd been invited in so the people in the room could sound off. A pension fund manager who had lost millions upon millions on an investment in AIG didn't want to hear what a good buy we were now; he basically wanted a chance to shout at us. So we sat through these sessions thinking about how we might fare better at the next one. The meetings were dispiriting but we got through them. It was simply a hazard of the tough assignment.

But many others were willing to listen. And what the road show turned into was a great opportunity for us to hone our message and give insight into the ways that a company can move out of a state of panic and back toward stability. We tried to spin as compelling a yarn as possible and I, in my folksiest manner, tried to put everyone at their ease.

Let me walk you through the portrait of AIG we were painting, because in dispelling the myths about the company, we were attempting to pre-empt the naysayers even as we laid out this extraordinary tale of recovery.

About the myth that all the top talent had left, I became a broken record. "Throughout 2010, we lost only 3 percent of our top people. That's sixty people," I noted in meeting after meeting. "That means 1,940 are still with us and working hard for the company. So I don't know where the idea of the brain drain came from. But let me ask you: What if the reporters got it wrong? What if all the people who've made AIG what it is—the people at all the parts of the company that didn't cause the problems we saw at Financial Products—what if they're still there? Because they *are* still there."

Myth No. 2: our customers were walking away. The truth was there was some slippage at Chartis in a few segments of our business, notably in what was known as our "D&O" coverage: we were the world's leading insurer of company directors and officers around the world, and we'd seen some attrition there. But the charts we pulled out during the presentations belied any significant declines: 97 percent of Fortune 1000 businesses—97 percent!—were current customers of some unit of AIG. Then, we'd show that one-third of the people on the *Forbes* list of the four hundred richest Americans were clients of some Chartis product.

Myth Nos. 3 and 4, which were interrelated: in the divesting of AL-ICO and AIA, we had sold off our crown jewels, with little left of value, and we still had troubled units on our books, especially FP. I talked here about the achievement of divestiture: we had managed to sell those companies at a record multiple of earnings—businesses which, by the way, had provided no dividends to help run the holding company. "If you look at the growth potential of what we do have—Chartis and SunAmerica, United Guaranty and even ILFC, you'll see we have tremendous earning power, and a tremendous franchise." As for the myth of too much remaining risk, I explained how several monitors from the Fed had been sitting in the Wilton, Connecticut, offices of FP every day for two years, "complaining that we're not selling fast enough." By going slowly, in fact, we were able to sell many of those tainted contracts at better prices, and as a result we'd amassed about $8 billion more than had been anticipated.

At every meeting, I refreshed everyone's memories of the debt we'd paid back in full to the Fed that past January. "Look, a condition of our loan arrangement with the Fed was that they would not accept final payment of the outstanding amount until they were absolutely sure that nothing further would happen at FP to embarrass them. 'How would it look if we allowed you to pay us back and then you convert the Treasury's preferred stock to common stock, and FP has a big blowup?' They weren't worried about us; they were worried about themselves! We would never have closed that transaction if the Fed had not been completely satisfied."

As we ticked off the myths one by one, the response was often: "But . . .

but . . . but . . ." Especially with regard to how really independent we could claim to be. At this point Moody's had us at a Baa rating, so we could claim to be an investment-grade company. But—if we got into further trouble, we were asked, couldn't we expect the government to step back in with another rescue? Weren't we certain to be severely downgraded by the rating agencies, once TARP was over and we were in dire need of additional assistance?

"There is no way on God's green earth that we're going to get another dime out of the U.S. government to support AIG if we can't make it on our own," I replied. "They would be *crucified* by the American taxpayer if they even contemplated intervening again."

And so, on May 24 Millstein and his people and my team and I negotiated the price of phase one of the AIG re-IPO. I lobbied for a share price of around $29.75, a full dollar over the amount that would set a course for a full payback. Treasury ended up setting a discounted price of $29 even. Four banks were to lead the offering—Bank of America, Deutsche Bank, Goldman Sachs, and JPMorgan Chase—but I'd not lost my sense of outrage over the way many of the banks had behaved toward us all through this years-long ordeal. No way were they going to take their usual cut of this deal, on the order of 2 to 3 percent. We pushed through a demand that meant they collectively got one-half of 1 percent on the stock offering. The banks agreed, in part because it was such a potentially huge transaction; the return would still be massive for them and they did not want to jeopardize their piece of it.

The rest was up to the investors. We waited anxiously to see how they would respond.

The first day was admittedly not fantastic, but it was good enough. Selling into a weak market, Treasury nevertheless reaped $8.7 billion and, in the words of Serena Ng and Randall Smith of the *Wall Street Journal*, "eked out a small profit for taxpayers."

"Eked out" was not the resounding milestone terminology I was after, but it would do for now. "AIG and the Treasury sold 300 million shares at $29 apiece, putting U.S. taxpayers in line to recoup at least $5.8 billon and reducing the government's stake in the insurer to 77 percent from 92 percent," they wrote on May 25. "More shares may be sold in the coming days, which could lower U.S. ownership in AIG to around 74 percent."

We could feel pleased about the billions we took in. Our road show had paid off. The results were a crucial validation of our ability to raise fresh capital on AIG's good name.

Yeah, I said that. Our good name.

In practical and psychological terms, the offering marked the return of AIG to respectability. That was in some ways a trickier goal even than profitability. We still had a ways to go in the vast public consciousness, but we were making inroads with the communities of investors and analysts and business leaders. Certainly, the company had unresolved issues: adequately managing our reserves, for example, in anticipation of insurance claims from unforeseen events, continued to be a troubling problem. And while we'd begun to deal with the redundancy in our operations, the duplications remained astounding: we had 153 separate human resources and payroll systems—one thousand people with the job of counting people!

Even so, that May 2011 offering was the first paving stone on a road that, over a remarkably short period of time, would take us all the way to a thrilling destination—a complete selling off of Treasury's stake in AIG, now in sight on such a relatively rapid schedule. It amazed me to think that I'd been at AIG for just twenty-two months.

And now I had a hankering to stay.

My repeated threats to walk away from this job were a thing of the past. I wanted to see this through. I'd talked about retiring in the spring of 2011, and of course, that deadline had come and gone. I'd since told the board that my cancer seemed to be under control and that I would be willing to remain aboard through the end of 2012. But my thoughts now, as we were really getting rolling and I might think creatively about other aspects of my post, shifted to staying my own course.

The era of internal combat at AIG was behind us, which made it a much more pleasant place to work. I told the board as much—although

I jokingly remarked at the time of the first stock offering that a few of the directors would not have been unhappy to see the back of me. I also knew by this time, however, that most of the employees of AIG had my back.

"I grow on you," I said, to laughter, at a town-hall meeting after the start of the re-IPO. Does it sound as if I was mellowing? Maybe, a bit. I still expected results, and when problems arose with, for example, the forecasting of our needs to build up our reserve funds to cover catastrophes around the world, I could still display fits of anger that terrified the troops. To the employees that day, though, I jokingly likened myself to Vegemite— the brown food paste Australians swear by, and the rest of us only slowly develop an appreciation for—if we ever do. "You know," I added, "it takes a while."

My appetite for doing the job was still robust. It was the cancer, no doubt, that would ultimately dictate the terms of my employment.

"I wanted to come in here, do what I needed to do, and retire," I told the employees that day in June. "You all knew that. I made that clear. Going through the illness I'm going through right now, I want more free time. I've talked to the board about how I could get a little bit more personal time for myself and better balance and so on.

"But I don't want to be, quite frankly, that inactive, because I think you've got to keep your mind going at this stage of the game, keep engaged. And I think that helps me healthwise. And so I'm not quite as willing to go back to retirement and worrying about my sickness. I'd rather enjoy being here with you."

I did continue to enjoy myself. In fact, the best was yet to come.

# FOURTEEN

# "YOU'RE WELCOME, AMERICA"

I WASN'T SURPRISED by the snowballing effect the successful stock offering of May 2011 had on our fortunes. The rest of the world, though, seemed to be living in the movie *Groundhog Day*: waking up to each bit of news of our progress as if any memories of the steady gains we were making had been erased in their minds the night before. Going forward from that May, and continuing over the next eighteen months, the pieces of AIG's turnaround were falling into place. Yes, a few bumps cropped up including one spectacularly ill-timed lawsuit that turned into a public relations disaster—but we were making headway at a pace that was astounding even our angriest critics. The things I'd been saying all along were turning out to be true. My assessment of AIG's intrinsic value and predictions about how the payback would proceed were proving remarkably accurate.

All told, we would return well over $40 billion to the federal government in 2011. The payoff of our loans from the Fed was completed two years ahead of schedule. Our net earnings for the year amounted to $1.2 billion—even during a period of record payouts for natural catastrophes. We were proceeding rapidly toward one of the most exciting days in the company's history—and maybe in American corporate history—when we would be able to tell the American taxpayer that the $182 billion they'd trusted us with was back in their hands. With interest.

Was it too much to digest for the average news consumer, who was led to believe that AIG was a haven for selfish people who put the entire economy at risk for their personal gain? The federal government had made a few supportive public statements in 2011 as our recapitalization plan progressed. But the pronouncements were fairly anemic and did little to temper the popular scorn for us. On behalf of AIG's employees, this stuck in my craw.

You may recall that from the beginning of my time at AIG I expressed a desire to steer clear of Washington. And as much as I possibly could, I did. So with regard to my irritation at the lack of on-the-record backing from Geithner and Obama, you may be thinking: What did I expect?

I wasn't looking for personal letters of congratulations or presidential medals; I wanted some help in taking the heat off the people who worked for me. I could say to the people of AIG that I appreciated their efforts until I was blue in the face. Hearing it from the commander-in-chief or one of his top lieutenants would have a different kind of effect on them, and naturally, on the public at large.

There was a noteworthy occasion when a message of encouragement was conveyed directly to me, back in early 2011, on the day that we closed the deal for the recapitalization. Jim Millstein arranged a lunch between Geithner and me at Treasury in D.C. Millstein remembers saying to the secretary: "You know, the guy's doing a hell of a job for you. Your personal reputation would have gone a different way if AIG turned out to be a complete disaster. So maybe we should have him in, you should have lunch with him, and we take him over to see the president and the two of you can thank him for his effort." Geithner recognized the value in this, Millstein said, and immediately agreed.

The political news site Politico got wind of our impending get-together on the morning of January 14, 2011, and revealed, "AIG CEO Robert Benmosche will dine with Tim Geithner at Treasury today to celebrate

AIG repaying its debt to the Federal Reserve Bank of New York and completing its complex recapitalization."

Millstein e-mailed me the item with a warning that we might receive questions about it from other reporters. Amazingly, it generated no further press ripples. I flew that morning on one of the company jets From Teterboro in New Jersey to Dulles Airport outside D.C. and was driven to the Treasury Building on Pennsylvania Avenue.

As for the lunch with Geithner and Millstein: mindful of the contentious issues I had stirred up at our last private meeting in the summer of 2009, I held my tongue, and my time with the secretary was cordial, a business lunch full of talk of what still had to be done. Afterward, we walked over to the White House to greet President Obama in the Oval Office. A more genteel fellow you'd be hard pressed to find. Although I respected his desire to do the right thing, as a leader he had disappointed me. I found him to be a timid advocate for American business, too subtle a thinker, as many others have noted, for the bruising battles that needed to be fought. I was a guy who—surprise, surprise—gravitated toward more decisive leadership, which is why I had liked Bill Clinton and especially Ronald Reagan.

The president sat in a chair, I on a sofa. He thanked me for having come out of retirement to formulate a plan that so quickly was returning billions to the country.

I couldn't let the moment with the leader of the free world pass.

I told him, flatly, that the business community needed more positive signs, more encouragement, from him. The messages about the financial health of the country, to my mind, were far too negative. We needed him to remind the nation more emphatically, I said, that the economic climate was improving. In terms of job creation and stimulating growth, we in the corporate world were part of the solution, not, as many seemed to think, the problem.

He listened. Was it the first time he'd heard this opinion? Probably not. I still felt compelled to underline it. So whether he took to heart what I said, I had no idea. We shook hands, I thanked him for having me in, and I was out of there. That night, a dinner was thrown for me at the Washington home of Tim Massad, the lawyer who had replaced Herbert Allison in 2010 as the assistant Treasury secretary overseeing TARP. To give the festivities a personal flavor, I brought along bottles of Benmosche Family wine. Not only did I want to share my product, I also thought a nod to my link to Croatia, after all the controversy about my excursions there, seemed slyly in order.

A nice picture of my sit-down that day with the president appears elsewhere in these pages. The Obama administration agreed to release it to us. This marks the first time, in fact, it has been published, because after the meeting, the White House did not distribute it to the press. Perhaps the optics of Obama conversing genially with the CEO of AIG were too radioactive at a time when re-election strategies were being batted around the West Wing.

I suppose I should have been pleased that the White House decided it was safe to meet with me at all. At the very least, the impression had been conveyed to the leaders of the land—thank you, Jim Millstein—that it was important to recognize that AIG had kept the faith after its government rescue. I just wish it had been a much stronger signal, and had come far sooner.

Millstein left Treasury a month later to return to the private sector and his New York–based consultancy, Millstein & Co., a financial services firm with a specialty in helping troubled companies. In a pinch, I can think of no man I'd turn to faster. He was a hero of the entire struggle to pull AIG out of the ash can, a great thinker and a brilliant tactician. Though we would remain friends and speak often, I was going to miss him at all those meetings.

As we gained momentum in late 2011 and then on through 2012, I had strongly positive things to report at virtually every quarterly earnings call—the conference call that public companies arrange with financial analysts to coincide with the release of their profit and loss results. (In some of our darker days earlier on, we refrained from the live presentations and disseminated recorded discussions of the relevant numbers instead.)

Treasury was selling off its AIG common stock at regular intervals and the Fed, too, was able to sell off the remaining securities that it had taken off our hands in the special vehicle called Maiden Lane II. By the middle of 2012, as our profits rose, AIG was buying back as many as half of the shares Treasury would put on the block. Treasury's stake was coming down so fast that year that the results were difficult for some people to digest: by August, reporters would be talking about the government as a minority shareholder in AIG. Investors were seeing our results and voting for us with their wallets.

Plans were moving forward for a sale of the remainder of AIA as well as of ILFC, our aircraft leasing division: we were looking to gain more capital, to meet our new tougher regulatory requirements, avoid the liquidity issues that caused such chaos before, and quite possibly provide funds for future acquisitions. We now had cash on hand, upward of $16 billion, due in part to our desire to pool our resources, and also because of our ability to mitigate our tax burden via the legally accepted practice of writing down some of the historic losses during the crisis. At the same time, we were engaging internally in a lively discussion of our employee performance-ranking system. This was a less than universally loved reform that I introduced, having adapted it from my experience years before as a human resources executive. And, get this, we were even mulling the possibility of offering dividends to shareholders for the first time in nearly five years.

In short, we were beginning to behave in ways that resembled any large, healthy, highly competitive American company. And a return to normalcy now amounted in AIG's case to something extraordinary.

How's this for a turnaround: we even had in the works a project to reintroduce the AIG name and logo as the central symbol of all of our branding. By the end of 2012, the words "Chartis" and "SunAmerica" would be eliminated, to be replaced by new umbrella titles for these vast operating units: AIG Property Casualty and AIG Life and Retirement. I liked to think Hank Greenberg felt as pleased as I did—well, almost as pleased, anyway.

With proof of progress mounting, we were devoting more thought to how we might spread the news of our recovery more widely. The arena of "free" media was tricky for us, given all the resentment in the country, but we were considering going to the press to tell our story more fully. One opportunity to get our message out beyond the business press came with the proposal for an in-depth profile in *New York* magazine. Sounded good to me; I even offered to host the reporter, Jessica Pressler, in Dubrovnik at Villa Splendid. With Christina Pretto, my vigilant communications chief, along to handle the introductions and be my backstop, we all met up at my Croatian home in mid-August 2012 to do the interviews for an article that would ultimately run in late October.

Denise, who was there, too, had a bad feeling about the whole thing. Not me. I was a news junkie myself; over the years, I'd developed a rapport with several of the reporters I respected, and I'd like to think some of them enjoyed our exchanges. (A few others, who I didn't think gave us a fair shake, earned my everlasting disdain.) But I knew that attempts to control what reporters saw or wrote were futile and foolhardy. So I tried to keep my expectations low and my worries to a minimum about how an article turned out. This particular piece was especially significant, though, in shaping how a reader who didn't necessarily follow the story day to day would think of AIG and, of course, me.

Since we were on home turf, Denise maintained she had some rights in terms of the ground rules.

"When she's interviewing me, some of the time, I don't want you to be here," I said to Denise before Pressler arrived.

Denise was having none of that.

"Wrong!" she replied. "There's nothing I don't know about our lives and if you have to tell her something for whatever the reason, then I want to know what you said."

So Denise was with us as Pressler conducted her interviews, whether while we were eating pasta in the shade of the outdoor living room, my favorite spot to lounge at Villa Splendid, or, in the van, driving up the Dalmatian coast to the Peljesac peninsula where my vineyards were, on the shoreline in the tiny village of Viganj and high on a hill in the Dingac region. We gave her the blue-chip Benmosche tour, the one I arranged for friends and family and even members of the AIG board. It had taken me six years to renovate the five levels of Villa Splendid, and I always enjoyed sharing it with guests. My showplace. I'd filled it with tapestries and antiques I bought in Switzerland, built a cabana into the rocks over the shoreline, turned a small adjacent building into a mini-villa that I named Lillian's Cottage, after my mother. The whole place was so spacious that we decided to turn the house into a part-time bed-and-breakfast, with five rooms available to visitors.

Pressler, who'd done her homework I was relieved to find, had a prickly way of starting a conversation. "People say you're taking your victory lap a bit too soon," she said at one point. It was the same naysaying I'd been hearing for years. It confirmed for me the reason for inviting a magazine reporter into my inner sanctum: yet another myth in need of debunking. The reality of the AIG story was straggling behind the erroneous conventional wisdom. Even now, the jabbering set didn't believe we'd pay every penny back to the government. "Wrong!" as Denise would say. No, it wasn't too early for a victory lap. In fact, I told Pressler: "We should be taking a victory lap!"

I'm a divulger—most of the time you ask me, and I answer. So we talked about everything that was public and some of what was private. I, as always, was just being myself. And as I've learned in life, being yourself is never a mistake. Even if what you say is sometimes taken the wrong way.

People at work often asked me, "How do you come across so real?" Now there's a question, one for which even I had no good answer. I do remember, though, some advice early in my executive career when I had to begin to take on a role as a communicator, having to get up and talk to people I hardly knew. I was so *not* polished in my approach that my boss at Paine Webber, Don Nickelson, ordered me to take a course on how to speak while making a slide presentation. That was helpful as a confidence-building exercise. But even better advice came from the wife of a business acquaintance of mine, back in 1982, who could sense how nervous I was in settings requiring me to get up and start talking.

"Bob," she said, "when you talk to people about what you're doing, just tell them the truth. Don't sugarcoat it. Tell it like it is. And if you manage to do what you say you're going to do, if you can pull that part off, it will pay off for you over and over."

Sometimes, the most obvious observations simply need to be verbalized. What I realized at the time was that most people were like me: when you sit and listen to someone, whether an acquaintance or a CEO, your antennae are up as to whether what you're being told actually means something. You want to get up and talk to people like there's nothing wrong? Okay, there's nothing wrong. But that's a waste of time. So I've always had this philosophy that if you know what you want to say, and why you want to say it, then just say it. Just stick to the truth.

And it's what I did, sitting for hours with Pressler.

We waited for the results to be published. In the meantime, Treasury put a new tranch of AIG stock on the market. And the wall kept a-tumbling down.

On September 11, 2012, almost four years to the day after the initial meltdown, a massive chunk of the wall came down. With AIG trading now for about $33 a share, the government unveiled its biggest AIG stock offering yet, selling 550 million shares. The $18 billion deal at a discounted price of $32.50 a share was well above the $29 break-even threshold. The sale would reduce the taxpayers' stake in AIG to just under 22 percent. As the presidential election was just two months away, the news that the government was unloading its AIG stock at a now accelerated pace seemed a boost to the administration's credibility, and just as importantly, to ours.

My team was feeling its oats. We would be further demonstrating our return to independence by using our capital, some of it raised from a sale of our remaining stake in AIA, to buy back some of those shares, about $5 billion worth.

"Few people would have predicted during the depths of the financial crisis—or even during the national outrage that followed news of bonuses being awarded at AIG after the bailout—that taxpayers eventually would turn a profit on the rescue of a company whose risky derivatives trades nearly sank the global economy," the *Washington Post*'s Brady Dennis wrote that day. "But that improbable outcome now seems probable. And an essentially nationalized company that seemed destined for failure is now a profitable, nearly-private enterprise once again, much smaller but with much less risk on its books."

Dennis reached out to the witty Millstein for comment. I had to laugh at his evaluation of the outcome. "Pretty good," Millstein observed, "even for government work."

Then the highest-profile piece laying out the story of my tenure at AIG hit the stands. The cover of the October 29, 2012, issue of *New York* magazine featured a grinning, bearded face that would surely fail to launch a thousand ships: mine. The tone of the piece was clear from the cover. Under the sub-headline, "AIG CEO," were emblazoned the words, in yellow capital letters: "YOU'RE WELCOME, AMERICA." Funny, right? Given the prevailing AIG story line, this gave you the impression that the guy in charge of the company ran the place with a bit of attitude. It conveyed guts, cojones, and maybe some recklessness.

It gave a lot of people around me a case of acid reflux. Do I have to spell it out? The idea it conveyed—that after practically bringing down the financial system AIG deserved the nation's gratitude—made me sound, to put it mildly, cavalier.

"There's nothing subtle about Bob Benmosche," Pressler began.

I loved it. And she quoted me correctly on the point I'd been hammering away at from virtually the day I arrived at AIG, more than three years before:

> *"Everybody said it's just not going to happen, they'll never pay it off," he goes on. "SIGTARP, Elizabeth Warren, Gretchen Whatshername in the* New York Times. *The fact is we now have succeeded in getting the Fed back all of their money, and we're just close to getting the Treasury paid back. And do you know," he adds, an indignant note*

*creeping into his voice, "neither of them have ever said 'Thank you'?*
*We have done all the right things. Somebody should say, 'By golly, those*
*AIG people made a promise and they are living up to a promise!' We're*
*left with a major part of the economy in America; they're going to*
*make a profit on top of everything else they've got," he finishes, settling*
*back into his chair. "God bless America. And God bless AIG. And*
*God bless Tiny Tim."*

Denise hated the piece, which she thought was snarky and gossipy; at
one point, it made mention of the fact that I had "various female compan-
ions." Which was true. My communications staff was wildly uncomfortable with how my candor was made to reinforce the long-standing "crazy
Bob" narrative. So yeah, it did go in heavily for the bull-in-the-china-shop
thing, and the focus could have been more on the rest of the AIG executive team and less on me. But it was a piece that to my way of thinking
helped to reset the conversation about the positive direction in which
everything was heading.

The piece was a lively document marking how far we'd come. The even
more meaningful one to me, however, was the letter I sent out on December 11, 2012, to our 62,000 employees around the world:

*Dear Colleagues,*

*We come together as a company to celebrate in good times and we*
*draw together in times of shared crisis. Today warrants a celebration*
*like no other in AIG's history and places well in the past a crisis none*
*of us will ever forget.*

*Today, the U.S. Department of the Treasury has priced an offer-*
*ing of approximately 234.2 million shares of AIG common stock at a*
*price to market of $32.50 per share. Upon the closing of this transac-*
*tion, expected this Friday, Treasury will have sold the last of remain-*
*ing shares of AIG common stock, receiving proceeds of approximately*
*$7.6 billion from the sale.*

*The closing of this transaction will mark the full resolution of Amer-*

*ica's financial support of AIG—with a profit to taxpayers of $22.7 billion to date. It marks one of the most extraordinary—and what many believed to be the most unlikely—turnarounds in American business history.*

*And you did it.*

*America invested in 62,000 AIG employees, and we kept our promise to rebuild this great company and deliver a profit to those who put their trust in us. You did this. Every single man and woman at AIG did this remarkable thing. There is a saying that in American life, there are no second acts. Well, take a bow, because today marks our second act.*

*We are not going to stop here and take a rest. We are not at the finish line. This turning around has been hard won, as you know. And, what a run we have had together.*

*Now, we have to exceed the expectations of our clients, our investors, our regulators, and our other stakeholders around the world. Since this is our second act, it is all about the quality, integrity, and power of our performance. Please know: my confidence in you is unqualified. You got us this far. I know you will take us—an independent company once again—to new levels of achievement.*

*This has been a long walk since September of 2008. Let's face it—it hasn't always been fun. Our next steps together are perhaps even more significant than all that you have done in the last five years to reconstruct what we nearly lost: our company.*

*My job now is to urge each of you to face tomorrow—bring on tomorrow—with the focus and determination that brought us to this point. I know that we will succeed together. But today, let's take a few moments to reflect and celebrate.*

*What a way to end the year. How are we going to top this next year?*

*Thank you from the bottom of my heart. I am so proud at this moment of each of you.*

*Sincerely,*
*Bob*

I can't tell you how terrific it felt, pressing the SEND button on that one. Victory lap in order! To be exact, Treasury sold the remaining 234,169,156 of its shares—the sixth and last of the Treasury sales of our stock. The $22.7 billion of government profit broke down this way:

- $5 billion was realized by Treasury in the stock sales, of which $4.1 billion came from the common stock and $900 million from the preferred stock holdings.
- $17.7 billion was accumulated by the Fed. Of that, $6.8 billion was loan interest; $1.4 billion came from the AIA and ALICO special purpose vehicles, and $9.5 billion was realized from the Maiden Lane II and III vehicles, which bought the toxic securities from AIG FP.

The headlines that day reflected the new reality. "Bailout Over," read the *New York Times*. "Taxpayers Wind Up Making $22 Billion Off AIG," declared the *Chicago Tribune*. "End of a Bailout: U.S. Sells Last AIG Shares," wrote the *Wall Street Journal*.

The story was carried everywhere, but I thought the news actually deserved to make an even bigger splash than it did. Did I detect only a grudging acknowledgment out there of our achievement? Maybe fulfilling a mission that much of the country found distasteful from the get-go simply would never be judged to deserve a victory lap.

We tried hard to capitalize on whatever momentum had been gained with a marketing campaign that included an element we rarely if ever produced—a TV spot that expressed our gratitude to the nation. The theme was the polar opposite of *New York* magazine's "You're Welcome, America." The commercial was titled, simply, "Thank You, America."

The sixty-second ad, created by the Boston-based Partners + Simons agency, was low-key. Several AIG employees were recruited to say, basically, that like trustworthy guests, we'd not only taken great care with America's money, placing it all back where we found it, but we'd given back even more than we'd been generously provided. It mentioned the service we provided in recent disasters: $144 million to the victims of a 2011 tornado in Joplin, Missouri, and $2 billion we expected to pay in claims resulting from 2012's Superstorm Sandy that ravaged the Northeast.

"We made a commitment to repay, and we did, and we gave America a profit. I'm pretty proud of that," one of the employees said.

I appeared in the spot to plant the idea that the taxpayers' help for us would have an ongoing payoff for people who bought our policies. "When we make guarantees for people's lifetimes," I said, "we have to act as a company that will make sure we are here for their lifetimes."

The spot ran from December 31, 2012, to mid-January 2013, and its message was carried on both electronic platforms and print ads. The gamut of exposures ranged from AIG's YouTube channel to airtime we bought during the Rose Bowl. All told, some 800 million impressions of the commercial were counted. Christina Pretto noted that through YouTube alone we got "340,000 hours of brand exposure and over 14,000 hours of brand interaction."

And then, *pow!* All that positivity was drowned out by the kaboom of an event in which we were an innocent bystander. On January 7, 2013, an article on the *New York Times*'s widely read DealBook blog—and printed on page A1 the following day—revealed that AIG's board would meet to consider joining Hank Greenberg's $25 billion lawsuit against the federal government, the one in which he was alleging Treasury's seizure of AIG stock had been unconstitutional.

Set aside the fact that we were not going to go anywhere near that lawsuit. The board felt it had a fiduciary obligation to hear Greenberg's lawyers out, and indeed, that Wednesday, January 9, lawyers for Greenberg and the government were invited to our boardroom to lay out their arguments for our joining, or remaining on the sidelines. But the way the *Times* laid it out in advance of the meeting, our position looked awful.

"Fresh from paying back a $182 billion bailout, the American International Group has been running a nationwide advertising campaign with the tagline 'Thank you, America,'" the story began. "Behind the scenes, the restored insurance company is weighing whether to tell the government agencies that rescued it during the financial crisis: thanks, but you cheated our shareholders."

I couldn't fucking believe it. The timing could not have been worse. It made me wonder once again if AIG would ever live down the turmoil from which we'd just emerged. We looked two-faced: the goodwill from the ad campaign seemed to evaporate, although a few news cycles later, after reports that we'd refused to sign on to the lawsuit, things simmered down. Still the damage had been done. Pretto, at a town-hall meeting in February, reported that the favorable social media response to the commercial was met by an equally negative reaction after the *Times* story.

The bad taste would linger as Greenberg's suit progressed; more than a year later, Jon Stewart would rag on us mercilessly in a segment about it on his nightly show. "Remember how we gift-wrapped 180 billion dollars to insurance giant AIG because of that company's terrible mortgage bets?" Stewart asked, laying out with withering sarcasm the circumstances of Greenberg's litigation—and then characterizing it all as the ultimate act of gall. "Yeah, you gave me CPR," he said, in the voice of a thuggish patient. "But would it kill you to take a breath mint?"

Stewart's audience roared. It just went to show that there would probably be segments of the media and the nation that would never completely forgive us, no matter how good for the money we proved in the end to be.

My job, for as long as I had it, would now focus on pumping as many of my leadership values into AIG's bloodstream as possible, and preparing the company for my successor. I was feeling healthy through much of 2013, running ten to fifteen miles a day, as the doctors began to marvel at my longevity. We'd streamlined AIG and with the closing down of FP and the sale of ILFC, divested ourselves of all the aspects of the company not associated with insurance. Our three-pronged core now was property and casualty, life insurance and annuities, and mortgage insurance.

"One AIG," my initiative to integrate the various branches of the company more fully and to reduce the corporate myopia that's come to be known as the "silo-ing" of American business, became a thrust. Leading Leaders, the intensive, off-site program I'd developed to encourage our managers across the world to think independently and hand off more responsibility to their own direct reports for implementing new ideas and creative decision-making, was picking up steam. I'd spend more and more of my time in small-group sessions around the country and the world, spewing Benmosche wisdom, listening to employees' dilemmas, and trouble-shooting.

In 2014, the cancer drugs that had prolonged my life for so long began to lose their effectiveness. As the tumors spread, especially to my brain, I tried some other treatments at Sloan Kettering in Manhattan and Massachusetts General in Boston, to no avail. I ultimately returned to NYU, where I underwent gamma-knife procedures in the spring of 2014 to remove the tumors. Though I was hoping to leave the job at the end of the year, I was asked by the board to leave earlier, on August 31, 2014, and I reluctantly agreed.

Peter Hancock succeeded me as CEO on September 1, 2014. I introduced him as my successor at my final town-hall meeting as chief executive, in London on August 5, 2014, a meeting beamed to employees around the world. There was an earnings call that morning, during which we talked about, among other things, the second quarter's $2.7 billion in profits from our insurance operations.

It had been five years since I'd taken this job, a job I said I really didn't need. And who could have imagined this outcome for me or AIG—who, in fact, imagined there'd still be an AIG?

"It seems like ancient history to me," I said at that meeting, as I reflected on all the days that had passed in my tenure as CEO. "I'm happy with my five years," I added. "And I'm happy it's done."

I reminded the audience that the work was just beginning, in terms of the creation of One AIG. My skills as an operations guy, going back to the beginning of my career, told me so. "We said, starting in May of 2011 after we re-IPO'ed the company and we got the first stock sold, that all of you have to start working on fundamentally rebuilding the company. And you all know that we had an enormous challenge in technology and process. A lot of you are struggling with the systems we work with, and I'm being kind by calling them systems. I guess 'antiquated systems' comes to mind. And whether it's finance, whether it's actuarial, whether it's the way we do our proposals, the way we price our products, the way we do our big data, and so on down the line, we have had enormous amounts of rebuilding to do as a company."

The new government scrutiny of our financial stability was altogether a good thing, but it would require a level of transparency that would challenge us going forward. Recall that before the meltdown, our regulatory overseers were state insurance agencies and the relatively lax federal Office of Thrift Supervision. Now, we were designated a SIFI—a Systemically Important Financial Institution—and answered to the Fed under the mandates of the Comprehensive Capital Adequacy Review mandate.

"We still have a long way to go," I said, referring to the organizational challenges of this post-bailout era. "Make no mistake about that."

At the end, many audience members raised their hands. So many still had questions and comments.

The first one came from Hancock, and in taking me back to the start of this five-year adventure, it reaffirmed the session's upbeat mood. "You get this call to be the CEO of AIG and you say yes," he said, adding: "What the hell were you thinking?"

"I was drunk," I said, as the room erupted.

A video was played in my honor, filled with the voices of employees around the world. "Bob," one employee said, "I just want to take a moment to say thank you very much for the focus and the drive and the leadership and the accessibility that you've shown us at the company. So, Bob, I would want to extend a thank-you to you for giving me the courage to be the leader that I always wanted to be."

That was further proof to me that the fire I had wanted to light under this company had indeed ignited.

The last question I took as AIG's CEO pleased me especially.

"Where are your wines available for purchase?" I was asked.

A question after my own heart. "Send me an e-mail and tell me you want some wine and we'll see what we can do at a reasonable price," I said.

"You know me," I added. "We'll give you discounts."

# EPILOGUE

Bob Benmosche
Leader. Hero. Friend.
1944 – 2015

MetLife    AIG    CREDIT SUISSE

Courtesy of Lyn Hughes © 2013

BOB BENMOSCHE DIED AT NYU Langone Medical Center on Friday, February 27, 2015, of complications of lung cancer. He was seventy. He exceeded the original estimates of his life expectancy by four years. In the words of his oncologist, Abraham Chachoua: "It was a remarkable run."

Tributes to him took note of his other remarkable run, at AIG. "Bob Benmosche was smart, tough, and intrepid," said former Treasury Secretary Timothy Geithner, "and deserves credit for doing a hard and unpopular thing well by navigating AIG back to safety."

"He stood up and fought for what he believed was right," said Hank Greenberg. "That's what a leader does, and he did that very well. I'm proud to have called him my friend."

In the months before his death, and even after his retirement, Bob continued his work at AIG, conducting his Leading Leaders seminars around the country. His energy flagging after some particularly grueling radiation treatments on his brain in the fall of 2014, he was still waxing optimistic about the future. One afternoon in late October, while relaxing under an umbrella on the beach in Boca Raton, he even mused about getting into politics. "If I can beat the cancer back again," he said, "I might run for Congress."

From South Florida, he explained, "As an independent."

Of course.

AIG celebrated Bob's life and career with a retirement party in Chicago on November 1, 2014. That afternoon, the company invited the two hundred guests to a rugby match at Soldier Field featuring the All Blacks, the renowned New Zealand national rugby union team for which AIG became global sponsor in 2012. That was followed by a dinner at the Hilton Chicago. The testimonials to Bob, some of them on videotape, paid tribute, in the words of then–AIG chairman Steve Miller, to "one of the greatest stories of business history." Remarks came from AIG colleagues and friends, as well as from Bob's allies in government, Sarah Dahlgren and Jim Millstein, and admirers in the media, including Fox Business's Maria Bartiromo, the *New York Times*'s Andrew Ross Sorkin, Bloomberg's Betty Liu, and CNBC's Jim Cramer. There was even a message from a onetime antagonist, Representative Elijah E. Cummings, a Maryland Democrat with whom Bob later became friends; at the congressman's behest, in fact, Bob traveled to Howard University in Washington, D.C., in the spring of 2014 to speak with business students about the lessons of the AIG crisis.

In her remarks at the retirement dinner, the Fed's Dahlgren talked about Bob fulfilling what she called the "five traits of great leaders": "These people, she said, "reduce complex ideas to simple messages, . . . are empathetic, . . . are optimists, . . . push their people, . . . and communicate emotionally."

When it came his turn to speak, Bob chose not to give a warm valedictory. His tone was instead cautionary. He talked plainly about his cancer: "My mother begged me not to pick up a cigarette, but there was not enough science to prove that it was a risk. I am to blame for what's happening to me." It was the sobering prologue to his offering one of his favorite bits of wisdom: "The hand that has been dealt you—deal with it."

He noted, too, his continuing worries about AIG slipping into old ways, because "People are nervous about change." He was concerned, he said, about the difficulties still facing the company, in terms of integrating its variety of complex systems and units. Invoking a sports metaphor, he said: "We're at halftime." His parting words, however, were those of the inspirational American orator William Jennings Bryan:

"Destiny is not a matter of chance; it is a matter of choice. It is not a thing to be waited for, it is a thing to be achieved."

The interviews for *Good for the Money* were conducted over the last year of his life in New York, Florida, and elsewhere. The last session occurred on Sunday, February 22, 2015, at the compound in Suffern, New York, where he and Denise raised their children, just a week before he died.

His funeral was held at Riverside Memorial Chapel on Sunday, March 1, and he was laid to rest in Monticello, New York, near his mother and father.

# INDEX